John and Anne Spencer have been active researchers of the paranormal for over twenty years. John is a former chairman and current Director of Research of the British UFO Research Association and they are both members of several international organisations researching into the paranormal. They are at the forefront of experimental work and research into many unsolved mysteries. Both John and Anne have lectured to paranormal groups around the world, and they regularly appear in the media. They have an extensive list of publications in the UK, many of which have gone into foreign translations and editions.

MYSTERIES
AND MAGIC

John and Anne Spencer

ORION

An Orion paperback
First published in Great Britain by Orion Media in 1999
This paperback edition published in 2000 by
Orion Books Ltd,
Orion House, 5 Upper St Martin's Lane,
London WC2H 9EA

A CIP catalogue record for this book
is available from the British Library.

ISBN: 0 75283 675 7

Printed and bound in Great Britain by
Clays Ltd, St Ives plc

CONTENTS

ACKNOWLEDGEMENTS

Special thanks are due to the following who have assisted and advised us, neither of whom are responsible for the opinions stated in this book, which are our own:

- Graham James, a white witch who assisted in the sections on *Magic and Witchcraft* and who provided information and examples of talismans, amulets and spells.

- The House of Jupiter for assistance with the section on *Astrology* and the provision of examples of 'readings' from its computer-based systems.

INTRODUCTION

If one word were to be used to sum up the contents of this book it would be the word 'secret'. This is a book about the secrets that people have held through the centuries, about why they kept those secrets and how they kept them. It is also about those who have sought to break the secrecy and discover the information contained therein for themselves.

It is a book about the occult, which means simply 'that which is hidden'. In modern day usage the term 'occult' has come to refer to the supernatural, to magic and even demonic activities. It does indeed encompass all of these things as described in this book, but it also offers a wealth of alternative knowledge and ways of living.

It is clear to any observer that 'the West' has become deeply fascinated with the paranormal in recent years. There has been a proliferation of magazines and television programmes, even films, based on mysteries of the world such as the debated existence of the Loch Ness Monster, the Yeti, and so on. Moreover, such programmes and films have placed emphasis on the powers and abilities that are now thought to exist within the mind.

Prominent within such debates is a strong belief that there are those who have access to secrets, and those who are being kept out. Indeed, in some 'branches' of the paranormal such thinking has unquestionably become paranoid; there is a strong belief that governments are keeping secrets of the paranormal from their citizens, or that there is a secret 'world government' that actually runs the politics, religion and finance of the world while the 'up front' governments serve only to detract attention from them.

It is an article of faith for followers of the UFO phenomenon that governments, and the US government in particular, have important knowledge of extraterrestrials that they are not releasing to the world; beliefs include the idea that the government and military have captured one or more crashed flying saucers and have even recovered from them dead – some say living – alien beings. More extreme beliefs suggest that the government and military are working alongside aliens in an alliance – a 'pact with the Devil', some might say – on schemes which allow both parties to abuse, and even kill, citizens. These groups of humans and aliens work together, it is suggested, in underground bases; the modern version of the 'underworld' of the demons. Despite the fact that the evidence for such extreme beliefs is flimsy to say the least, modern distrust of governments is one of the unifying forces of 'ufology'. A group of UFO-interested people with very different, even conflicting, views can be easily united when the subject under discussion is distrust of government.

Such distrust is perhaps most typified in the beliefs that followed in the wake of the Kennedy assassination of 1963. Two-thirds of the American population believe that the Warren Commission's conclusion that a lone gunman – Lee Harvey Oswald – killed the president is wrong, a conclusion brought about by either the result of incompetence or, as more generally asserted, a cover-up. It is fascinating to study the reasoning behind such belief: that Kennedy was the first Catholic president; that he was too liberal towards civil rights; and so on. These same views can be found throughout history; the justification for extreme political acts being religious or racial/cultural.

The belief in a secret world government, or 'New World Order', has been a persistent one. The basis of the belief, though there is a lack of consistency and much debate between its proponents, is that there is a world-wide network of elite people who actually control the financial institutions and the religious bodies. From those positions they dictate economic and political policy, even the exact opposite of the stated political policies of the established governments. The evidence in support of the claims is tenuous; the fact that this is a belief of emotion rather than rationality is shown by the language used by its advocates; vicious, unyielding and extreme. Government statements are 'crap', people who cannot see their reasoning are 'fools' or 'conspirators'; their suggested responses are replete with destruction, punishment and retribution. Much of the literature is laced with expletives. Humour is virtually non-existent. Anyone wanting to see this kind of thinking in action need only look into the websites relating to UFO 'chat' and 'discussion' areas.

Although this kind of thinking abounds at the present time, it is not unique, nor indeed new. There has always been a belief that someone, or some group, knows more than is being admitted to and that that something is responsible for the ills of those 'out of the know'.

The arguments for or against the existence of a New World Order aside, it is very clear that throughout history groups of people have sought to keep secrets, or to imply to others that they have secret knowledge to which only they have access, and which they alone control. No wonder then that beliefs in conspiracies exist; even where there is no conspiracy someone has a vested interest in pretending that there is.

But why? What is gained by having, or pretending to have, a secret?

For the answer to that we need only go back in our memories to the school playground. How wonderful it was to have a secret, to be begged by others to tell it, to be able to swear others to secrecy before imparting it. (And it had to be imparted; the whole point of a secret not to be revealed is to reveal it!) How lonely and disturbing it was to know that others were sharing a secret and that you were not included. (And how quickly did you come to the conclusion – rightly or wrongly – that it involved you!) As children groups of boys, and groups of girls, would get together in gangs. There would be secret passwords, secret rituals and so on. Often, it seems, the only apparent point of the gang was to have the rituals and the passwords; once you were 'on the inside' you realised there was nothing else there. But actually there was something; it was the view of others from the outside. You were there, inside, and they were outside, and you could enjoy the envy of others.

Is it so different in the so-called conventional world? As we become adult and enter the world of work we find secret 'gangs' and rituals again. This time we dress them up differently; closed-door meetings at work, membership of this or that committee which has no published minutes; the jargon and technical language of professions: law, accountancy, engineering, computer-programming. Membership of an exclusive club with a special jargon that says to other 'initiates', 'we are members of the same club' and says to the rest of the world 'and you are not'. Perhaps much of it is subliminal, unintended; but it is clear that it is a part of the work-fabric that is dearly clung to by each 'initiate'.

The basis of it all is the old adage: 'Knowledge is Power'. We seek to have power over others, and to ensure that others do not have power over us. The secret is the key to this.

In the modern day, science and the scientist often represent the dichotomy of hope and fear. We hope that science will provide a better future for us, indeed we trust it to ensure our very survival. Limitless, cheap, non-polluting sources of energy; spacecraft to take us to other planets – a lifeboat in times of cataclysm on Earth; cures for cancers, AIDS and other diseases; the ability to prolong life, and so on. But the fear is that science is either running too far ahead of the ability of humankind to control it – the atomic bomb is virtually the universal symbol of this fear – or that there are scientists who might abuse their position of power. The classic image of the 'mad scientist' of 1950s B-movies was the embodiment of that fear during the birth of the atomic age.

But this is just new lipstick on the old face. The same dichotomy existed in earlier centuries; only the 'secret holders' have changed. Scientists are the modern day inheritors of the old occult skills. Chemistry's birth was within alchemy; astronomy's birth was from astrology; and so on. In earlier centuries the holders of the occult secrets were 'special' people, they were largely unapproachable by the masses; most astrology, for example, was in the control of a priesthood or royalty. Since the masses were illiterate they would have to believe what was fed to them by 'their betters' so the learned clergy – virtually the only people of earlier times who could read or write besides royalty – had a monopoly on thought. They could dictate the only path to God, or to knowledge, from their pulpits. All they had to do was stop anyone getting into an alternative pulpit.

With the advent of the printing presses in the mid-fifteenth century, books became widely available and literacy increased dramatically. The priesthood lost its singular control over people's thinking and was forced to use a combination of threats and suppression to keep its positions of power. Even today there is censorship. Publishers come under pressure to publish what is 'politically correct', for example, and become afraid to publish extreme or alternative views. Those that do become labelled 'radical' in the worst sense of that word. But a step away from the printed word is changing this: now the Internet is providing what amounts to censor-free literature. There is apparently no power that can prevent material being placed on websites around the world and accessed by computer from anywhere else. How the established institutions will react to that is yet to be seen.

But the basic requirement for a group seeking to be special, to have some sort of claim to have been ordained by the gods, and to control the flow of information to what it regards as the 'uninitiated', is still very present. We see it today in the UFO literature; that so-called contactees and abductees have been contacted by aliens – the modern day equivalent of the gods – and that they claim to have a mission to bring the wisdom of the extraterrestrials to the world. They are, they claim, specially chosen. Because they have been selected to meet with these aliens then they must, *ipso facto*, control the flow of information from the extraterrestrials to the human race. And of course this arrangement meets the old occult rules. To acquire the knowledge of the occult required special learning, initiation and determination because the knowledge could not be attained in our normal, physical world. The knowledge was in other dimensions, on other planes; it could only be accessed via alternative states of consciousness brought about by drugs or other techniques, or by purity of spirit that gave access to the divine, to the world of gods. In the modern version the knowledge is claimed to be literally out of this world – on other planets – only to be accessed by those who have a relationship with the aliens and who, we are told, are taken by them to visit such worlds.

This book is not about UFOs, or these modern versions of old qualities. It is about the originals; the alchemists, the occultists, the shamans, the witches and the manipulators of magic. It is especially relevant, in a world that is now searching for new meanings, to see how our ancestors dealt with the same needs.

The book starts with a review of Hermeticism, a term used to describe the interconnected approach of learning that was promoted in the seventeenth century. It is thought to date back to the first century.

Hermeticism is a starting point of understanding alchemy, a good deal of astrology and divination and to understanding the motivations of secretive cults such as the Knights Templar, the Freemasons and the Rosicrucians. In these occult traditions the seekers of hidden knowledge sought to learn from texts and oral traditions that they believed had direct lineage to God or the gods. The following section examines witchcraft and magic, assessing the efforts of those who wish not just to know of but to utilise the forces of the cosmos to their own ends. The remaining three sections of the book look at the beliefs that have developed in tandem with these quests: beliefs that have sought to read the minds of the gods by divination, prophecy or informed observation. Section three looks at the major divinatory systems: cards (the Tarot), stones (Runes) or interaction with chance and change (the *I Ching*). The fourth section considers the work of Nostradamus, probably the best-known prophet in the western world, and contrasts it with that of a contemporary clairvoyant. The final section looks at astrology, the most familiar and accessible of divinatory systems.

Hermeticism's resurgence in the seventeenth century was a part of the revolution of that period known generally as the

Renaissance. This too is especially significant to the modern day; many scholars believe that the youth revolution (encompassed by the term 'the Sixties') was a second Renaissance, the initiation of a 'New Age'; a revolution that promoted a belief in taking a wider view, an interconnected view of the world as a whole. In the spiritual sense this has also come to us through a 'cousin' of Hermeticism; known as holism, the idea that mind, body and spirit are interconnected and that the personal has resonance with the universal. In healing, in particular, we are encouraged to take a holistic approach, and this can be extended to all aspects of life.

Psychic and spiritual healing have become commonplace subjects of discussion. And alternative and complementary treatments are manifold: acupuncture, acupressure, reflexology, aromatherapy, rebirthing, hypnotherapy, past-life therapy, modern mesmerism, crystal healing, shiatsu, chiropractic, biodynamic massage, kinesiology, Rolfing, chelation therapy, Reiki, aura therapy; the list is almost endless. But if there is a common theme amongst all these it is the holistic approach, the idea that mind, body and spirit must all be cared for and treated as a whole.

Indeed that reasoning is fast becoming generally accepted; the world must be seen as a whole. That to understand even mundane aspects of everyday life requires not the divisional teachings that have dominated the last century and a half but the comprehension of the world as an interconnected 'One'. Teaching and scientific discipline have created specialists whose apparent knowledge of individual subject areas is very detailed and very deep but whose application, outside of their singular field, is often very limited. Politics is seemingly undertaken in isolation of its effects on individuals; religion seems often to have little to do with people's everyday needs; science appears to act without moral code or ethics (consider the line in the film *Jurassic Park*: 'Your scientists were so preoccupied with whether or not they could, they didn't stop to think if they should'). Even science itself is fragmented into physics, chemistry, biology etc with specialist divisions even within those disciplines. Teaching has become highly compartmentalised and the resurgence towards a holistic approach seems to be a reaction to that.

We can trace the emergence of this thinking back to the emergence of the so-called New Age in the 1960s which largely rejected the priciples of earlier generations – which were seen to have created wars, the atomic threat and racial and prejudicial disharmony – and attempted to replace it with something more meaningful.

But this New Age revolution was far from the first of its kind and indeed amounts to the rediscovery of a general set of beliefs which had effectively been embraced by the Renaissance centuries before. It is the concept of Hermeticism.

As is often the case, science fiction predicted the re-emergence of this 'New Age' Hermeticism. The best example is in the book *The Voyage of the Space Beagle* by A. E. van Vogt (1951), where the concept is called 'nexialism'. On board the *Space Beagle* (clearly a reference to the HMS *Beagle* that had carried Charles Darwin on the original 'five year mission to seek out new lifeforms') the ship's only nexialist, Grosvenor, describes the concept as 'applied whole-ism', the science of joining in an orderly fashion the knowledge of one field of learning with that of other fields. The nexialist rises above the ordinary scientists who make up most of the rest of the crew by seeing the connections between their disciplines that they do not see. Grosvenor makes it clear that he regards himself as 'better' than the other scientists – as many Magi of earlier centuries claimed to be.

There is a telling phrase in the book that is the true echo of the attitude of centuries-old suppression of those who have sought out occult knowledge. Grosvenor had knowledge that the others did not have – 'knowledge is power' – and he could apply it in ways the others could not. One man sees the power of the nexialist and tells him '... you are potentially the most dangerous man on this ship.' In that phrase is the fear of the occult that has caused the religious and political oppression of occultists over the centuries.

And in the 1960s the 'youth revolution' met with just such a reaction from the Church and politics. The Church either sought to condemn (witness the sermons from the pulpit against the 'sinful gyrations' of Elvis Presley), or sought to find a reconciliation wherein it could 'tame' the emerging new faiths (long-haired vicars playing guitars in church). Politics was similarly divided between those who stood up for the old values and those who sought to embrace the new, such as British prime minister Harold Wilson's many attempts to associate himself with the Beatles. When The Beatles were granted OBEs a handful of those individuals of the old values returned their own honours to the Queen as a protest against this new recognition. (Significantly, one of those who sent back his honour asked for it back again after John Lennon returned his – that individual had clearly identified which of the Beatles he believed was more magician than musician!)

During the earlier centuries, the emergence of Hermeticism, alchemy and the prominence of the Knights Templar, Freemasons and other groups, history is replete with the almost schizophrenic attempts of the Church and other authorities to condemn and reconcile in almost equal proportions.

What we are seeing in the modern world is the logical extension of earlier beliefs, a moving backwards towards those old beliefs and modern ways of carrying them into the next millennium.

1

SEEKERS OF HIDDEN KNOWLEDGE

If secrets hold knowledge and knowledge is power then it is inevitable that there will be many who will seek out that knowledge in order to control the power within. The original secrets are alleged to be the secrets of the divine; the secrets of the gods. Those who claimed to have access to them then became the secret-holders, and others sought to understand their methods and their histories in order to gain access to that same power. Hermeticism is the start of our exploration into the secrets, and those who seek them.

HERMETICISM

The basis of Hermeticism, the belief that everything is interconnected, comes from what is known as Alexandrian syncretism originating in the Egyptian city of Alexandria in the first century. At that time, Alexandria was under Greek rule and the intellectual centre of the Western world. Hermeticism is named for and attributed to the writings of Hermes Trismegistus, an Egyptian who, it is said, lived at the time of Moses (see page 27). Michael Baigent and Richard Leigh in *The Elixir and the Stone* (1997) describe Hermeticism thus:

> Theology and philosophy were more or less interchangeable – or overlapped to such a degree that the lines of demarcation between them were indistinguishable. And thus the intellectual ambience of Alexandria was alive not only with diverse faiths

and creeds and their attendant theologies, but also with what we today would call philosophical systems; and these enjoyed a comparable respect, a comparable exalted status. Cults, sects, mystery schools and religions in Alexandria were complemented by philosophical teachings. ... In Alexandria, then, cults, sects, religions, philosophical schools and systems jostled against each other, contended with each other, cross-fertilised each other, nourished each other in a dynamic and constantly mutating intellectual bouillabaisse.

Within these Alexandrian systems were 'dualists' who saw a distinction between spirit and matter. The dualist contended, basically, that matter was inherently evil and that the material world was the creation of, if not the Devil, then at least a lesser god. Spirituality, on the other hand, was the handiwork of the true God and therefore the goal of humanity was to transcend matter and to reach spirituality in order to reject that which was evil and to unify with that which is good. (In the New Age of the modern world we have seen a great deal of rejection of materiality and a commensurate emphasis placed on developing spirituality.)

Baigent and Leigh make the point of Hermeticism and alchemy that there seems evidence of a 'time being right' for their emergence in the first century. As they state:

Hermeticism had much in common with Chinese Taoism, which originated much earlier but which was still flourishing around the same time. And indeed, adherents of Hermeticism would often speak of the 'Way of Hermes', implying not just a corpus of teachings, but their practical application. The word 'Tao' also means 'Way', and Taoism incorporated a similar practical dimension. There is no evidence of any cross-fertilisation between Taoism and Hermeticism. China is a considerable distance from Alexandria; and the distance was even more considerable in the first centuries of the Christian era. But it is, at the very least, striking that Taoist alchemy should appear in

China at the same period that Hermetic alchemy appe
Alexandria.

In the emergence of Hermeticism an emphasis was placed on a
change, particularly with regard to religion and spirituality, from
the passive to the proactive. Prior to the emergence of Hermeticism, humankind's role in the cosmos was regarded as largely
passive. The gods dictated the course of events on Earth and
humanity could only watch. At best a person could pray for, and
seek, change but whether or not it was granted would be at the
behest of the gods. Hermeticism allowed humankind to actually
play a proactive role in changing the world. People feared the
occultists in the belief that they seemed to control occult and
alchemical powers and had in their mortal hands that which
previously only the gods had been able to command.

This emergence through Hermeticism is well shown by the
work of Marsilio Ficino (1433–99). He had been a student at the
University of Bologna and in 1459 was summoned by Cosimo de
Medici to run his Platonic Academy in Florence. Ficino had been
educated in the humanities, in music, Greek language and Greek
philosophy and ran Cosimo's academy from a Medici villa in
Careggi. One of the tasks Ficino undertook was to translate Plato
from the original Greek but he was abruptly diverted from that
task in order to translate an eleventh-century copy of *The
Hermetica*, the corpus of Hermetic texts, which Cosimo had
acquired. Both Cosimo and Ficino saw the Hermetic text as life
changing and a foundation for their future work. Cosimo died
within the year but Ficino worked on, combining Plato's work
and *The Hermetica* as a religion which he saw as an alternative to
Judaeo-Christianity.

As part of the magic contained within this philosophy Ficino
believed in a proactive use of astrology. Using the right blend of
planetary influences an individual could, in effect, correct
problems in their horoscope and rebalance their characteristics
and qualities. So, for example, an individual particularly influenced by Saturn (which was said to produce melancholy) could

be aided by invoking the neutralising or counterbalancing effects of the optimistic Jupiter. As such, therefore, even astrology, which is largely seen as a matter of divining the truth, i.e. understanding what is inevitable, suddenly becomes a proactive force for change. Ficino's translation of *The Hermetica* in 1463 was one of the bases of the Renaissance. Yet it might never have had quite the impact it had but for the invention of the printing press around the same time. The economics of the printing press were that thousands of copies of books could be produced far more easily than the individual, written copies of previous years. The result was inevitable, and economy driven. Mass production needs a market and that market was the mass of people around the world. As a consequence literature and learning became the purview of not only the learned, the scholars, the rich and the clerics but of a much wider population. The Church could no longer contain its monopoly on knowledge. The upper classes could not prevent the middle classes from acquiring an equal standard of learning.

As we have come to learn today the genie cannot be put back into the bottle but at the time the Church thought that it could be. Since it tried to retain control over its own learned texts it was the new 'occult' writings which began to proliferate during the Renaissance. Since the Church understood very clearly the loss of political power it was about to suffer it sought to retain its control over its own sacred writings by condemning the alternatives.

The extent of these prohibitions is demonstrated by, for example, the Index of Prohibited Books which was created during the Council of Trent between 1545 and 1563; the Index was not abolished until 1966. The decrees of the Council were confirmed by Pope Pius IV on 26 January 1564 setting a standard of faith and practice for the Catholic Church until the mid-twentieth century.

Hermeticism, then, was an all-embracing philosophy of the hidden sciences and hidden knowledge. Now we must explore the deeper worlds of the mystic; in particular alchemy which featured prominently in the Hermetic texts, and the Cabbala, both of which represent the same spiritual search. In the later part of this section we shall then look at the leading figures and institutions that have set out on the quest for that knowledge.

ALCHEMY

At face value alchemy is the art of metallurgy and transmutation. Many believe it to be the forerunner of modern chemistry.

Alchemy was first observed in Egypt in the last centuries BC and into the early centuries of the first millenium. The quest for changing base metal into gold probably first arises here as an extension of metalworking techniques of the time. About 200 BC Bolus of Mendes described the making of gold, silver and precious stones using specific recipes. These techniques changed the colour of metals, yellowing or whitening them to look like natural golds and silvers. The colour changes were believed to be the actual production of gold and silver from these 'base' metals. By AD 300 according to the writings of Zosimus of Penopolis alchemy incorporated Greek philosophy, magic, astrology, Gnosticism and Christianity as depicted in occult symbols.

It is probably from Egyptian religious beliefs that alchemy derives its basic formula. Their belief was that the gods created the world from a dark mass of confusion which was not actually matter but which was potential matter and which contained the potential for all life. (Some theorists believe that this may have been drawn from local creation myths which probably arose from seeing life developing along the banks of the Nile from black silt deposited during the annual flooding).

On this basis matter was not so much created as 'grown'. The belief was that all matter was composed of a limited number of components in different proportions and that by changing the proportions the end product is changed. Greek alchemy, according to Aristotle, determined that matter was composed of fire, earth, air and water in various combinations. Later alchemists added a fifth element, a mystical blend of the other four. Aristotle's concepts were modified by Arab alchemists who suggested that all materials were composed of sulphur, representing the soul, and male energy, and mercury, representing the spirit and female energy. European alchemists added a third component, salt, corresponding to the material body. Later translations of this alchemy have looked at the four states of matter: gas, liquid, solid and electro/plasma. Transmutation consisted first of 'killing' the existing material by first stripping it down to its essentials and then regrowing it with the components in different combinations.

In the seventh century Egypt and the eastern Mediterranean were conquered by the Arabs who imported alchemy into their own beliefs and then further spread them to Europe. Alchemy comes in fact from an Arabic word *al-kimiya*, in turn based on the Greek word *chemeia* (fluid). Probably the most famous Arab alchemist, a Sufi mystic who died about AD 815, was Jābir ibn Hayyān who is generally known as Geber (see page 36).

One of the aspects of alchemy is the turning of base metal into gold, symbolising the purification of the human soul. Each of the then known planets was believed to influence the development of particular metals and they constituted a 'ladder of perfection' going upwards from Saturn at the base (lead) through Jupiter (tin), Mars (iron), Venus (copper), Mercury (mercury), the Moon (silver) and at the highest point the Sun (gold). Gold was the purest metal; alchemy consisted of attempting to rid other metals of the impurities that prevented them being gold, in order that they could become so.

The quest for turning base metal into gold naturally attracted many so-called alchemists whose only concern was to produce wealth for their own acquisition. They became known by the derogatory term 'puffers', a reference to the bellows used on their furnaces. These were the pseudo-alchemists who concentrated entirely on the physical and chemical properties of metal, ignoring the spiritual dimension of the true alchemy. Some commentators have, perhaps somewhat cruelly but with good reason, pointed out that it is the puffers who are the true forerunners of modern day chemists rather than the alchemists.

The Flemish chemist Jean Baptiste van Helmont (1577–1644) claimed that he had successfully transmuted mercury into gold. In 1782 an Englishman named James Price, a Fellow of the Royal Society, made similar claims and so impressed the Society that they asked him to conduct experiments in front of trained observers. He arrived for the experimentation and promptly committed suicide, casting severe doubt on his claim.

The Philosopher's Stone

The quest for the Philosopher's Stone derives from ancient Chinese alchemy and is the supreme goal of the alchemist's art. Quite what the Philosopher's Stone is intended to be is itself shrouded in mystery. Generally it is regarded as a compound that can turn all metals into gold and that is also the Elixir of Life; a universal medicine capable of curing all disease and conferring immortality on individuals.

These two concepts are not actually different; metals that were not gold were regarded as somehow impure and therefore 'sick' and alchemy believed that the transmutation of base metals to gold was actually curing illness in the malformed substances. The derivation of this probably comes from a combination of both Middle Eastern alchemical thinking and Chinese thinking which used gold as a part of medicine.

Richard Cavendish has pointed out the contradictory nature of the description of the Philosopher's Stone: 'It is a stone and it is not a stone, it exists everywhere in nature but is ignored or despised, it is unknown and yet known to everyone, it is made of fire and water, it is a fluid without weight, it comes from God but does not come from God.' (*The Encyclopedia of the Unexplained*, 1974)

Interestingly, Professor F. Paneth, a non-resident lecturer in Chemistry at Cornell University, USA believes that radium may well be the Philosopher's Stone or at least bears comparison. 'In a way, radium possesses the first and principal property ascribed to the Philosopher's Stone; it has the power of transmuting elements – if not metal. And even in its second property of being a valuable aid in the curing of diseases, radium seems to be closely related to its fabulous predecessor. So in a very remarkable degree, radium produces the twofold effects of the Philosopher's Stone–transmutation and healing.'

The seventeenth-century English alchemist Eirenaeus Philatethes in *A Brief Guide to the Celestial Ruby* described the Philosopher's Stone as: 'A certain heavenly, spiritual, penetrative, and fixed substance, which brings all metals to the perfection of gold and silver. ... It is the noblest of all creative things after the rational soul, and has virtue to repair all defects in animal and metallic bodies, by restoring them to the most exact and perfect temper. ...'

There have been many claims of success in finding the Philosopher's Stone. The Swiss physician Paracelsus (see page 41) was alleged to have located the Philosopher's Stone though it has been pointed out that he died without having amassed the fortune which might have been expected from one who had found so obviously valuable a product. On the other hand Pope John XXII who died in 1334 having denounced alchemists as swindlers was believed to have been an alchemist precisely because when he died he left a very wealthy estate.

Nicolas Flamel (see page 40) who died in Paris in 1418 was alleged to have found the Philosopher's Stone with the result that his house was ransacked immediately after his death by looters searching for it. He died phenomenally wealthy and many believed this was a result of his alchemical work. Having spent twenty years attempting to unravel the mysteries of alchemy he claimed that on a pilgrimage to Santiago de Compostela in Spain he met a converted Jew who interpreted the original Hebrew of the text. After apparently succeeding in alchemical transmutation Flamel gained the patronage of Blanche de Navarre, the daughter of the King of Navarre and subsequently the wife of Philippe of France. Rumours of immortality – conferred by the

Philosopher's Stone – pursued Flamel even after his death. He was supposedly seen attending opera in Paris in 1761.

The Elixir of Life

Of the 'Elixir of Life' probably the most famous story is that of Count Cagliostro. The story has it that an ageing noblewoman who sought to recover her youth consulted Cagliostro who gave her a small phial of substance to be taken when the Moon had entered its last quarter. As this was still in the future, the phial was locked up in a cabinet and the woman told her maid that it was only a cure for the colic so as to minimise her potential interest in the substance. But the story goes on that the maid then suffered a bout of colic and drank the contents of the phial. In the morning she found that she had changed from a 50-year-old woman to a beautiful young woman, presumably much to her employer's annoyance.

Alchemy: the Hidden Levels

However, just about everything that has preceded this paragraph under the heading of alchemy could well be nothing more than what is known as an 'occult blind'. An occult blind is the use of the hidden and symbolic meaning within the Language of the Birds (described in Section Four page 232) to satisfy the idly curious allowing them to believe that they have understood a meaning and wander off to their own devices, leaving the true meaning available only to the most devoted. Although there is no doubt that alchemy has some basis in metallurgy and chemistry of ancient times and in the coloration and changing of some metals, even perhaps the production of some alloys, it is highly unlikely that that search was the true purpose of alchemy. It is certainly unlikely that the quest for the Philosopher's Stone or the Elixir of Life was intended to be a 'genuine' quest, at least taken at face value. It is in the hidden meanings and deeper understanding of the Language of the Birds where we probably find the truth of alchemy. Essentially alchemy was a spiritual quest.

In Alexander Seton's *The New Light of Alchemy* (1604), the Scottish occultist offers a description that reconciles this:

> ... the sages have been taught of God that this natural world is only an image and material copy of a heavenly and spiritual pattern; that the very existence of this world is based upon the reality of its celestial archetype; and that God has created it an imitation of the spiritual and invisible Universe, in order that men might be the better enabled to comprehend His heavenly teaching, and the wonders of His absolute and ineffable power and wisdom. Thus the sage sees heaven reflected in nature as in a mirror; and he pursues his Art, not for the sake of gold or silver, but for the love of the knowlege which it reveals; he jealousy conceals it from the sinner and the scornful, lest the mysteries of heaven should be laid bare to the vulgar gaze.

This would seem to put the puffers in their place; they fell for the obvious meaning of the quest for the transmutation of base metal into gold, set about trying to profit from it and completely failed to understand that they were wasting their time.

The beginning of the reconciliation of metallurgy and the spiritual comes from the concept that in order to pursue alchemy, and particularly in the quest to create the Philosopher's Stone, the individual, the alchemist, will not succeed if he is not spiritual and high-minded in his quest. As the fifteenth-century alchemist Nicolas Valois stated: 'The science is lost if purity of heart is lost.'

With a deeper understanding of alchemy we see that the true quest is to turn the base material of humanity into the purity of spirit and spiritual oneness. The ladder of metals referred to earlier becomes a ladder of spiritual growth that the alchemist endeavours to climb to reach a nearness to God. As Valois also commented, after what he believed was a successful transmutation: 'Thou wilt do as I did if thou wilt take pains to be what thou shouldest be – that is to say, pious, gentle, benign, charitable and fearing God.'

The German alchemist and philosopher Heinrich Cornelius Agrippa von Nettesheim (1486–1535), commonly known as Agrippa, believed that the alchemist was the only real subject of his own experimentation and that all magic represented personal transformation. He stated: 'The world is a certain whole body, the parts whereof [are] other bodies of all living creatures'.

One of the earliest recognitions of this deeper meaning of alchemy was suggested by the esotericist Mary Anne Atwood who published *A Suggestive Enquiry into the Hermetic Mystery* in 1850 which suggested that the goal of alchemy was spiritual perfection. The German-born occultist Frans Hartmann in *Magic White and Black* made similar comments that base metal was an occult blind for animal energies that 'could be transformed into the pure gold of true spirituality, and how, by attaining spiritual knowledge and spiritual life, souls could have their youth and innocence restored and be rendered immortal.' There in a nutshell is both the Philosopher's Stone and the Elixir of Life as well! The psychologist Carl Gustav Jung (1875–1961), regarded alchemy as a form of psychology. He saw alchemical symbolism occurring in the dreams of his patients many of whom had never heard of alchemy or any of its images. Jung believed that the symbols came from what he termed the collective unconscious and regarded alchemy as the process of the development of an individual personality from a universal whole. One of the alchemical texts Jung read comments: 'The soul is only partly confined to the body, just as God is only partly enclosed in the body of the world.' This confirmed Jung's belief that 'the psyche is only partly identical with our empirical conscious being; for the rest it is projected and in this state it imagines or represents those things which the body cannot grasp.' Jung was given a Chinese mystical and alchemical tract called *The Secret of the Golden*

Flower in which he found the bridge between gnosticism and the psychology of the unconscious. Jung believed that although the language was different both Eastern and Western alchemy was a matter for the transformation of the soul. In 1935 Jung delivered a lecture at Villa Eranos on Lake Maggiore in Switzerland entitled 'Dream Symbols and the Individualisation Process' and the following year lectured on 'The Idea of Redemption in Alchemy'. In 1944 he published *Psychology and Alchemy*. One of the most enduring influences on Jung was that of the great German poet Johann Wolfgang von Goethe (1749–1832). It was a family tradition that Jung himself was descended from one of Goethe's illegitimate offspring. Jung regarded Goethe's work *Faust* (written between 1775 and the poet's death) as a work of Hermetic magic and Goethe himself as an alchemical magician. Jung described: 'I regard my work on alchemy as a sign of my inner relationship to Goethe. Goethe's secret was that he was in the grip of that process of archetypal transformation which has gone on through the centuries. He regarded his *Faust* as an *opus magnum* or *divinum*. He called it his "main business" and his whole life was enacted within the framework of his drama. Thus, what was alive and active within him was a living substance, the superpersonal process, the great dream of the *mondus archetypus* (archetypal world).'

The Eastern Tradition

The alchemical process (base metal into gold) may be referring to the purification of 'life forces' that Eastern philosophies have embraced over the centuries. There are references within Chinese alchemy.

No one is certain when the oral traditions of Chinese alchemy began but they were first written down in AD 320 by Ko Hung in the text *Nei P'ien*. The Chinese alchemical process purifies the universal life force, *Chi*, by feeding the body the correct balance of purified substances. Chinese alchemy therefore was largely concerned with the production of pure elixirs. Indian yoga refers to the life force as *Prana*. Yoga and meditation purify the life force by clearing the body's *chakras* – channels of energy through which the life force moves. In yoga the ultimate result is the controlled release of *kundalini*, a stored-up force of sexual energy depicted as residing at the base of the spine. *Kundalini*, to be powerful, must be stored and not released. There seems to be a link between this belief and the belief, which also originates in the East, that the withholding of orgasm or ejaculation strengthens the life force. It is essential in many Eastern philosophies and was practised by, for example, Mahatma Gandhi as a way of generating his own internal strength. For many centuries the practice has been part of Western religious or spiritual belief. In the West many witches held back from orgasm in order to develop their abilities; monks and nuns abstained from sex in order to better focus their minds on God.

The purification of the life force (by elixir or by meditation and yoga) may be further linked to sexuality. Indeed, alchemy may be describing the act of union itself. Indian alchemy itself represents the union of the male (Shiva) and the female (Shakti) producing the enlightened being, Jivan.

Bearing in mind the belief that base metals grew in the ground just as a child grows in the womb, so alchemy becomes the process of developing that base metal, or that child, into the purest form attainable.

In Seton's *The New Light of Alchemy* it states: 'Take the living male and the living female and join them in order that they may project a sperm for the procreation of a fruit according to their kind'. Other alchemical texts refer to the union or sacred marriage of the King and Queen, of the Sun and the Moon, of the Red Lion and the White Eagle and so on. (This is also explored in the examination of witchcraft in Section Two, page 161).

Whether actual sexual union or techniques were employed in alchemy is doubtful though there is a close link between Chinese alchemy and sex magic. However, some European alchemical texts suggest that the presence of a woman, or 'mystic sister', is essential to alchemy.

THE CABBALA

The Cabbala (there are many spellings of the word; we shall use 'Cabbala' here except where directly quoting) is the ancient Jewish body of mysticism and theosophy handed down to the prophets and holding the secrets of the Universe. Cabbala means 'knowledge handed down by tradition'. It was embraced during the Middle Ages and Renaissance by Christian mystics as enthusiastically as by the Jews.

It contains elements of Gnosticism (see page 124) and gives a powerful symbolic interpretation of the Torah and the commandments. Its origins were in small and elite circles but developed into a major popular movement after the expulsion of the Jews from Catholic Spain in 1492.

The Cabbala distinguishes seventy-two names for the Deity, thirty-two Ways of Wisdom and fifty Doors of Knowledge. Alchemists, magicians and other 'seekers of the truth' turned to the Cabbala in the hope that it would provide them with the answers they sought, in particular to the development of the Philosopher's Stone or the Elixir of Life.

Although the Cabbala was originally passed on orally it was later written over an extended period of time. For example, the *Sefer Yetsarah*, the Book of Formation, was probably written between the third and sixth centuries AD whereas the Book of Splendour or Brightness, the *Zohar* (or *Zefer Ha-Zohar*), was probably written in the late thirteenth century in Spain, most likely by Moses de León of Guadalajara.

According to Dr C. Ginsburg in *The Kabbalah*, the Cabbala existed before creation and was handed down by God to the angels. His interpretation is as follows.

The Kabbalah was first taught by God Himself to a select company of angels, who formed a theosophic school in Paradise. After the Fall [of humankind, in the garden of Eden, as a result of Adam's succumbing to temptation] the angels most graciously communicated this heavenly doctrine to the disobedient child of earth [Adam], to furnish the protoplasts [humankind] with the means of returning to their pristine nobility and felicity [i.e. to find their way back to God's favour]. From Adam it passed over to Noah, and then to Abraham, the friend of God, who emigrated with it to Egypt, where the patriarch allowed a portion of this mysterious doctrine to ooze out. It was in this way that the Egyptians obtained some knowledge of it, and the other Eastern nations could introduce it into their philosophical systems. Moses, who was learned in all the wisdom of Egypt, was first initiated into it in the land of his birth, but became most proficient in it during his wanderings in the wilderness, when he not only devoted to it the leisure hours of the whole forty years, but received lessons in it from one of the angels. By the aid of this mysterious science the lawgiver [Moses] was enabled to solve the difficulties which arose during his management of the Israelites, in spite of the pilgrimages, wars and frequent miseries of the nation. He covertly laid down the principles of this secret doctrine in the first four books of the Pentateuch, but withheld them from Deuteronomy. ... Moses also initiated the seventy elders into the secrets of this doctrine, and they again transmitted them from hand to hand. Of all who formed the unbroken line of tradition, David and Solomon were most initiated into the Kabbalah. No one, however, dared to write it down, till Simon ben Jochai, who lived at the time of the destruction of the second Temple.

God, called *En Soph*, was an infinite and incomprehensible concept in space and time beyond human understanding. Indeed it was a tenet of the Cabbala that it [*En Soph*] could not be understood. In order to create or change the world *En Soph* employed intelligences, the *Sephiroth*, as its agencies. These ten agencies were known as: The Crown; Wisdom; Intelligence; Love; Justice; Beauty; Firmness; Splendour; Foundation and Kingdom. In one of the texts of the Cabbala, the *Zohar*, the importance of humankind is expressed. 'Man is both the import and the highest degree of creation, for which reasons he was formed on the sixth day. As soon as man was created everything was complete, including the upper and nether worlds, for everything is comprised in man. He unites in himself all forms.'

It is a tenet of the Cabbala that the human being represents the whole Universe, a distinctly Hermetic belief. Indeed the shape of the human being was believed to be a physical representation of the Hebrew word for God. As the *Zohar* states: 'Just as we see in the firmament above, covering all things, different signs which are formed of the stars and the planets, and which contain secret things and profound mysteries studied by those who are wise and expert in these things; so there are in the skin, which is the cover of the body of the son of man, and which is like the sky that covers all things above, signs and features which are the stars and planets of the skin, indicating secret things and profound mysteries whereby the wise are attracted who understand the reading of the mysteries in the human face.'

The human soul existed before and beyond man and was used to finalise the creation of the human being. The soul inhabited the World of Emanations in a state of unity of both the male and the female. When the soul becomes part of the human being it is divided into male souls and female souls and marriage becomes the quest to reunite the two souls (also the origin of the New Age expression 'soul mate'). The Cabbala states that all the souls must live lives and return to the World of Emanations spiritually developed. When this work is complete all sin and suffering will have been eliminated.

As we can see, the God referred to in the Cabbala is less of a being and more of an 'Infinite'. The God of the Cabbala did not make the world in the sense of creation but rather the world and everything else flows from God and is in a state of constant growth. As such therefore the emanations from God contain good and evil, infinity and finite boundaries, spirit and matter and so on. The *Zohar* offers:

> The Aged of the Aged, the Unknown of the Unknown, has a form and yet has no form. He has a form whereby the Universe is preserved and yet has no form because he cannot be comprehended. When he first assumed the form [of the first emanation] he caused nine splendid lights to emanate from it which, shining

28

through it, defused to bright light in all directions. ... So is the Holy Aged, an absolute light but in himself concealed and incomprehensible. We can only comprehend him through those luminous emanations which again are partly visible and partly concealed. These constitute the sacred name of God. [As interpreted in *The Kabbalah* by C. D. Ginsburg.]

Christian Cabbalism which resulted as a union of interest by Christian writers formed the basis of a great deal of the work of such as Agrippa (see above), the English alchemist and astronomer John Dee (1527–1608) and the mystic Robert Fludd (1574–1637) and as such has therefore influenced a great deal of European occultism.

Perhaps the Cabbala has been most noticeably influential of all in the development of the occult alphabets such as the Gematria, Notaricon and Temurah, all based on the Hebrew language.

Gematria

Gematria was basically developed by German Cabbalists in the thirteenth century but it had been used in much earlier cultures. For example, King Sargon II, Babylonian ruler of the eighth century BC, used the numerical value of his name to calculate how high the wall of Khorsabad should be built (16,283 cubits).

The Gematria is a system of numerical writing based on the twenty-two letters of the Hebrew alphabet each being given a numerical equivalent. This results in every word having a number value derived from the sum of the numerical equivalent of each letter in the word. Gematria 'word play' generates the system of hidden meanings which are an inevitable factor in most occult writings. For example, the Hebrew word for serpent and for Messiah both have the same numerical value (358). This suggests to Cabbalists that when Moses carried the image of the brazen serpent he was predicting the coming of Christ, the Messiah. (*Numbers 21:9* 'And Moses made a serpent of grass, and put it onto a pole, and it came to pass, that if a serpent had bitten any man, when he beheld the serpent of grass, he lived').

Early Christians derived the image of Christ as a 'dove of peace' using the method above because the Greek letters *alpha* and *omega* (which represent the first and the last word of Christ) and the Greek word for dove, *peristera*, have the same numerical equivalent, 801.

Genesis 18:2 refers to 'and lo, three men'. This is believed to represent the archangels Michael, Gabriel and Raphael because the numerical equivalents of 'and lo, three men' and 'elo Michael, Gabriel ve-Raphael' each have the same numerical equivalent, 701.

The Notaricon

The Notaricon is an encoding system where every letter of a word is regarded as the abbreviation of another word. As an example 'agla' is Notaricon for the Hebrew phrase *Atha gibor; leolam Adonai* – meaning 'Thou art mighty forever, oh Lord'. Modern Rosicrucianism acquired its name by the use of the Notaricon. The word *cromaa* means 'in truth' using the ancient Egyptian word 'maat' for truth. By reversing the word it forms 'TAAMORC' – an acronym for 'The Ancient And Mystical Order Rosae Crucis'.

Temurah

Temurah interprets text by analogy. One letter is exchanged for another or the ordering of lettering is changed according to a set of principles.

These and other principles are similar to those used by Nostradamus (see page 221) in encoding his quatrains, as described in Section Four.

The Sephirothic Tree

The essence of Jewish occult law and the Cabbala is the Sephirothic Tree, or Tree of Life (see page 32). It is held to represent a three-dimensional visualisation of the spiritual world and is usually shown as a tree growing downwards with its roots in Heaven. The tree grows through the four worlds which start in the World of Pure Spirit and descends to the World of Matter.

- The first world is *Atziluth*, the World of Origins. The ruler of Atziluth is the Adomai Malakh, also known as the Lord King.

- The second world is the *Briah*, World of Creation. Briah is ruled by the archangels and is the source of ethical and moral reality. The ruler of Briah is Sandalphon, the archangel of Presence.

- The third world is *Wetzirah*, the World of Formations where the archetypes form. Wetzirah is the domain of the Cherubim, who represent the four elements and are symbolised by their zodiac images, Taurus, Leo, Scorpio and Aquarius.

- The fourth world is *Assiah*, the World of Expression which is our familiar material world. Assiah is the World of Man, formed by the creative powers of our own senses.

The tree has ten spheres or *Sephiroth* penetrating these four worlds representing aspects of the divine personality, aspects of God's revelation of himself. The ten aspects or levels are believed by occultists to spell out his only true name.

- The highest level of the tree is *Ain Soph*, the nothingness out of which everything arises. The highest Sephiroth is *Kether*, the Supreme Crown which is dominated by the being called the Metatron and is the source of First Motion which created the Cosmos.

- The second level is *Chokmah* (or *Hokmah*), the level of Wisdom which is inhabited by the spiritual being Ratziel.

- The third level is *Binah*, Understanding, governed by Aralim and represents Saturn.

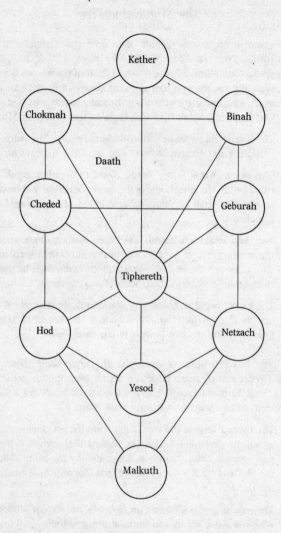

THE SEPHIROTHIC TREE

- The fourth level is *Chesed* (or *Hesed*), the level of Mercy or Love represented by Jupiter and ruled by Chesmalim.

- The fifth level is *Geburah*, the equivalent of Mars, representing Severity or Power and is ruled by Seraphim.

- The sixth level is *Tiphereth*, Beauty, ruled by Michael and is the equivalent of the Sun.

- The seventh level is *Netzach* (or *Netsah*), the equivalent of Venus the Victory or Endurance, ruled by the Archangel Auriel and the Elohim.

- The eighth level is *Hod*, Splendour or Majesty, the equivalent of Mercury and ruled by the Beni-elohim.

- The ninth level is the foundation, *Yesod*, ruled by Aishim and the equivalent of the Moon.

- The lowest level *Malkuth* is the equivalent of the Earth, is the Kingdom, and is ruled by Cherubim.

Between the third and fourth levels is the Abyss, known also as *Daath*, the Bridge of Knowledge.

There are twenty-two possible paths between the ten Sephiroth. The layout of the 'levels' is such that they form triangles of opposing and harmonising forces connected by the paths. An Initiate must travel the paths from one level to another as part of his or her meditation.

The tree serves as a highly effective tool for meditation which is aided by the subliminal representation that the tree is a growing, developing organism in which Man can see himself as part of that growth.

The tree is based on the fundamental belief that the human soul came from God and descended to the physical plane by way of the planets, attracting characteristics from the planets in turn, a link to astrology. After death the soul would return back to God discarding these characteristics along the way but the journey could be made using mystical techniques during life, through meditation and spiritual development. Impeding characteristics could be shed and the individual in life could ascend the tree towards God.

If we now examine the tree, the levels and the paths with their triangular linked representations we begin to see the real complexity of the Sephirothic tree.

- The highest triangle is formed from *Kether* from which emanate the two main opposing forces, *Hokmah* and *Binah*. *Hokmah* is the active male force, dynamic and thrusting which is the impetus for all growth, movement and evolution. *Binah* is the female force containing wisdom, understanding and intelligence and is passive and inert. *Binah* represents stability as opposed to *Hokmah's* evolutionary characteristics.

- Having then crossed the abyss, the next triangle holds the opposing forces of *Hesed* and *Geburah*. This triangle represents the powers which impose form and give substance to concepts. *Hesed* is the constructive force. In the human body this is the force of growth; in the family it is the protecting, guiding father. *Geburah* is the controller and limiter of growth. It can be destructive, authoritarian. Together they represent construction and destruction, all phenomena derive from their interaction. They are united in *Tiphereth* which combines both elements as represented by the Sun: the Sun can warm and nurture or can wither and kill. In the body, *Tiphereth* is the human heart, in the mind it is the enlightened consciousness.

- The third triangle, *Netsah*, is the force which binds the Universe together represented by Venus, the goddess of Nature, Love and Desire. This drives the instincts and passions, the instinctive reactions and is balanced by *Hod* which represents intelligence, communication, in other words deliberate and premeditated responses. These two, instinct and premeditation, are reconciled in *Yesod*, the foundation of all active forces. *Yesod* is also the link between *Tiphereth*, the Sun and *Malkuth*, the Earth and is represented by the Moon.

To ascend the tree, modern occultists believe that the journey is made on the astral plane; a dimension of reality which allows for dreams, thoughts and imagination to become real. Through meditation and spiritual enlightenment those imaginations become the very qualities that allow the shedding of planetary influences as the ascent is made. The state of body needed to allow for this journey is the meditative state typically represented by yoga. It is the mental processes, the devotion to occult understanding, which make astral travel different from 'mere' out of body travel.

To ascend the tree requires a certain purity of spirit attained only through determination and focus. This brings us back to the true basis of alchemy, as described earlier.

DRAMATIS PERSONAE: THE PROMINENT OCCULTISTS

There have been many leading seekers of wisdom, of which the following are those that have most influenced the progress of the subject.

Hermes Trismegistus

Hermes Trismegistus has been known by various names and spellings: Hermes Trismegitus; Hermes Tris Megetus; Thrice-Great Hermes; Thoth-Hermes; or just Thoth.

Plato debated whether 'Thoth was a God or just a divine man'. He was believed to be an Egyptian who lived at the time of Moses, and may have been Moses' mentor. As the Egyptian god Thoth, he was the god of Magic. Alexander the Great is thought to have discovered his tomb in a cave near Hebron. The tomb is said to have contained the emerald tablet, the *tabula smaragdina* (smaragdine tablet). This tablet is held to have contained the basic doctrine of alchemy. 'Thou shalt separate the Earth from the fire, the subtle from the gross, gently, with great industry. It rises from Earth to Heaven, and it receives the power of things above and of things below. By this means shalt thou obtain the glory of the whole world, and all darkness shall depart from thee. It is the strong power of every power, for it will overcome all that is subtle and penetrate all that is solid. Thus was the world created.'

In all probability Hermes Trismegistus did not exist as a single person, at least as the writer of the Hermetic texts, but was probably based on one or more Egyptian sages and a composite of the Greek god Hermes and the Egyptian god Thoth with most of 'his' writings anonymously composed by others. The surviving fragments of the forty-two books allegedly written by him, *The Hermetica*, probably combined Cabbalistic and Christian elements interwoven into Egyptian philosophy.

The myth that developed around Hermes Trismegistus is that he was a king who reigned for over 3,000 years, who carried an emerald containing all philosophy and who vanquished the dragon of ignorance, Typhon. Most of his writings were allegedly stored in the great libraries at Alexandria and were possibly destroyed when the libraries were burned. In 48 BC Julius Caesar laid siege to the city of Alexandria and set fire to both the Egyptian fleet and the buildings on shore. In subsequent centuries the Alexandrian libraries were further decimated by Persian invaders and zealous Christians, in particular Theodosius II, who destroyed most of the 'pagan' buildings in AD 391. Works that have survived include *The Divine Pymander* which describes that divine wisdom was shown to Hermes Trismegistus, the 'vision' which tells of the wisdom of the Egyptians and of the spiritual development of the soul.

Geber (Jābir ibn Mayyān, c. AD 721–815)

Geber was possibly a native of Mesopotamia. He is thought by many to be the first practising alchemist (presumably by those who believe Hermes Trismegistus was not a 'real' person or that he was a theologian). His work largely involved metallurgy and chemistry seeking the transmutation of metals. He wrote several important works including *The Sum of Perfection* and *Investigation into the Perfection of Metals*. The former, though, has been challenged by Professor Marcellin Berthelot (1827–1907) as being a forgery composed long after Geber's death.

Michael Scot (1175–1234)

Scot studied at Oxford University and afterwards in Paris. He settled in Toledo, Spain, in order to study Arabic. He later became Court Astrologer to Emperor Frederick II. It is said that he provided the Emperor with several astrological predictions for both the buildings of towns and cities and for action during military campaigns. In 1223 Pope Honorius III wrote to the Archbishop of Canterbury asking him to provide a living in England for Scot who returned there in 1230, bringing with him the works of Aristotle, hitherto unknown in England. It is said that he died and was buried at Melrose in the Scottish Borders after completing several important works on the subject of alchemy. In one rather curious account concerning Scot it is said he invited friends to dine but failed to provide any cooked food and instead caused spirits to bring dishes to the table, insisting that they had been brought from the kitchens of the Pope and from various sovereigns of Europe, including of France and Spain. It is also said he sailed in a demonic ship and rode through the sky on a demonic horse. In Dante's *inferno*, Scot is one of the Magis condemned to eternal torture.

Albertus Magnus (1193–1280)

Albertus Magnus was a Dominican alchemist who became Bishop of Ratisbon before retiring at Cologne. He was born at Lauringen on the Danube and entered the Dominican order as a result of a vision of the Madonna. He furthered the study of the works of Aristotle and was mentor to Thomas Aquinas (see below). Albertus Magnus has been heralded as the most important figure in thirteenth-century science and learning. He published works on pure sciences as well as magic and alchemy. It was he who differentiated between evil or black magic and so called natural magic which he believed could be reconciled with Christian theology. Far from offending conventional religion he was canonised in the twentieth century.

Thomas Aquinas (1225–74)

Chief disciple of Albertus Magnus was the Italian scholar Thomas Aquinas who is regarded as one of the great theologians of his day. He was educated by Dominican monks at Monte Cassino and went on to study at the University of Naples. At the age of seventeen he joined the Society of Preaching Friars. This was against the wishes of his family, who imprisoned Aquinas in his father's castle for two years. Considered slow in his youth (he was known as 'the Dumb Ox'), he began teaching under his mentor Albertus Magnus in 1248, initiating a career as scholar, philosopher and teacher which transformed the 'Ox' into 'the Angelic Doctor', revered throughout Europe.

Although best known for his theological and philosophical treatises, Aquinas was not immune to the fascination with the occult which permeated thirteenth-century European culture. One story of his occult practices was that he was so disturbed by the sound of horses passing by on the road outside his window he made a small brass model of a horse imbued with magical powers and buried it beneath the road after which no horse would pass along the road despite any amount of cajoling.

Roger Bacon (1214–94)

Arguably the most famous of English alchemists, Bacon believed in the concept that all matter was composed of mercury and sulphur and that all matter was intended to be gold but that some was made imperfect. He studied mathematics and science at Oxford and Paris, turned his attention to theology, philosophy and astronomy and indeed is credited with the inventions of the telescope and gunpowder. He was conversant in Latin, Hebrew, Arabic and Greek. He believed in the existence of the Philosopher's Stone and that there would be a way of banishing all disease and prolonging life. He had entered the brethren of St Francis but because of his beliefs was regarded as a sorcerer and was expelled. Pope Clement IV banned him from writing; the ban being lifted in 1266. Unfortunately Bacon's attempt to write a book on philosophy again offended his masters and he was imprisoned for fourteen years as a result. His studies of alchemy are said to have produced an oracular brazen head which could predict the future; in addition he used scrying glasses and a crystal ball. Many people believed that these strange legends were constructed falsely about Bacon though they point to the fact that in his writings he did predict boats propelled without oars, vehicles moving without horses, and others that fly.

Arnold de Villanova (c. 1250–1310)

De Villanova was educated at the Sorbonne in Paris. In medieval times this was the main centre for physicians in Europe and de Villanova went on to become a significant physican and alchemist. He moved to Italy and was appointed Physician-In-Ordinary to Pope Clement V and indeed it was only with Papal protection that he survived without significant oppression as he was widely known to be an alchemist and, by implication, a sorcerer. After his death many of his manuscripts were ordered to be destroyed by the Inquisition.

Raymón Lull (1230–1315)

Lull (sometimes Lully) was the son of a Spanish nobleman born on the family estates on the island of Mallorca. After a youth of sexual excesses, generally with married women, he became chaste and entered the Chruch and later studied Arabic in order to embark on missionary work in the Middle East. His excursions, which did not have the Pope's consent, failed and he returned to Europe to seek new support. His second excursion to the Middle East was no more successful and he ended up in prison in Tunis. Not being one to give up, when he finally was released from prison he had a third attempt during which time he was so severely injured that he died shortly afterwards in 1315. Although the Pope had not consented to his expeditions there was an enormous uprising of people who admired his religious fervour and who sought to have him canonised. Canonisation was refused on the basis that Lull had been interested in alchemy. His writings on alchemy were extensive and knowledgeable including *De Secretis Medicina Magna* and *Alchemia Magic Naturalis*. As in the case of so many alchemists there are also a number of tracts in existence which are thought to be forgeries attributed to his name.

Nicolas Flamel (c. 1330–1418)

Nicolas Flamel worked originally as a copyist in Paris. His occupation exposed him to books and documents on painting, poetry, science and architecture and also, to his deep interest, on alchemy. According to legend one night he dreamed that an angel stood before him holding a book and told him: 'Look well at this book. At first you will understand nothing in it, neither you nor any other man. But one day you will see in it that which no other man will be able to see.' It was shortly after this that a manuscript came into his hands which transformed his life. At the age of around 30 he came across an alchemical text which he could not read as it was written in a language with which he was not familiar but he believed it transformed his life. This was entitled *Abraham the Jew, Prince, Priest, Levite, Astrologer and Philosopher to the Nation of Jewes, by the Wrath of God Dispersed among the Gaules, Sendeth Health*. Flamel embarked on a quest to learn the language and, as stated earlier, it was while journeying in Spain that he met a converted Jew who was able to translate the text for him.

Even in the eighteenth century his work was being revered by such as Sir Isaac Newton (see page 48). Flamel's tombstone was created during his life and depicts a sun above a key and a closed book. The tombstone is now in the Musée de Cluny, France.

Paracelsus (1493–1541)

One of the most well known alchemists of all time is Aureolus Philipp Theophrastus Bombastus von Hohenheim who is known as Paracelsus. He was born near Zurich, the son of a physician. Paracelsus, an only child, was instructed by his father in surgery, medicine and alchemy as a youth. At the age of 16 Paracelsus entered the University of Basle, left almost immediately and began studying Hermeticism and alchemy further inspired by the teachings of the Abbot of St Jacob at Wurzburg.

Paracelsus was arrogant, dogmatic and egotistical and managed to alienate almost every member of the medical profession that he came across. Nor was he modest about his involvement in alchemy. 'I ... am endowed by God with special gifts for this end, that every searcher after this supreme philosophic work may be forced to imitate and to follow me ...' He rejected contemporary medical wisdom, instead creating what we would now recognise as a holistic approach to healing, treating the human being as a whole. His approach was classically Hermetic, believing man to be a microcosm of the cosmos and all aspects of man a microcosm of the whole of man. He did not believe in specialisation and held that true healing could only come from being master of a wide range of subjects including medicine, chemistry, alchemy, astrology and so on.

His restless quest for knowledge took him far across the world from Spain to Europe to Russia visiting Palestine, the Middle East and even India. He was present at the siege of Rhodes in 1522 working as a military surgeon in the army. He worked as a physician in Salzburg in 1525 and settled in Basle in 1527. However, he managed to offend the medical establishment there as well and was soon touring the world again. He died in 1541 in mysterious circumstances; many believe he was poisoned by one or more of the many medical experts he had opposed. It was not until twenty years after his death that his prolific writings were published. Effectively they had been suppressed during his lifetime by his enemies.

Apart from being recognised as an early founder of holistic medicine Paracelsus is generally regarded as the father of all modern medicine. For example, he recognised that many bodily functions were linked to chemical reactions and that chemical medicines could be used to correct imbalances in those functions.

His experiments with poppies produced laudanum which for 400 years was a regularly prescribed painkiller and is still used today in the form of morphine. He examined the properties of other drugs and the therapeutic values of sulphur which was generally used as an antidote to infection before the invention of antibiotics. He was one of the first to identify the fact that blood circulated round the body.

Paracelsus explored the use of magnetism in relation to the human body and laid down the foundation for the work of such as Friedrich Anton Mesmer (1734–1815). He also laid down the foundations of modern psychology recognising the connection between the psyche and the physical body. He was one of the first to examine the phenomena of hysteria and psychosomatic disorder, rejecting a belief in demonic possession.

John Dee (1527–1608)

Dee was born of Welsh ancestry and studied at Cambridge reading Greek and Mathematics. He had widespread interests in the sciences, mechanics, cartography, navigation and indeed was a close associate of the Flemish cartographer Gerardus Mercator (Gerhard Kremer, 1512–94), who devised the Mercator Projection used in most map-making to the present day. In 1546 Dee became a Fellow of Trinity College where he taught Greek.

After several years touring in Europe Dee returned to England and became associated with Lord Burghley who founded the early Elizabethan espionage networks. Between 1552 and 1555 Dee served both the Earl of Pembroke and the Duke of Northumberland and numbered among his friends the Earl of Warwick and Robert Dudley, later the Earl of Leicester. In 1555 he was imprisoned for treason against Queen Mary which served him in good stead when her half-sister Queen Elizabeth ascended the throne. Indeed, it was Dee who used astrology to select the most propitious moment for the Coronation. In 1564, already having acquired the title of 'Great Conjuror' from his enemies he published his celebrated work on Hermetic and Cabbalistic magic, *Monas Hieroglyphica*. He established at his home in Mortlake near Richmond what amounted to an Italian style academy for students of Hermeticism which included laboratories and a library of most of the works of early alchemists.

The gravitas Dee acquired by being a favourite of the queen allowed him to spread his beliefs widely to an influential circle of people including the spymaster Sir Francis Walsingham, Sir Philip Sydney, Walter Raleigh and others.

Dee was always passionate about exploration, travelling across the Atlantic in the search for the much fabled 'Northwest Passage' (a sea route linking the Atlantic and the Pacific). He suggested the creation of a permanent British Navy and is believed to have been one of the sponsors of Drake's circumnavigation of the world (1577–80). Dee also promoted a vision that amounted to an early British empire. Between 1582 and 1588 he had a disastrous association with a con-man known as Edward Kelley who convinced Dee that he was an occult adept. Despite being taken in by Kelley, Dee's work continued at a pace. He toured the continent and for a time worked under the patronage of the Holy Roman Emperor Rudolf II (1552–1612) who himself was strongly inclined towards Hermeticism and alchemy.

The Church was, needless to say, alarmed at an allegiance between a Catholic emperor and a magician from Protestant England and set about a policy of 'divide and conquer'. In May 1586 the Pope sent a complaint to Rudolf which stressed Dee's 'conjuring'. The Pope ordered both Dee and Kelley to be sent to Rome for interrogation but Rudolf effected their escape to Bohemia where they lived for two years protected by a Bohemian nobleman, Count Rosenberg. Dee became an espionage agent, not only undertaking assignments himself but running a team of other agents.

Dee's favour waned with the death of Elizabeth and the ascension of James VI of Scotland to the throne of England. James was hostile towards magic and very soon those of Dee's friends who were still alive were out of favour. Dee died at Mortlake in 1608.

Count Cagliostro (1743–95)

Born Giuseppe Belsamo to a poor but historically aristocratic Sicilian family Cagliostro was, from the start, a rebel. He studied chemistry and medicine but was expelled from one school after the other for insubordination. At the age of seventeen he worked in Rome as a draughtsman, also carving out for himself a reputation as an accomplished forger. He gradually moved towards an interest in alchemy and the occult. He took as his most influential mentor a Greek scholar named Altotas. They travelled extensively through Africa and Asia with lengthy stays in Egypt where Altotas educated Belsamo in the secrets of clairvoyance. Belsamo was introduced to the Grand Master of the Order of the Knights of Malta from whom he learned much science, philosophy and astrology. Some say he was initiated into the order.

Clearly he was one of those people with that almost indescribable quality of charisma and presence. One of his earliest supporters, Baroness D'Oberkarch believed that he was 'possessed of a demonic power; he enthralled the mind, paralysed the will'. He was also a friend, and disciple, of Comte de Saint-Germain.

As he pursued the occult he adopted the name Count Alessandro Cagliostro (the name Cagliostro came from his godmother). He travelled with his beautiful young wife, Lorenza Feliciani, across Europe practising clairvoyance, telepathy, fortune telling and spiritual healing and attracted important and powerful people in all the countries he visited. Stories that sprung up about him included his conjuring up the archangel Michael, predicting the winning numbers in a lottery three times in succession and entertaining the ghosts of deceased royalty to dinner.

He claimed that while visiting London in 1776 he came across a manuscript describing mystical rites of Egyptian masonry though since no such tract has ever been located it is widely thought that he made up the whole thing himself. It allegedly described an order of Freemasons in ancient Egypt founded by the prophets Elijah and Enoch, known as the Grand Copt. Cagliostro began using that title for himself. As this alleged manuscript indicated that members of this order were immortal Cagliostro announced to the world that he was himself several thousand years old. He founded the Egyptian Rite of Masonry with himself at the head; his wife presided over the women's lodges as the Queen of Sheba. His seance room in Paris was decorated with statues of Isis, Anubis and Apis; his servants were dressed as Egyptian slaves and the walls covered in Egyptian hieroglyphics.

He was admitted to the Esperance Lodge of Freemasons on 12 April 1777 in London and toured the Freemason lodges around Europe, lecturing and demonstrating his occult abilities. Now wealthy and honoured throughout Europe he teamed up with Johann Lavater, Swiss theologian and friend of Goethe who became one of his most ardent supporters.

The Catholic Church did not view Cagliostro favourably and regarded him either as a crook or a challenge to their authority.

His downfall, however, was ignominious, tangled up in fraud and forgery. Queen Marie-Antoinette had long expressed a desire for a particular diamond necklace that was so expensive even she could not afford it. Comtessa de la Motte convinced the jeweller who owned it that the queen wished to buy it in secret and without the knowledge of Louis XVI. Forged letters for this purpose, purportedly signed by Cardinal de Rohan were presented. Believing himself to be dealing with the queen's own agents the jeweller released the necklace before being paid for it and when he was not paid complained to the king. The king saw that the letter signed by Cardinal de Rohan was a forgery. De Rohan happened to be one of Cagliostro's close friends and the Comtessa insisted that it was Cagliostro who had stolen the now missing necklace. Whether he actually had any hand in this scam is uncertain but we must remember that he had in his youth had a history as a forger. He was locked up in the Bastille for a year and later released, exonerated. His fame was so great amongst the people of Paris that when he was released a crowd of 10,000 people turned out to acclaim him. However, for the rest of his life he was treated with suspicion because of the affair.

Now without the support he had previously enjoyed he went somewhat recklessly to Rome to practise Freemasonry, was arrested by the Inquisition in 1789 and sentenced to death, a sentence later commuted to life imprisonment. He spent the remaining six years of his life in a small dark cell where he was allegedly strangled by his jailer. There were, however, rumours for years across Europe, Russia and America that he had lived, possibly because of his claim for immortality, and he was supposed to have been seen for many years afterwards. One person much later in history believed he had the answer to Cagliostro's ultimate fate. That was Aleister Crowley whom we shall come to later. Crowley listed Cagliostro amongst many of his claimed previous incarnations.

Modern interpretation of the occult has not been kind to Cagliostro. Richard Cavendish in *A History of Magic* (1977) refers to him as 'a ludicrous figure'. Grillot de Givry in *Witchcraft, Magic and Alchemy* (1931) refers to him as 'a mere superficial Cabalist' and Julian Franklyn in *A Survey of the Occult* (1935) refers to him as 'one of the world's greatest medical charlatans'.

Giovanni Casanova (1725–98)

Cagliostro was a charismatic enough character, but one of his protégés managed to eclipse even him. In his early years Cagliostro met the Italian adventurer Giovanni Giacomo Casanova. He introduced him to Cabbalistic and astrological magic which Casanova in turn used to impress women and con money out of them. Casanova had been intended for the priesthood but, reminiscent of Cagliostro, he was expelled from a seminary for misconduct at the age of sixteen. He pursued a 'career' as soldier, preacher, alchemist, gambler, violinist, lottery director and spy. He was often involved in political and sexual scandals. In 1755 he was imprisoned by the Venetian authorities for practising magic but escaped and travelled throughout Europe winning the influence of a great many powerful people.

One of Casanova's victims was the wealthy and eccentric Marquise D'Urfé who owned an alchemical laboratory and occult library. She sought to be reborn as a man and Casanova persuaded her that he knew the way to achieve this. On his instructions she wrote to the Spirit of the Moon, posting the letter by burning it in an alabaster cup. Shortly afterwards a reply from the Goddess of the Moon was received written in silver ink on green paper; it appeared, as Casanova had predicted, floating in the Marquise's bathwater. Casanova had persuaded her that both he and she should be together in the bath. Following through the instructions given by the Goddess Casanova and one of his mistresses performed ceremonies of sexual magic with Madame D'Urfé in order to impregnate her with a baby son into whom her soul would be transferred. She did not, however, get pregnant and Casanova fled the scene. He was favoured by Louis XV (1710–74) and became the lover of the Marquise de Pompadour.

In 1785 he retired to write his memoirs in twelve volumes, many aspects of which were considered so racy that they were not published unabridged until 1960.

Sir Isaac Newton (1642–1727)

When scientists defend the scientific principle they will often invoke the spirit of Isaac Newton in their defence. 'Newtonian physics' is a byword for the practical and the real. Newton, whose laws of physics govern the movement of spaceships and put men on the Moon, is held by many to be the very personification of science itself. What those same scientists tend not to mention is that Newton, one of the founding fathers of modern science would, to quote Michael Baigent and Richard Leigh in *The Elixir and the Stone* (1997), 'have bridled in horror at any such status, and would vehemently have repudiated it'. Newton saw himself not only as scientist but as natural philosopher. He was a Hermeticist and deeply involved in alchemy. Most of his work was dedicated to alchemy, prophecy and the like with only a small amount of his writings dedicated to science. As BettyJo Teeter Dobbs comments, in *The Foundations of Newton's Alchemy* (1975), it is 'a curious anomaly ... that Newton's studies in astronomy, optics and mathematics only occupied a small portion of his time. In fact most of his great powers were poured out onto church history, theology, "the chronology of ancient kingdoms", prophecy, and alchemy.' Science insisted that having claimed him for their own, Newton's other, and more important work, should be censored. All of his non-scientific work, after his death, was suppressed, marked 'not fit to be printed'. It was not until 1936, two centuries later, that the material came to light. John Maynard Keynes, commenting on the suppressed work once it had been revealed said in *Newton, the Man* that Newton's 'deepest instincts were occult, esoteric, semantic'. Keynes regarded Newton as 'not the first of the Age of Reason. He was the last of the magicians.'

THE KNIGHTS TEMPLAR

Alchemy and the occult were not entirely the purview of individuals, even such charismatic ones as Cagliostro and the cults he formed. There have been a number of constructed, lasting, organisations that have pursued the 'hidden knowledge'; we must examine the impact they have made down the centuries. The first of these is the Knights Templar.

The Knights Templar was a medieval religious and military order formed in Jerusalem sometime between the year 1114 and 1118 with the ostensible purpose of protecting pilgrims visiting Palestine after the First Crusade. The order was formed by two French knights, Hugh des Payens and Godfrey of St Omer. Founding members also included André de Montbard, the uncle of Bernard of Clairvaux (see below). In its first ten years the Order was believed to consist of only nine knights though there are records of additional recruits.

The order was strictly known as the Order of the Poor Knights of Christ although they were popularly known as the Knights of the Temple of Solomon, or the Knights Templar, as their initial headquarters in Jerusalem was adjacent to Solomon's Temple. Unlike the two other major religious societies of the era, the Knights of St John of Jerusalem (also known as the Knights Hospitalers) and the Teutonic Knights, both of which had begun as charitable institutions, the Knights Templar was a distinctly military order. The order received Papal sanction and in 1128 at the Council of Troyes they were given monastic rules. This formally bound them with a legal constitution and combined their military and religious purpose. As the writer Seward, in *The Monks of War* (1974), states: 'For the first time in Christian history, soldiers would live as monks.' It is clear that from the outset this was part of a design. The Council of Troyes was conducted under the supervision of Bernard of Clairvaux. Bernard was a French ecclesiastic who in 1113 became a monk in the Cistercian monastery of Cîteaux and shortly afterwards became Abbot of a monastery at Clairvaux. Under his guidance the monastery became one of the most prominent of the

Cistercian Order. Bernard's influence was enormous, with something like ninety monasteries established on the basis of the one at Clairvaux, and indeed the Order of the Knights Templar was designed on a pattern which closely followed the monastic order of Cistercians.

The Order of the Knights Templar was a phenomenal success from the start and immediately after the Council of Troyes began taking in a large number of recruits as well as donations of money and property. By the end of their first year as a constituted Order they owned property in France, England, Scotland and the Iberian peninsula. Eventually they would come to own land in Italy, Austria, Germany, Hungary and Constantinople. Within a short time the Knights Templar had established itself 'as the single most wealthy and powerful institution in Christendom,' as described by Michael Baigent and Richard Leigh in *The Temple and the Lodge* (1989), 'with the sole exception of the Papacy'.

In England the Knights Templar enjoyed favourable and close rapport with the monarchy. Henry I embraced the knights warmly. His successor, the usurper Stephen of Blois, had been active in the Crusades and furthered the relationship with the Knights Templar because of their association with the Holy Land. Indeed he encouraged the proliferation of preceptories (subordinate communities of the Order) across England.

Henry II, who came to the throne in 1154, maintained the close association; but the closest of all relationships was with Henry's son, Richard Cœur de Lion (Richard the Lionheart, 1157–99). Indeed several authors have commented that Richard was secretly a Templar, or was at least treated as an honorary member of their number, so much respect did they have for him. On his death in 1199 his arch rival and brother John took the throne and continued the close relationship.

The Order was exempt from taxes in England, had its own courts, was allowed to grant right of sanctuary in the same way as a church, had its own markets and fairs and was represented in Parliament. The powerful financial and political power given to the Knights Templar allowed it to effectively establish the formula of modern banking. The Templars regularly moved money and supplies from Europe to Palestine and developed an efficient banking system which became used by the rulers and nobility of all of Europe. Ultimately the Knights became bankers for most of Europe and inevitably amassed even greater wealth. Over time the English monarchy became deeply in debt to the Order. Henry III, at one time, even pawned the English crown jewels to the Templars.

It was part of their banking system which produced the first 'secret code' of the Templars. Rather than carry money which could be stolen by highwaymen the Templars devised a system of carrying specially constructed IOUs or letters of credit. Money could be deposited in one area, the IOU transported to another part of the world and 'cashed in' locally. In order to prevent the IOUs from being stolen they were given a series of elaborate codes to which only the Templars had access.

Inevitably in their 200-year existence the wealth and power of the Templars created enemies. But of all their enemies no one proved as formidable as Philippe IV of France (1268–1314). His ambition was matched only by his ruthlessness, probably best demonstrated by the fact that he single-handledly split the Papacy asunder and divided the Catholic Church for nearly seventy years.

Philippe had sought direct control of the Papacy and in order to achieve this arranged the kidnapping of Pope Boniface VIII and almost certainly arranged the murder of his successor, Pope Benedict XI. Conflict arose when Philippe imposed levies on the church to finance his armies and Boniface responded with a Papal Bull forbidding the collection of taxes from the clergy without Papal consent. Philippe retaliated by forbidding the transfer of gold or currency to Rome and Boniface withdrew. Later Boniface issued a further Bull accusing Philippe of exceeding his royal powers when the king had accused a French bishop of treason and imprisoned him. Philippe announced his intention of deposing Boniface and the Pope responded by threatening to excommunicate Philippe. Ultimately the Pope was kidnapped and held prisoner at Anagni and died three weeks after his release from the mistreatment he had suffered during captivity. In 1305, following the murder of Benedict XI, Philippe installed on the Papal throne the former Archbishop of Bordeaux as Pope Clement V. He created a seat for the Papacy in Avignon in France where it remained until 1377.

Once he had dealt with the Papacy, Philippe moved against the Knights Templar; he feared their military strength, he envied their wealth and he resented the fact that they had not admitted him into the order even as an honorary member. Furthermore, he believed that they were preparing to set up a virtually independent state within France which would deprive him of part of his country and place a religious order theoretically more powerful than 'his' Papacy very near to home.

He produced a list of charges gleaned from spies he had managed to infiltrate into the Order, and then drew up arrest warrants and seizure orders which were distributed to authorities all around the country, sealed. At an appointed moment all sets of orders were to be opened simultaneously and immediately acted upon. In dawn raids on Friday 13 October 1307 the king sought to arrest every Knight Templar in France, to occupy their properties and to confiscate their wealth. In one sense the raid was successful in that it effectively destroyed the Knights Templar as a force. But from Philippe's point of view success was only partial. The Templars had been tipped off and had managed to secrete their wealth away. Prior to the raid many of the Order's most secret documents were destroyed by the Grand Master. A group of Templars dealing with the Order's treasury escaped and the Preceptor (head of the Order) of France took a fleet of eighteen galleys to sea presumably containing a great deal of Templar wealth. The location of the galleys was not discovered then and indeed has never been; nor has the vast Templar wealth ever been found.

Because the Knights Templar are removed from us by seven centuries it is difficult to describe the impact that Philippe's virtually instantaneous destruction of them produced. Considering that they were established over two centuries and across most of the known world as a powerful, wealthy and respected religious order then the analogy that has been offered by Baigent and Leigh in *The Temple and the Lodge* is reasonable: that it was similar to us in the modern day watching the destruction of the Papacy and the Catholic Church from greatness to nothingness in just a short spread of years.

Under extreme torture captured Templars confessed to a wide range of strange practices, many of which were almost certainly trumped up, falsified or at best confessed to only to satisfy the accusers. Since the Templars had no interest in promoting the detail of their rituals and secrets and since Philippe had every motive in promoting his extracted confessions we probably have a very distorted view of the Templars coming down to us through history as the majority of recorded accounts of their so-called activities are from those confessions extracted under torture.

It is from these confessions that we hear that the Templars worshipped the demonic 'Baphomet', and that they rejected Christ, regularly spitting on the cross. While it seems true that the Knights Templar had become immersed in Middle Eastern philosophy and religion, and it is believed that they sought to reconcile Islam, Judaism and Christianity, it is evident that they maintained a respectful relationship with all three beliefs, which may have been regarded as heretical in conventional religious quarters. The general description of the Knights Templar as anti-Christian heretics is unlikely to be anything more than exaggeration.

However, the Templars knew the value of 'image' and they had promoted some of the stranger beliefs for their own ends. They had encouraged the widespread public perception that they possessed occult secrets; even that they were somehow 'more than human'. They had promoted the belief that they were the reincarnation of the army that brought down the walls of Jericho centuries before and they encouraged the popular belief that they were somehow custodians of the Holy Grail. They had promoted themselves as Magi, alchemists and sorcerers creating the awe which protected them but also engendering fear in their enemies. They knew the value of myth and they had promoted these beliefs knowing that they would gain fear and respect in equal measure, both of which were of use to them.

Over the next seven years the persecution and destruction of the Knights Templar spread out from France under the direction and authority of Philippe's 'tame Pope' and was furthered by the Inquisition (see below). Although some countries, such as England, attempted to resist or at least play down the persecution of the Knights Templar the pressure from Philippe and Avignon was too great. On 22 March 1312 the Order was dissolved by Papal decree. Two years later, in Paris, the Grand Master Jacques de Molay and the Preceptor of Normandy, Geoffroi de Charmay were roasted to death over a slow fire.

Around the world those Knights that survived did so by adapting. In Germany many entered the Knights Hospitalers or the Teutonic Order. In Spain they were brought into a new order created especially for them, Montesa. In Portugal they changed their name to the Knights of Christ and as such survived into the sixteenth century playing a significant part in history. The navigator Vasco da Gama, for example, was a Knight of Christ and it was under the Templars' flag that Columbus sailed to the New World. A large number of the Knights are alleged to have gone to Scotland, and possibly this was the destination of the fleet that fled France. Some commentators believe they assisted Robert the Bruce in the battle of Bannockburn in 1314 which effectively secured Scotland's independence for almost the next 300 years.

The Order of Knights Templar formed the blueprint for similar groups to follow. For example, in 1445 the French King Charles VII created the Scots Guard which was clearly based on, and indeed had many similarities to, the Order of the Templars.

And in 1540 the Spanish soldier-priest Ignatius Loyola deliberately modelled his own 'religious soldiers' on the Templars, forming what was to become the Society of Jesus, generally known as the Jesuits.

These Orders cannot claim direct descendency from the Knights Templar. However there remains a strong belief that there is a direct lineage from the Knights Templar to a modern day secret society. This is the Fraternal Order of Freemasons.

FREEMASONRY

Rather as the Knights Templar deliberately perpetuated a belief in their own mystical powers and true origins, so Freemasonry seems to enjoy the controversy that its own secrets and closed meetings generate. The origins of Freemasonry are obscure. Masonic myth takes the origin of the Freemasons back to the building of the Temple of Solomon in Jerusalem and therefore to the Old Testament of the Bible.

It is certainly probable that guilds, virtually trade unions, of stonemasons have existed throughout time as indeed they have done for many crafts. It is also inevitable that as stonemasonry would have been the primary craft involved in the building of cathedrals and churches there would have been religious overtone and belief. No doubt some of those masons will have seen themselves as undertaking 'God's work' just by virtue of the buildings they were constructing. The Freemasons themselves point to an English origin from the time of the Saxon King Athelstan (c. 895–939), which has no doubt some basis in truth as there was an extensive building programme during his reign evidenced by the constructions in York in particular. Another possible origin is believed to be that of the Comacine Masons, a college of architects based at Lake Como, in northern Italy. Again, this Masonic group is highly likely to have existed. In all of these strands we seem to be considering a guild of craftsmen with a trade to ply, albeit one that will have commanded enormous respect.

However, it is clear that in the early seventeenth century there was a new influx of recruits to the Guild of Masons, men described rather vaguely as 'of wealth or social status'. Basically they were the Hermeticists, alchemists and other occultists with particular beliefs who interwove their own learning and beliefs into that of the stone-cutters guilds. To examine this we must examine the Hermetic connotation of 'God as architect'. Renaissance Hermeticism treated architecture and the sacred geometry as a means of spiritual closeness to God and indeed of expressing tribute to God. Because Judaism and Islam forbid the making or worshipping of graven images, expression of worship through the form of buildings was very prominent. John Dee described architecture as 'an art whose essence is to be found in abstract principles of mathematical proportion and cosmic harmony'. The Franciscan friar Francesco Giorgi, a Hermeticist who brought together his interpretation of the Christian Cabbala, sacred geometry and Platonic and Pythagorean thinking, saw architecture as a harmonious link between microcosm and macrocosm, a fundamental principle of Hermeticism similar to the general theme of 'as above, so below'. Robert Fludd (1474–1637) is probably responsible for the architecture of the Globe Theatre which housed many of Shakespeare's plays and designed it on Hermetic principles. Thirteenth- and fourteenth-century art followed through this image depicting Christ or God as 'divine architect'. Illustrations would often show the figure of Christ or God holding an architect's compass. The architect's compass (known today as dividers) is one of the Three Great Lights in masonry, the others being the Volume of the Sacred Law and the Square; no Masonic lodge may meet unless these are present and displayed. Probably the earliest reference to the creator as 'Architect of the Universe' is in Plato's *Timaeus*.

Sir Christopher Wren (1632–1723) is believed to have been a Grand Master of Freemasonry from 1685. Certainly he was a member of the 'Invisible College' (a secret group of intellectuals formed during the Cromwellian Protectorate in the 1650s) and a founding member of The Royal Society, all of which emphasise his Hermetic interests. Of course, as one of the most famous architects in English history he is regarded by some as the most important link between the practical side of stone-cutting masonry and the Hermetic wisdom that was incorporated into Freemasonry.

Masonry became a centre for Hermetic and alchemical belief. The spiritual quests of the occultists became enmeshed with the work of the stonemasons in building temples and churches as objects of worship. God was being revered as an architect; the Architect of Humankind.

Candidates join the Freemasons as 'apprentices' which is the first degree of membership. The second degree is Fellowship, and the third is Master Mason. Each level has its working tools and tracing boards (visual aids which are used to illustrate the teachings of each degree). The tracing boards and tools are in effect aids to contemplative learning, setting out in symbolic representation the spiritual dimension of the Masonic quest in the same way as the Sephirothic Tree of the Cabbalists represented their learning journey to the spiritual (see page 32).

In the first degree the candidate is encouraged to learn about himself and his place in the world. This is as much a learning of his inner mind as the outer world. In the second degree he is beginning to enter 'the Temple'; learning more of himself such as about his morality, and the exercise of his free will. In the third degree he develops his spirituality. This involves going through a symbolic death in order to be reborn as a 'new and enlightenened person'.

One of the earliest references to Freemasonry occult knowledge is in the 1638 poem 'The Muses Threnodie' by the Scottish occultist and poet, Henry Adamson:

> For we be brethren of the Rosie Crosse;
> We have the Mason word, and second sight,
> Things for to come we can foretell aright ...

Slightly earlier is the entry in the Scottish Earl of Rothes' diary for 13 October 1637 where he refers to 'the Masone word'.

Four guilds, called lodges, united in London on 24 June 1717, forming a Grand Lodge which within six years became the Grand Lodge of England. This is the heart of Freemasonry around the world and it is recognised that all Grand Lodges have been derived from it in the years since.

There are many Masonic Rites which developed over the centuries of which only a small number of consequence survive today. Most important from the point of view of this study is the York Rite which was formed in the eighteenth century and which is currently described as holding the existing membership of the Knights Templar. But, as mentioned earlier, the legend of

Masonry goes back to the Old Testament and the building of King Solomon's Temple. Central to this belief and to some features of Masonic practice is the murder of Hiram Abiff.

Hiram Abiff, who was probably the king of Tyre at the time of Solomon (tenth century BC) was an expert in architecture – for which we can presumably infer 'architecture in praise of God'. Having been taught the principles of sacred geometry, directly from God, according to tradition, Hiram became a centrally important figure and architecture and sacred geometry became an important link to the divine.

It was Hiram who put together the huge manpower necessary to build the Temple. Some of the workforce, at least according to Masonic tradition, were free men paid for their work although most were slaves. The professionals were ranked in three levels: Apprentices, Fellows and Masters. Each level was given its 'code word' and a particular sign or handshake. Each worker would, when seeking his wages for his work, give his code word and make the appropriate handshake to indicate his rank and would then be paid at the correct rate. This would be the origin of the so-called secret handshake of the Freemasons. However, Hiram was murdered by members of the lower ranks who were attempting to extract from him the code word for the rank of Master so that they could use it to collect higher wages. The 'traditional' details of the murder all form part of Masonic ritual. Hiram had been blocked from leaving the Temple through the west door, was struck by three blows to the head, failed to leave by the north or south door and died at the east door. In a modern Freemasonry meeting the Master always leaves by the east door.

The murderers buried Hiram's body under a clump of acacia but it was discovered. The acacia is a much revered plant in Freemasonry. Hiram's body was then buried with great ceremony with all those present wearing white aprons and white gloves to show that they did not have the blood of their Master on them. At present day meetings of Masons the apron, now patterned with meaningful symbols and images, is worn ceremonially.

The impact of Freemasonry in the seventeenth century should

not be understated. Baigent and Leigh in *The Temple and the Lodge* suggest: 'Freemasonry was to act as a kind of adhesive, a binding agent which served to hold together, in a way that the Catholic Church no longer could, the diverse elements and components of a fragmenting world, a fragmenting world view.'

The reconciliation between stone-cutting and Hermetic wisdom was probably most emphasised by Scottish-born French writer Andrew Michael Ramsay (1686–1743), one of the leading individuals of Freemasonry in France. On 20 March 1737 he delivered a speech which became known afterwards as 'Ramsay's oration'. He stated:

> The word Freemason must therefore not be taken in a literal, gross, and material sense, as if our founders had been simple workers in stone, or merely curious geniuses who wished to perfect the arts. They were not only skilful architects, desirous of consecrating their talents and goods to the construction of material Temples; but also religious and warrior princes who designed to enlighten, edify, and protect the living Temples of the Most High.

The references to 'material Temples' and 'Temples of the Most High' come very close to pinpointing an origin from the Knights Templar, though to have been more specific might have been dangerous given the prevailing Catholic politics at the time in France. However, Ramsay's further contention that Freemasonry had begun in the Crusades probably came even more dangerously close to the Templars. He stated:

> At the time of the Crusades in Palestine many princes, lords and citizens associated themselves, and vowed to restore the Temple of the Christians in the Holy Land and to employ themselves in bringing back their architecture to its first institution. They agreed upon several ancient signs and symbolic words drawn from the well of religion in order to recognise themselves amongst the heathen and Saracens. These signs and words were only communicated to those who promised solemnly and even

sometimes at the foot of the altar, never to reveal them. This sacred promise was therefore not an execrable oath, as it has been called, but a respectable bond to unite Christians of all nationalities in one confraternity. Some time afterwards our Order formed an intimate union with the Knights of St John of Jerusalem. From that time our Lodges took the name of Lodges of St John.

As a final link in the chain Ramsay quite certainly linked the Freemasons and the Scots Guard, referring to: 'Those Scotsmen to whom the kings of France confided during many centuries ...'

Modern Day Distrust of Freemasonry

Freemasonry has always generated some opposition. Clearly there has been the opposition of the Roman Catholic Church though in fact in the present day there are many Catholics belonging to Lodges in Latin America and the Philippines. There has also been political opposition: for example, in the northern states of the United States of America the Anti-Masonic Party was formed which for years was regarded as the only serious opponent to the Democratic Party. There is a great deal of distrust based on the anonymity of Freemasons in public service. In England in February 1998 it was indicated that the Commons Home Affairs Select Committee intended to force Freemasons to name members who may have been involved in miscarriages of justice. The thinly veiled threat was that if this was not complied with their entire membership rolls would be forced into the public domain. This arose because the United Grand Lodge of England had, as reported in the *Mail on Sunday* of 15 February 1998: 'declined to reveal the names of policemen, judges, magistrates and journalists who may have figured in three high-profile cases'. These cases were the 'Birmingham Six' (a group of men falsely convicted of terrorist bombing), the activities of Deputy Chief Constable of Greater Manchester John Stalker, and the disbanding of the notorious West Midlands Regional Crime Squad. As reported by the newspaper, 'Since appearing before the committee last summer, the Masonic leadership has provided the numbers of members involved in the cases, but has persistently refused written requests to name names.' Just a few days later it was reported that the Home Secretary, Jack Straw, intended to set up a register of Freemasons working in the criminal justice system. It was suggested that existing judges would not be forced to admit their allegiances but that anyone joining the bench would have to disclose membership of any 'secret societies'. The basis of the fear would seem to be that police and criminals who were both members of Freemasonry would assist each other over and above the demands of the law. In an article in the *Daily Mail* of 18 February 1998 one example was given. 'Kenneth Noye, launderer of the Brink's-Mat bullion money, acquitted of the murder of a police officer in the grounds of his country estate and wanted for the M25 road rage killing, was certainly at one time a Mason. It is clearly a matter of public concern to know if policemen and judges consorted with him in his Lodge, too.'

We therefore have a clear chain of interwoven Hermetic and alchemical beliefs which have run through the secret Orders of the Knights Templar and the Freemasons. It is worth examining one further Order which arose from the same stem and to which we have already obliquely referred in quoting Henry Adamson's 1638 poem where he refers to 'Brethren of the Rosie Crosse': the Rosicrucians.

THE ROSICRUCIANS

The Rosicrucians, or the Order of the Rosy Cross, is probably the organisation with the most uncertain of origins. There is a school of thought which argues that Rosicrucianism dates back to 1489 BC. This theory is promoted by Harvey Spencer Lewis, the founder of the Ancient and Mystical Order of Rosae Crucis (AMORC) in the United States between 1909 and 1916. Although this is an extremely unlikely origin it is a foundation of Rosicrucian belief and it would be simplest to set out that belief first and then examine the likelier beginnings afterwards.

According to Lewis's proposals Rosicrucianism began with mystic scholars working under the direction of Pharaoh Thutmose III (1504–1450 BC) who demanded that their work be kept secret and referred to only as the Order of the Brotherhood. Thutmose's successors continued as Grand Masters of the Order through to Amenhotep IV (1372–54 BC), otherwise known as Akhnaton. Amenhotep is said to have built a temple for the Order in the shape of a cross at El Amarna in Egypt. During the reign of Amenhotep the Order flourished but when he died more conventional Egyptian religion was reinstated and the Order was restricted to the temple at El Amarna. It is said that from there its influence worked through the centuries passing on teachings to King Solomon, Plotinus, Pythagoras, Plato, Solon and Ammonius Saccas. The effective founder of Hermeticism, Hermes Trismegistus, is said to have served as a Grand Master. According to Lewis, Freemasonry dates back to when this Rosicrucian order taught the Masons how to build Solomon's Temple.

However, a more certain – and oddly enough equally mythical – origin for the Rosicrucians surrounds the person of Christian Rosenkreutz ('Rose Cross'). This story tells us that he was born in 1378 in Germany, and that at a young age he was sent to study humanities at a convent and later travelled through the Middle East learning the mixtures of magic and occult that proliferated there. In Spain he sought out the Moors who had a strong mystical tradition, but was rebuffed by them. He eventually returned to Germany and began the Rosicrucian Order. The order built its headquarters in 1409; it was known as the House of the Holy Spirit, or Spiritus Sanctum. Rosenkreutz died in 1484 at 106 years of age and was entombed in a special vault in the Spiritus Sanctum. It is said that the tomb was discovered, in 1604, resplendent with magical symbols, ritual objects, an artificial sun, and Rosenkreutz's body, perfectly preserved.

This story emerged around 1614 in Kassel, Germany in anonymously circulated pamphlets: The 'Fama Fraternitatis dess

Loblichen Ordens des Rosenkreutzes' and the 'Confessio Fraternitatis'. In 1616 a third pamphlet appeared, 'The Chemical Marriage of Christian Rosenkreutz' which was allegedly written by Rosenkreutz in 1459 and describes a wedding ceremony (not his own) surrounded by occult and alchemical symbolism and including the creation of Homunculi – magically created artificial human beings. These pamphlets sought out membership of the Rosicrucians but despite the number of people who applied to join the Order, none ever received a reply. It is now widely accepted that this story is mythical, and that all three pamphlets were the invention of a German Lutheran pastor, Johann Valentin Andrea (1586–1654).

In the early eighteenth century there were several books and manifestos published detailing the activities and beliefs of the Order of the Rosy Cross. They were often political or religious tracts, promotion of causes such as the support of the arts, the creation of universal brotherhood and the unification of Europe.

An origin of Rosicrucianism can be linked to Bohemia. The Emperor Charles IV (1316–78), whose court was held in Prague, was believed to be one of the originators; he has been described as the last Initiate ruler on a European throne.

The German town of Heidelberg was the main centre of Rosicrucianism in the seventeenth century and contains the castle used by the alchemist and Rosicrucian King Frederick V of Bohemia (1596–1632). Even the gardens are designed on Rosicrucian and Hermetic principles and they contain a bust of the figure regarded by many as the greatest Rosicrucian of all, Wolfgang von Goethe (Perhaps more cynically, some commentators have suggested that if Goethe had not publicized his belief in and membership of the Rosicrucian Order, the group would have died in obscurity).

Another leading Rosicrucian was almost certainly John Dee (see page 42) who spent a good deal of his time in Bohemia and was deeply immersed in the various beliefs which Rosicrucianism embraced.

From whatever dubious origins the Rosicrucians may or may not stem it is clear that a brotherhood of the Rosy Cross did indeed form from a group of those who had been deeply involved in Hermeticism and alchemy and whose numbers almost certainly included Roger Bacon, Agrippa, Paracelsus, René Descartes, Francis Bacon, Christopher Wren, Robert Fludd, Thomas Vaughan and Goethe. The descendants of that group have led to modern day Rosicrucianism. Rosicrucianism has always been concerned with alchemy, promotes stress-free healthy living, abstinence from meat, alcohol and tobacco and the promotion of self-healing through what can now be called holistic approaches.

In 1866 the English Societas Rosicruciana in Anglia was founded by Robert Wentworth Little. Prominent members of this society later formed part of the founding membership of the Order of the Golden Dawn (see below). Dr William Wynn Westcott, Supreme Magus, and his colleague, Samuel Liddell MacGregor Mathers, were influential in this development. They were alleged to correspond with Anna Sprengel in Nuremburg who furnished them with outlines of Rosicrucian rituals and authorised them to set up a temple in London. Many believe that Anna Sprengel was a figure of Westcott's imagination.

Rosicrucianism in England was largely concerned with Hermeticism and alchemy but in France its membership tended to be basically artists who, in strict Hermetic tradition, expressed their pathway to the occult secrets through their art. One of the leading figures in French Rosicrucianism was Joséphin Péladan. In 1885 he declared himself Grand Master of the Rose-Croix and three years later 'revived' (though in fact created) its *Ordre Kabbalistique de la Rose-Croix*. Péladan was an outrageous character who eventually took for himself the title 'Sar' (Syrian for king) and issued increasingly eccentric proclamations. Needless to say many members were disaffected and there was a general fracturing of Rosicrucianism in France into several smaller groups.

One of the most influential Rosicrucians was the Austrian social philosopher Rudolf Steiner (1861–1925) who said that Rosenkreutz 'felt it to be his mission to make it possible for every human being, no matter where he stands in modern life, to rise to spiritual height'. In 1906 Steiner was head of a Masonic Lodge called Mysteria Mystica Aeterna in Germany and interpreted Rosicrucianism through his own personal beliefs based on the esoteric theories of Goethe. Steiner believed that clairvoyance was the only pathway to higher knowledge and had a tendency to condemn all other Rosicrucians as charlatans.

All Rosicrucian groups have as their symbol a combination of the rose and the cross. The cross represents death, suffering and ultimate resurrection and of course derives its symbolism from the death of Jesus Christ; but it is sometimes shown in the shape of an *ankh*, reflecting the theory of an ancient Egyptian origin and a belief in reincarnation. The rose has always been the emblem of secrecy. According to Greek mythology Eros, the god of love, gave the rose to the god of silence. In Roman taverns there was usually a rose above the door to signify that anything said in the tavern in drunkenness must remain confidential. (This is the origin of the term *sub rosa*, or 'below the rose'). Some of the roses used by Rosicrucians are complex and deeply symbolic. For example some have twenty-two petals symbolising the twenty-two secret paths of Cabbalism.

Modern Rosicrucianism includes:

- AMORC founded by Harvey Spencer Lewis and based in San José, California where it houses the Rosicrucian Egyptian Museum and Art Gallery allegedly containing the largest collection of Egyptian, Babylonian and Syrian artefacts on the West Coast.

- The Rosicrucian Fellowship founded in 1909 at Oceanside, California by Max Heindel which houses a Temple of Healing, built to correspond to the zodiac. Members of this organisation actively promote spiritual healing and astrology.

- The English Societas Rosicruciana in Anglia which demands that members must be Freemasons.

- The Societas Rosicruciana in the United States founded in 1907 by Sylvester Gould.

- The Fraternitas Rosae Crucias, the first established in the United States founded in 1858 by Pascal Beverly Randolph which traces its ancestry back to the French occultist Eliphas Lévi.

THE HERMETIC ORDER OF THE GOLDEN DAWN

The Order was founded by two Rosicrucians, Samuel Liddell MacGregor Mathers and Dr William Wynn Westcott, and Dr William Robert Woodman in 1887. It was heavily promoted by the poet William Butler Yeats (1865–1939) who was very attracted to both it and the general occult and mystic traditions.

Mathers adopted the title Comte de Glenstrae indicating an alleged descent from a Scots clan. Mathers drew from the Cabbala, the Keys of Solomon and the writings of John Dee and with a small group of others, all Freemasons like himself, produced a document which was a basic instruction for occult rituals and the understanding of Cabbalistic wisdom. This document was the basis of the founding of the Hermetic Order of the Golden Dawn. The Order seems to have been at least in part an alternative to Madame Helena Blavatsky's Theosophical Society (see page 74); Mathers had settled permanently in London where she had her headquarters.

The Hermetic Order of the Golden Dawn was in effect supposed to be a branch of a Rosicrucian order in Germany based on documents relating to Anna Sprengel. However, it is probable that neither the Order there, nor Fräulein Sprengel, existed. The Order of the Golden Dawn attracted over a hundred members from England and Scotland and had a Lodge in Paris. Membership eventually embraced such notables as: Yeats; Aleister Crowley (see below); the Irish Nationalist Maud Gonne; Annie Horniman, tea heiress and the founder of the Abbey Theatre in Dublin; Florence Farr, mistress of both Yeats and George Bernard Shaw; Constance Wilde, wife of Oscar; Gerard Kelly, later President of the Royal Academy; and William Crookes, scientist and psychic researcher. It had a religious basis but soon moved more towards magic and indeed towards so-called black magic. In Paris, Mathers claimed he was in contact with 'the Secret Chiefs of the Third Order', supernatural beings, who shared with him the true meaning of the Tree of Knowledge and conferred on him Perpetual Head of the Order. Mathers believed these beings to be 'human and living upon this Earth; but possessing terrible superhuman powers'.

Mathers became increasingly authoritarian. The Order attracted figures who became controversial, such as Crowley and is held to have lost both purpose and direction. Yeats believed that the destruction of the Order resulted from a feud between Mathers and Crowley (who claimed to have released forty-nine demons against Mathers).

Crowley had been initiated into the Outer Order in 1898 and now sought initiation into the Second Order in London, but this was rejected. Crowley therefore appealed to Mathers in Paris to initiate him, which he did. The London members of the Order expelled both Mathers and Crowley (and a few others of dubious loyalty) leaving themselves without a chief, a vacuum which was quickly filled by Yeats. He became imperator of the Outer Order's Isus-Urania Temple. He maintained a peace of sorts for around a year but then resigned in February 1901, although he maintained membership of one of its offshoots, the Order of the Morning Star (Stella Matutina) until 1923.

Other difficulties had arisen with Annie Horniman, the daughter of a rich tea importer who had been a member of the Golden Dawn since January 1890. She had provided a great deal of financial support for the Order and her disputing the authority of Mathers had caused the first most severe fracture in the order. There has even been the suggestion that Annie Horniman and Mathers' wife, Mina, either enjoyed a lesbian relationship or that tensions were caused by their unconscious recognition of their attraction to each other.

A. E. Waite (an enthusiastic Freemason) took control of the Hermetic Order of the Golden Dawn in 1903 and retitled it the Holy Order of the Golden Dawn, replacing the Egyptian heritage with Christian writings and discouraging the practice of magic. It did not attract great attention and Waite ended it in 1914.

ALEISTER CROWLEY

Having mentioned his rather destructive role in the Hermetic Order of the Golden Dawn it is worth examining the life of this extraordinary character once dubbed by the media 'The Wickedest Man in the World'.

Crowley started his life in occult groups as a member of the Hermetic Order of the Golden Dawn but quickly took a quite different path from its original object and styled himself the Great Beast (or Beast of the Apocalypse) after the horned monster from the Bible's Book of Revelations.

He was born into a wealthy and religious family in 1874. His father made a fortune in the ale business and then became a preacher in the Plymouth Brethren, a strict Christian sect. Crowley's father died when Crowley was eleven and almost immediately the son turned away from the Bible to the darker side of magic.

Some of the writings of the Hermetic Order of the Golden Dawn indicated that a period of seclusion and purification was required in order to devote the proper energies to magic and Crowley sought out Boleskin House on the shores of Loch Ness in Scotland as the site of his seclusion. He adopted the title Lord Boleskin for the duration, one of many impressive titles he gave himself in life including Count and Prince. In addition, he claimed to have had various previous lives including as Count Cagliostro, Pope Alexander VI, Edward Kelley (assistant to John Dee), Eliphas Lévi (who died on the day Crowley was born) and an Egyptian priest of the 26th Dynasty, Ankh-F-N-Khonsu.

During this time Crowley claimed to have conjured up demons. He described his workroom as becoming so dark even on bright, sunlit days that he could only work with the lights on twenty-four hours. After his acrimonious divorce from the Hermetic Order of the Golden Dawn, he travelled to Cairo. There he saw a depiction of the falcon-headed Horus, the Egyptian sun god, bearing the number 666 – the number of the Beast. He was fiercely attracted to the image. While in Cairo 'a messenger from the forces ruling the Earth at present' came to him and gave Crowley the philosophy with which he was later to dominate his life: 'do what thou wilt shall be the whole of the law'. This no doubt justified Crowley's appetite for drugs, sex and almost every other indulgence. He did, however, insist that the true meaning of this phrase was not to do as you please but rather to 'do what you have to do, and nothing more'. (This would seem to be more related to the Taoist belief of letting events take their own course without interference).

Throughout Europe and later in America Crowley pursued activities of magical and sexual sadism. He appears to have been astonishingly charismatic. He filed his teeth to sharpened points and would bite his disciples. He founded the Order of the Silver Star and called himself Magus, the master magician.

In his writings he insisted on spelling magic 'magick' to distinguish it from what he believed was just stage magic. He added the 'k' from the first letter of *kteis*, the Greek word for the female genitals.

During the First World War Crowley lived in the United States writing anti-British propaganda for the Germans. In 1916, living in New Hampshire, he affirmed the title of Magus through a ceremony of his own design, baptised a frog as Jesus Christ and then crucified it.

After the war he moved to Sicily and established a community there. There he spent his time in sexual abuse and heroin addiction and published a book, *The Diary of a Drug Fiend*. He also published a novel, *Moon Child*, in 1929 fictionalising his own accounts to create a child by magic. The final straw came when police broke up the community following the death of one of the followers of Crowley, apparently poisoned after drinking the blood of a ritually-killed cat. Crowley was evicted from the villa and expelled from Italy by Mussolini.

In 1934 he sued the sculptress Nina Hammett for libel because she had stated in her biography of him that he practised black magic and indulged in human sacrifice. The testimony at the trial was so repulsive that the judge apparently stopped the trial and found in favour of Hammett.

In his later years he met Gerald Gardner, recognised by many as the father of modern witchcraft (see page 104). Crowley died in 1947 and was cremated in Brighton, having virtually returned to the place of his origins. At his funeral service a sexual poem written by him, 'Hymn to Pan', was read out which so disgusted the Brighton Council that they passed local laws to ensure it could never happen again.

DION FORTUNE

Another seeker of occult wisdom who has had an influence on the way we perceive the history of the occult is Dion Fortune. She also had links with the Hermetic Order of the Golden Dawn. Her lifelong interest in the paranormal allegedly arose due to her contact with the teachings of the Christian Scientist Mary Baker Eddy (1821–1910).

Fortune was born Violet Mary Firth in 1891 near Llandudno, Wales. Her family were Christian scientists. She adopted the name Dion Fortune from her family motto *Dio non Fortuna* (which means 'by God, not by chance'). From an early age she was very interested in the spiritual. At the age of four she had visions of the drowned city of Atlantis and she later came to believe she had lived there in a past life as a temple priestess.

At the age of twenty Fortune believed she had been the target of a curse. She was convinced that the principal of the educational institution in which she worked, who was known for her developed abilities in yoga, had turned the yoga energies into a malign and destructive force targeted at Fortune herself. It was a life-changing event. 'It was this experience which led me to take up the study of analytical psychology, and subsquently of occultism', she wrote. She became a psychologist and indeed wrote several books on the subject but came to the conclusion that psychology could not explain all the facets of the human mind and sought the remaining answers in the occult. She was briefly involved with a Theosophical movement but left it believing it was foolish. She did, however, believe in the existence of the Masters, not in the flesh as Theosophy would have it but on the 'inner planes'. She joined an off-shoot of the Hermetic Order of the Golden Dawn, the Stella Matutina, and only after her initiation did she believe that the psychic attack by her former employer was finally repelled and cured.

However, she soon fell out with Mina Mathers. Dion Fortune reported that she and Mrs Mathers engaged in a psychic and magical battle. She was plagued by an infestation of tomcats and found that her enemy had taken the form of a gigantic tabby cat on the astral plane. It became her mission to create a way in which she could help others to be protected from the same fate. In 1930 she published a book *Psychic Self Defence*. She became adept at scrying (divination by crystal gazing), out of body travel and well versed in the Cabbala.

Although her attitude towards the occult was benevolent she once accidentally almost invoked the forces of evil. While resting and thinking of a person who she felt had done her harm she became angry and resentful. Then,

there came to my mind the thought of casting off of all restraint and going berserk. The ancient Nordic myths rose before me, and I thought of Fenris, the Wolf horror of the North. Immediately I felt a curious drawing-out sensation from my solar plexus, and there materialised beside me on the bed a large wolf ... I could distinctly feel its back pressing against me as it lay beside me. ... I knew nothing of the art of making elementals at the time, but had accidentally stumbled upon the right method – the brooding highly charged with emotion, the invocation of the appropriate natural force, and the condition between sleeping and waking in which the etheric double readily extrudes.

Having released this creature into the world she felt she had done wrong and sought out a mentor – many believed this was probably Aleister Crowley – for advice. She was told to reabsorb the creature which could only happen if she was able to forgive the person who had done her harm.

Fortune recognised this as a defining moment in her life. 'I had enough sense to see that I was at the dividing of the ways, and if I were not careful would take the first step on the Left-Hand path.' She recalled the wolf and reabsorbed it. 'The tension relaxed, and I found myself bathed in perspiration'. For the remainder of her life she devoted herself to avoiding evil and following the path of research.

Prior to the First World War she had a dream in which she believed she met two of the Masters, Jesus and the Comte de St Germain, and that she was accepted as a pupil by Jesus. She was granted a vision of her past lives which amounted to an unbroken line of priestesses from Atlantis to her present life. She believed that she was able to remember everything she had ever learned in all her lives.

Late in life, in 1924, she formed the Fraternity of the Inner Light, devoted to esoteric Christianity. It was originally a part of the Order of the Golden Dawn but became independent after the breach with Mina Mathers. Fortune was one of the first people in the West to explain the interaction of the *chakras* which are a basic part of Eastern philosophy.

In the winter of 1923 Dion Fortune went to Glastonbury and contacted three more Masters; Socrates, Lord Erskine, who she believed was a reincarnation of Thomas Moore and David Carstairs, a young officer killed at Ypres in the First World War. Throughout her life Fortune periodically returned to Glastonbury and immersed herself in Arthurian legend. She also believed she came in contact with another Master, Merlin.

In addition to the Fraternity of the Inner Light, Dion Fortune ran the Challis Orchard Club, a pilgrimage centre in Glastonbury and founded the Belfry, a temple in London dedicated to Isis. After her death in 1946 it is alleged that she continued to run the Lodge through mediums but was eventually banished by magical ritual as she was deemed no longer necessary.

Dion Fortune is often regarded as having been a witch and is certainly popular in modern witchcraft. However, the Society of the Inner Light (into which the Fraternity of the Inner Light transformed) always maintained that Fortune was not a witch and that the Society was never connected with witchcraft.

MADAME HELENA PETROVNA BLAVATSKY

Madame Helena Blavatsky is one of the modern occultists who helped form the modern image of the quest for hidden knowledge.

Blavatsky was born Helena Hahn in 1831 in Ekaterinoslav, Russia, the daughter of an Army colonel. Like many of the leading figures in the occult she was rebellious from an early age. At seventeen she married an older man, a Russian government official but took off on a world tour before, so she claimed, the marriage was even consummated. She travelled through India, Canada, Mexico and Tibet. In Tibet she had to disguise herself as a man as she would have been forbidden to travel as a lone woman. The years between 1848 and 1858 were spent, she claimed, in an unspecified Himalayan retreat learning from Eastern spiritual masters, although there is no documentary evidence of this. She claimed that her magic powers came from the Mahatmas of Tibet (Mahatma means 'Great Soul') and the Egyptian goddess Isis.

In 1871 Madame Blavatsky went to Cairo where she formed the Société Spirite for occult phenomena along with Emma Coulomb but this was shut down after clients alleged fraud.

After her travels around the world she returned to her native Russia and practised as a medium and later travelled to the United States where she became part of the spiritualist movement that was begun by the Fox sisters (Maggie, Katie and Leah) in

1848. Within a short period, along with William Judge, an American attorney, and Colonel Henry Steel Alcott, she was able to found the Theosophical Society which has endured to the present day.

The basis of Theosophy was, Blavatsky maintained, drawn from the Cabbala, from Hinduism, Buddhism and western occult tradition. Its objectives were to form a universal brotherhood of Man, to study the ancient religions and philosophies and to investigate the laws of nature and the powers inherent in the human mind, body and spirit. In effect then the Theosophical Society was designed to further the seventeenth century Rosicrucian beliefs of reconciling science and religion through the investigation of human ability.

As Richard Cavendish states in *A History of Magic*, 'In the history of magic, as distinct from the wider area of occultism, the Theosophical Society's importance lies in the stimulus which it gave to magicians, many of whom joined it and left it again.' In 1877 Blavatsky wrote her first book *Isis Unveiled*, claiming that it was 'a plea for the recognition of the Hermetic philosophy, the ancient universal wisdom'. In her book *The Secret Doctrine* she maintained that all religions came from one source, a truth which was only fully understood by the Tibetan Mahatmas with whom she maintained a psychic link.

In 1878 Madame Blavatsky became the first Russian woman to acquire US citizenship; she apparently took the step in order to prevent the English in India thinking she was a Russian spy. Following this she left for India to study Hindu and Buddhist religions.

Madame Blavatsky and those around her were impressed by the influence of astrology. Alan Leo (William Frederick Allen), arguably the most successful of British astrologers, joined the society in 1890 and promoted astrology through the Theosophical Society as a way of relating to the true nature of man and the Universe. He was, amongst other things, the pioneer of the mass produced horoscope.

Blavatsky's attraction was at times somewhat showman-like and often consisted of the generation of apports (objects made to appear as if by magical means) not dissimilar to those claims more recently related to Sai Baba. There is an interesting story which arose at a dinner party. She had previously claimed that during a picnic she made a cup and saucer appear in her hand 'miraculously'. Two men at a dinner party poured scorn on the claim and Madame Blavatsky became very angry. She turned to the hostess and asked her to imagine something that she really wanted; the hostess mentioned a brooch she had lost years before. Blavatsky told her to envisage it as clearly as she could. Then she told the guests to go to a flower bed outside claiming that her Mahatmas had now deposited the brooch therein. After digging, the brooch was found.

She came to believe, from her spirit guides, that the world was inhabited by seven 'root races'. The first, invisible, inhabited the North Pole. The second lived in Northern Asia and are alleged to have invented sexual intercourse. The third were large ape-like creatures who occupied a lost island in the Pacific called Lemuria. They communicated by telepathy. The fourth were the occupants of Atlantis which Blavatsky maintained had been destroyed by black magic. The humans – as we know them today – were the fifth and will apparently be replaced by a race that will once again populate Lemuria. The seventh and last race will take over when the Lemurians die.

Blavatsky died at the Theosophical headquarters in London in May 1891. After her cremation one-third of her ashes stayed in Europe, one-third went to the United States and one-third went to India where they were scattered on the Ganges.

In 1884 Richard Hodgson of the Society for Psychical Research in London investigated her household in Adyar near Madras. He had been alerted to claims of paranormal phenomena there and produced a scathing report alleging fraud and trickery. It was over 100 years later, in 1986, when the SPR published an article admitting that they believed the report was prejudiced and that Hodgson had ignored favourable evidence.

Madame Blavatsky, like so many leaders in the occult, was somewhat eccentric. Her eccentricity was probably best summed up by W. E. Henry who said: 'Of course she gets up to fraudulent miracles, but a person of genius has to do something; Sarah Bernhardt sleeps in her coffin.'

GEORGEI IVANOVITCH GURDJIEFF

The last of the principal players in the occult to be examined here is Georgei Ivanovitch Gurdjieff. Gurdjieff was born in 1847 at Alexandropol (now Gyumri) in Armenia, near the Turkish border. He came from Greek stock who had lived for a time in Turkey before moving to Armenia.

At a young age Gurdjieff left home and was absent for a period of some twenty years during which he seems to have toured Asia, Europe and Africa. It appears he visted Tibet, the centre of Asia, India, Arabia and Egypt. He studied hypnosis and yoga and eventually returned to his home with the basics of the occult system that was to drive him for the remainder of his life. The fascination for his followers no doubt lay in his apparent reconciliation of 'West' and 'East'. He had been brought up in the Western ways, read books on medicine, neuro-pathology and mechanics and used the language of Western science to explain his beliefs about the nature of man and the Universe. In Moscow in 1912 he began collecting followers and a group was set up with the assistance of a Finnish mental health specialist, Dr de Stjoernval in St Petersburg. Gurdjieff was soon to meet a most important disciple, Peter Demianovitch Ouspensky (1878–1947). Ouspensky had been influenced by theosophical work and was seeking a teaching that would satisfy his questionings. Ouspensky found in Gurdjieff exactly the kinds of answers he had been seeking.

The basis of Gurdjieff's system is that man is asleep and must be woken up. He is not just a creature of habit but he is actually a machine subject to mechanical laws. The man who seeks to be enlightened or aware must wake himself up, become master of himself and learn how to alter the laws so as to affect himself. This is done by self-observation and self-remembering. Man as a machine does not possess a soul. Gurdjieff believed that by intense work on himself he could create something akin to one. He called the system the fourth way or 'the way of the cunning man'. The fourth way indicated that it was an alternative to the other three, the ways of the fakir, the monk and the yogi.

In many ways Gurdjieff's beliefs were the basis of much of the so-called New Age and New Age language. For example, when we speak of negative energies or negative people it is based on Gurdjieff's belief and writings in the doctrine of negative emotion. In the 1960s Gurdjieff's legacy continued in the hippie movements and other alternative cultures. Indeed in many ways his thinking permeates the present day. Modern day shamans bringing the teachings of North and South American Indians and other non-technological cultures to the West use similar terms when they describe awakenings. They refer to the fact that you cannot enter an altered state until you leave the one you are already in, in effect that all states are some kind of altered state; it appears Gurdjieff had views similar but expressed differently.

Gurdjieff died in 1949 but it is probably significant that his most powerful book *Meetings with Remarkable Men* came out posthumously in 1960 and had significant influence in triggering the youth revolution and bringing many of the ancient mystical traditions directly into the 'New Age' in which we are still presently living.

2

WITCHCRAFT AND MAGIC

To attain the sanctum regnum, in other words, the knowledge and power of the Magi, there are four indispensable conditions – an intelligence illuminated by study, an intrepidity which nothing can trick, a will which nothing can break, and a discretion which nothing can corrupt and nothing intoxicate. TO KNOW, TO DARE, TO WILL, TO KEEP SILENCE – such are the four words of the Magus.

This was the description of the essential qualities of those pursuing the occult given by Eliphas Lévi (born Alphonse Louis Constant) in his 1855 publication *The Doctrine and Ritual of Magic*. Lévi has himself been referred to as the last of the Magi.

The Magi were originally a priestly order in ancient Persia. They were the followers of Zarathushtra (Zoroaster), prophet of the Parsee religion. Religion and rituals of the Magi eventually incorporated Babylonian rituals, astrology, demonology and magic. Indeed the word magic is derived from Magi. By the first century AD the Magi were regarded as wise men and it is believed that three of their number were the 'three wise men' who came from the East to worship Jesus at the time of his birth. The three Magi – Caspar, Melchior and Balthasar – are held to have travelled to Bethlehem and been converted from their pagan religion to Christianity. Legend has it that their remains are buried in Cologne Cathedral.

The Magi were known for their gift of prophecy and were consulted by the leaders of the known world on religious and political matters. Theirs was the search for truth and the quest

81

for the divine, symbolised by the building of their temples on the highest peaks, i.e. near to God.

As the so-called civilised world grew bigger so the influence of the Magi migrated reaching the West with variances that included the Jewish Cabbala and early Christian theology. Magicians of the West gradually developed a combination of alchemy, astrology, divination, metaphysics and more.

The sixteeth-century magician Agrippa (Heinrich Cornelius Agrippa von Nettesheim) described the Magus as an individual 'who has cohabited with the elements, vanquished Nature, mounted higher than the heavens, elevating himself to the archetype itself with whom he then becomes co-operator and can do all things.' The Magus sought to call down divine power from above and project the energies beyond himself to influence the action of others. As such therefore the Magus channelled divine energy into the physical world.

We might think of the Magus as magician; perhaps Merlin is the classical 'image', and in the modern day that magic is worked by the group we call witches.

THE HISTORY OF WITCHES AND WITCHCRAFT

Who was the first witch? When did witchcraft begin? These are frequently asked questions, impossible to answer. The history of witchcraft is not the history of a group or an Order such as the Knights Templar. Neither is it the history of a religion; its origins cannot be traced from a clear starting point and through an evolution, as can be done with, say, Christianity.

This is most clearly demonstrated when we consider the present day proponents of the Craft. There is no Supreme Witch. There is no single set of criteria to be a witch. There is no ruling or governing body which registers witches and 'de-frocks' them for inappropriate belief or behaviour. To be a witch is as near as can be to the sixties adage: 'do your own thing'.

But there are widely held views in the public domain about what people believe witches are, what they do, how they act. And they are mostly wrong and frankly, for the most part, based on the excesses of the tabloid media. To read the red-bannered 'Sundays' it would be easy to imagine that witches spend their evenings either dancing around naked, engaging in orgiastic behaviour or sacrificing children to the devil. Such prejudicial attitudes created disgraceful witchhunts and legalised murders in former times; today at least the worst they seem to create is an air of distrust or ridicule. There have also been landmark moments such as the repeal of the Witchcraft Act, and key figures who have shaped some aspects of modern witchcraft.

The history of witchcraft will, therefore, be at least two histories somewhat intertwined. One is the history of a belief system. The other is the history of a political expedient pursued for power and greed.

So who *was* the first witch? When did witchcraft begin? Picture a lone figure sitting in the barren and dry veldt near the equator that would one day be called Africa. Somewhere between seven million and twenty million years ago, the primitive ancestors of humankind were widely distributed on the African and, later, Eurasian continents. Somewhere along the line they acquired the beginnings of what we regard as humanity; they started to become recognisable as human beings. During that evolution there came a time, probably quite early on, when they believed they could influence their own environment. They developed tools, created shelters, formed into groups with social structures and established farming practices.

They were essentially creatures of nature; dependent on nature for food, for warmth and for safety. During the warm seasons they probably fared better than during the cold. They might occasionally be devastated by flooding or volcanic activity. During the night they were probably more vulnerable to animal predators than during the day; the night became a time of terror, or at least of caution. When they learned to farm and harvest they recognised that their crops were sometimes better than at other times. Sensibly, they sought to control their environment so that they could better guarantee their survival. Some of that effort went into technology – developing better tools and even weapons. Some went into learning better farming practices, better hunting tactics. But some of it looked towards the gods.

It is a fact, for whatever reason, that we know of no culture that has ever existed, or exists today, which does not have some belief in what we might loosely label the supernatural: a belief in gods, in a realm such as heaven, and in powers greater than humanity. We do not really know why that should be the case, although there are many reasonable assumptions. One is that it gives us someone to depend on when we are in need – 'there are no atheists on a sinking ship' as someone once said. Perhaps it also gives us someone to blame rather than ourselves when things do not go well. It offers hope; if we are unhappy with our lot on Earth at least there is something better to come later. It offers salvation; if the Earth were truly in trouble our gods would come down from the skies and save us. (Nor have we changed much in this regard over the last few million years; take a look at some of the beliefs currently held about UFOs and Alien Visitation!) But let us not be overly cynical; for every culture to have developed such beliefs suggests at least one other possible reason, that the so-called supernatural exists. In fact, whether it does or does not, whether gods and heaven or reincarnation or aliens actually exist is less important than the fact that there is a widespread belief that 'something' does. Humanity is largely shaped by belief, not by objective reality, even if that could be defined.

And so inevitably some of our lone figures sitting in the veldt looked around them and wondered if there was something else that could be done to better their conditions. If these gods existed then perhaps they could be appealed to for assistance. If nature had 'intelligence' then perhaps it can be persuaded to use it to the benefit of the tribe. Was there some way to 'make contact' with the gods? Was there a particular set of rules – rituals – that should be gone through to bring positive influence on the tribe's conditions? So somewhere in a tribe in the far distant past was the first witch, the first person who started on the road to believing that they might be able to gain the positive influence of the gods. And in the same moment is the birth of magic; the belief that certain rituals and approaches can bring about change.

Witchcraft therefore describes the principal vehicle for magic; the power to bring about change by the exercise of will, employing supernatural means.

In this we have also the beginning of mythology. Not in the sense we tend to use it today of something that is 'unreal', but rather in the sense of a way of defining the inner, deeper, belief systems of a society and culture. It is mythology, not reality, that defines every culture. Even when we take a product of science such as the atomic bomb, it is our beliefs which dictate whether we will or will not use it: its availability for use is far more significant than its actual use. As Richard Cavendish in *Mythology: an Illustrated Encyclopedia* (1987) says: 'Myths are the imaginative traditions about the nature, history and destiny of the world, the gods, man and society.' Myths allow a people to express their beliefs, to impose and justify behaviour and to weave a social structure. They allow a people to understand the importance of customs and values.

And in competitive societies struggling for survival where it is believed that gaining the gods' influence is seminal, then it would follow that the society that had the most effective rituals, the society that could arrange the most favourable influences, or the society that is 'closest' to the gods, would be the winner.

So from the very earliest times, the society with the best spiritual leaders believed themselves to be potentially the best-surviving culture. (Neither has that attitude changed over time both the Allied and Axis powers in the Second World War believed that they were the most favoured by God in their 'crusades'.) These early leaders we would probably call shamans, witch-doctors or medicine-men, but essentially they were the first witches.

The shaman uses a variety of techniques, drugs, rhythmic drum-beating and so on to enter an altered state which enables him or her to commune with the gods, or to enter the gods' realm. This is the basis of the spiritual leadership of their group. It is the same with what we today call witches; various rituals and techniques are used to commune with the gods.

In this scenario we also see the beginning of religion, but there is a difference. Religion implies the existence of a god or gods to whom people will pray, seeking divine intervention. Witches do not plead to their gods to intervene but seek magical power to bring about changes themselves. They seek to 'tap into' the natural powers around the Earth. The witch therefore does not merely call for assistance but brings about change personally. To the extent that witches, with the use of rituals, acquire supernatural skills, there is an overlap with sorcery and magic.

If we come much further towards the present day in time we find that most communities had a 'wise woman' or 'wise man' who represented this tradition. They would practise spells and incantations, they would engage in divination for local people, especially for the local farmers, and they would be sought to ward off evil or unexplainable illness. They were probably regarded as a 'bit strange' and no doubt formed the basis of some local prejudice, but in the main there is every evidence that prior to the 'witchhunt' days they were accepted with little concern or fear. They provided a focus for the community and no doubt served a purpose of being one of many central figures for cohesion similar to the local community hall, the village green and pond, or the local church.

And we can trace such figures up to the present day. Even in our hi-tech lives there are similar people, and many of them actually describe themselves as witches. But whether or not they are – and we shall look at modern witchcraft later – they perform that function. They offer 'counselling' that is akin to spiritual advice rather than the 'mainstream' advice of the church. Many work within the professions of 'alternative' or 'complementary' healing – aromatherapists, reflexologists, stress counsellors and so on – and while some might balk at the idea of being regarded as 'witches' many use the term quite specifically. How appropriate or inappropriate the term might be we shall see later.

There is a widespread belief that witches co-operate with each other, act as a group and meet in secret covens or other groupings, usually at night. To some extent this is true. Ancient beliefs about witches included the conviction that they could fly – traditionally on brooms – a belief that was prevalent in tribal Africa, Asia, America and throughout Europe.

The earliest records of witchcraft in Europe, constructed from diverse writings of the Greeks and Romans and a variety of fiction often orally transmitted through the generations, show two separate traditions.

The shamanic tradition already mentioned was particularly prevalent in the far north, from Iceland to Russia. The shaman travelled – presumably 'out-of-body' – to the world of the spirits. The shaman were usually, though not always, male. Further south witches learned magic and divination, undertook spiritual healing, and learned how to work magic with a series of rituals. Most witches, again not all, were women.

Because witchcraft was relied on as a powerful tool for a community the witch was expected to 'win' for the tribe. A witch that could not bring about the right results in the harvest, or the right types of weather, was a liability. Across Europe, in pagan times, witches were regularly punished or executed for their failures. It was the coming of Christianity which ended such sacrifices with the simple logic that if the one, omnipresent, omnipotent God was responsible for the world, and all that happened within it, then witches were not effective, and must have been deluding themselves and their communities. Hence, they were no longer a threat and could be safely ignored by God-fearing Christians.

The Witchhunts

During the late Middle Ages a sea change occurred in Christianity. While the early concept had been that God was a Master in control of everything, the change made room for the belief that the Devil had been allowed by God to test humans, to offer them free will. Therefore humans could become followers of the Devil, and devout followers of Christianity sought to weed out those who chose this path. It was decreed that witches had chosen to serve the Devil, indeed had made a pact with him. Witches therefore had enormous powers, and it took equal power of God-fearing Christians to do battle and defeat the forces of evil.

The truth is, however, that while some no doubt held this view sincerely, for the most part it was a political expediency subscribed to by an acquisitive and greedy Church that sought to establish itself as the most powerful political force in the world. In order to defeat enemies it had to have enemies; what better than the servants of Satan. In order to unify the devout there needed to be an enemy, and the easiest target was a sub-section of the community; these strange and generally harmless women practising as witches. (It happened again in America in the 1950s when America needed an enemy to replace those defeated in the Second World War; they chose to root out Communists. Not for nothing, and very appropriately, was this called a 'witchhunt'; the similarities were disgracefully clear.) Lastly, to control a community the established powers needed to control the thoughts of others; a tenet well explored in George Orwell's novel 1984. So the witchhunts were prepared to persecute not only those who claimed to be witches, but those who were accused of being witches on often the flimsiest evidence. The reason was clear; people were being moulded and forced into the Christian tradition and even to suggest any other belief was not allowed.

Witchcraft was never the same thing as Satanism; but for the medieval witchhunt the two became temporarily synonymous. The huge division in religion, philosophy and learning that we have since come to call the Reformation (begun in 1517 by Martin Luther) shook the very foundations of the Church. It fought back, believing, or claiming at least to believe, that the Reformation was a sign that Satan had 'pulled the stops out' and was seeking world domination. Christianity embarked on a purification crusade. And witches were to be the example set to those who wavered in their beliefs.

The Inquisition

The Inquisition was a judicial body created during the Middle Ages by the Papacy with a view to locating and bringing to trial anyone thought guilty of the crime of heresy. Heresy refers to any view which is contrary to mainstream belief; in this case anyone who believed anything other than that preached by Rome. If found guilty the usual punishment was excommunication from the Roman Catholic Church, i.e. exclusion from the Church.

The origin of the Inquisition is in Pope Innocent III's crusade against the Albigenses of southern France, regarded by many as the most important single group of heretics during the Middle Ages. They were dualists who believed in two gods, one of good, usually associated with Jesus and the God of the New Testament, and one of evil identified as either the Devil or the God of the Old Testament. They were thought by some to have equal power, though that was a matter of debate even within the belief system. The physical world, though, represented the darker, evil side. Everything material – wealth, food, the physical body – was evil. The Albigenses believed that the devil had imprisoned the human soul – which was of light and goodness – within this evil physical body and that salvation could be found by leading a spiritual and pure life. Those who lived appropriately would secure freedom after death when the soul was released into the spiritual realm. Leading an unworthy life would result in reincarnation, possibly as an animal. Most heretic of all was their belief that the established Catholic church was an agent of the Devil, as demonstrated by its immense wealth and corrupt priesthood.

At first the Church believed that it could convert these heretics through reason, and that such conversion would be peaceful. But they could not, and Pope Innocent III (1160–1216) launched the armed Albigensian Crusade against them between 1209 and 1229. That crusade violently suppressed the Albigenses, and in doing so desolated much of southern France. Although the spirit of the Albigenses was defeated small groups survived in isolated areas and were still being hunted by the Inquisition into the fourteenth century.

It was in 1231 that the Inquisition formally came into being with the constitution 'Excommunicamus' of Pope Gregory IX (1148–1281) nephew of Innocent III. The war against the Albigenses had concerned him and his edict placed the prosecution of heretics under papal authority. This was the formal founding of the Inquisition.

The Inquisition was administered for practical purposes by the Franciscans and Dominicans who were regarded as learned in theology and devout in their beliefs. Each tribunal was headed by two inquisitors of equal power supported by a team of police, counsellors and others. Their powers were great – they could excommunicate even ruling princes – and as such it is inevitable that there were many accusations of corruption and cruelty. That said, there was a general recognition that many of the inquisitors acted fairly and reasonably, and gained a reputation for both justice and mercy.

At the outset the Inquisition consisted of 'normal' trial procedures where, for example, the testimony of two witnesses was considered sufficient for a guilty verdict. But in 1252 Pope Innocent IV approved the use of torture to extract confessions from those accused.

Typical penalties for the guilty were penances such as a pilgrimage, being forced to wear a cross, a public whipping or a fine. In some cases there was confiscation of property or imprisonment. Contrary to popular conception the most severe penalty available to the Inquisition was life imprisonment. Execution could only be authorised by a civil authority.

Having dealt with the Albigenses (see page 89) the Inquisition went on to confront other similar heretic groups such as the Waldenses and the Fraticelli. Finally they began to seek out witches, though with less vigour than in the early days.

The Inquisition came into its own again with the rise of Protestantism, particularly when it confronted the Catholic church in Rome itself. In 1542 Pope Paul III (1468–1549) revived it, establishing the 'Congregation of the Inquisition', sometimes known as the 'Roman Inquisition', and also established the Holy Office. It amounted to the birth of the Counter-Reformation, a reaction to the Reformation which had brought the occult to the fore. (In fact this Pope was responsible for many of the landmark acts that have come down to us through history: he negotiated the Treaty of Nice in 1538; excommunicated Henry VIII of England in the same year; created the Council of Trent; and authorized the establishment of the Jesuits in 1540.)

Under Paul III the Inquisition was relatively mild, but under his successor, Paul IV (1476–1559) it became active and vigorous. It was Paul IV who approved and published the first Index of Forbidden Books in 1559. Later Popes again scaled down the vigour of the Inquisition but they allowed it to become a normal instrument of Papal regulation and control of the orthodoxy. As such it became more fearful once it became more 'ordinary'. It would not be until Pope Paul VI in 1965 that a sweeping redesign of papal authority was made, reorganising the Holy Office, renaming it the Congregation for the Doctrine of the Faith, and lifting the ban on certain books.

The Spanish Inquisition

Distinct from the Inquisition above, and perhaps more commonly known, was the Spanish Inquisition. King Ferdinand V of Spain (1452–1516), and his equally powerful wife Isabella I sought to strengthen their royal position and created, to do so, the *Santa Hermandad*, or Holy Brotherhood, virtually a military police force. One of the demands made was for religious conformity. The Pope, Sixtus IV (1414–84), saw the confluence of interests and in 1478 issued a Bull which empowered the monarchs to appoint three inquisitors to seek out and persecute heretics and other offenders against the Church. This was the formation of the Spanish Inquisition. This Inquisition was, from the start, less of a religious instrument and more of a political device designed to secure the powers of absolute monarchy. Within just a few years the Papacy transferred all power to the monarchs, although it was always administered by churchmen.

This Inquisition was organised on much the same lines as its namesake, but it quickly became notorious for its cruelty and violence. Its first and most infamous Grand Inquisitor, Tomás de Torquemada (1420–98), executed thousands of claimed heretics. In certain countries, such as Mexico and Peru, it was clear that the Inquisition was seeking out sorcerers far more than religious heretics who might have been a direct threat to the Church's authority. The Spanish Inquisition did not come to an end until 1834.

The Heresy-Hunting Machine

To return to the specifics of the witchhunts. There is a further suspected reason, cynical though it may be, for the emergence of the witchhunts. The Church had perfected a 'heresy-hunting' machine that had scourged Europe for what might be called 'genuine' competition. The power of the Knights Templar, for example, had been very potent and had been stamped out. That machinery still existed, however; all it needed was a new purpose.

Researchers suggest that the first emergence of this new belief system arose in the Western Alps in the 1420s. The first persecutions were in Switzerland in 1428. These persecutions did not become a major event until much later; but between 1560 and 1632 such oppression was rife across Britain, France, Germany, the Netherlands and Denmark. Although it virtually came to an end in north-west and central Europe the influence then moved on to Sweden, Poland, and Austria.

But the religious argument alone cannot account for these persecutions. Religion was merely the vehicle, and the opportunity, of the time. Europe in particular had undergone a huge population explosion in the late Middle Ages and was facing the inevitable problems of crowding and supply shortages. (In Germany in the 1930s and 1940s the persecution of the Jews was also based on the same idea; that Germans needed food and 'lebensraum' – living room – and the persecution of European Jews was similar to the witchhunts.)

In the final analysis no-one knows the number of witches, mostly women, who died as a result of the persecutions but it is generally agreed that a figure around 40,000 is appropriate. In 1589, in Quedlinburg, Germany, 133 women were burned at the stake in one day.

However, despite the appearance of a holy crusade the witchhunts were conducted more by the small bureaucrats than by the Establishment proper. The Establishment may have given the 'nod' in order to centralise and strengthen its power but it depended a great deal on the interpretation at local level of the position in order to conduct the witchhunts.

A high percentage of witchhunts and executions were carried out in Germany which at the time did not have centralised government, consisting instead of a collection of small, self-governing states with many local leaders seeking to display their power. Similarly, there were a high number of such executions in Scotland where authority was not, at that time, centralised. In the more 'organised' and developed states such as Spain there was not the same need for individual power and the witchhunts were virtually insignificant. In any case the Spanish Inquisition had other work to keep it occupied and in the end actually banned witchhunting as a waste of time. Nor did witchhunting occupy the Papacy to any degree; they also had a different agenda at the time, as noted above.

The general pattern of the witchhunt was for a person to accuse a suspect of witchcraft who would then be arrested and brought before the local magistrate. Trials were generally held with the same propriety and thoroughness as any other trial; suspects generally had an approximately 80 percent chance of being found not guilty. However, there were many times when local conditions prevailed, when the magistrates were a close part of the community and shared its prejudices; in those instances it was thought that the accused stood only a 20 percent chance of acquittal. Such local magistrates, seeking to demonstrate their powers, having prejudicial viewpoints in the first place, and often belonging to communities where religion became the defining focus, would often authorise the use of torture to obtain confessions and to extract the names of other witches. In such circumstances the conviction rate was greatly increased for obvious reasons. The first accused would be tortured until they confessed, implicating others, and those they accused were already starting from a **weak** position because they had been denounced by an already convicted witch.

No doubt the witchhunters tried and convicted those who practised witchcraft, in the sense of merely following a nature-religion rather than entering into a diabolical pact. But it is known that a good many non-witches were implicated and often executed; midwives, spiritual healers and so on. In fact, any woman – most of the convictions were of women – who was in any way thought non-conformist.

It is also evident from the records of the witchhunts that many of those who confessed did so genuinely believing themselves to have been involved with the Devil. They had become convinced that their dreams, which we now would recognise as fears or strange fantasies, actually reflected some part of them unknown even to themselves. They died believing themselves to be evil; convinced by those with a political and ego-driven axe to grind.

Religion was undoubtedly the catalyst for the witchhunts, and approval came 'from the top'. However, the demographic studies of the persecutions show, as noted above, that it varied according to the degree of centralisation of government of the countries involved. This was clearly because of the respective power of local magistrates and their equivalents; the genuinely powerful people having better things to do and local 'minor-machos' using the authority they had for their own ends. Some no doubt pursued the witches with genuine religious fervour. But it is clear from other aspects of the witchhunts that other motives abounded.

Sexual power was unquestionably one of those other motives. Most witchhunters and people in authority were men; most witches were women. It is obvious that, in order to avoid the prejudicial accusations and trials, some women gave their favours to those who might be in a position to, effectively, let them live or die. There is the clear indication of such in some accounts, though perhaps not as many as might be expected. But there were more subtle motivations. For example, one way to find a witch was to find the 'Devil's mark' which the Devil was obliged to place on the witch; on men it was often in the hairline on the head, for some reason; with women it was usually concealed on the breasts or in the pubic hair. And it had to be sought out and examined in detail. Witchhunters presumably were thorough in their duties!

A second motivation for some witchhunts was financial. In many of the countries where the witchhunts were most zealous anyone convicted of witchcraft and sentenced to death forfeited their goods and property. Such wealth was then shared out between the Church, the local councils and the lawyers involved in the prosecution. Furthermore, in some countries the law required the victim to pay for the expenses of their torture, imprisonment, trial and execution; the money going, of course, to the authorities.

To take an example of this: Nicholas Remy (1530–1612), Attorney General of Lorraine, France, who boasted that he had burned nine hundred witches in fifteen years, signed the death warrant of one George de Haut stating 'so that at least he will feel the flames keenly before being suffocated, his goods to be declared forfeit and confiscate to whom they belong, reasonable expenses for the trial first being deducted'. Indeed, there were cases of property being confiscated before trials had even been conducted. In Offenburg in Germany, in 1628, it can be shown that the town council made a very lucrative habit of arresting wealthy individuals on the basis of witchcraft and offered financial inducements to anyone who would accuse a witch. The percentage of wealthy victims speaks for itself; seventy-nine of the wealthiest people in the locality were convicted of witchcraft. Every one of the confessions had to be extracted by extreme torture which, apart from securing the necessary admission of guilt, also probably settled a good many feuds between the rich and the would-be powerful. Even more disgraceful was the reason for a temporary halt in the persecutions in that year; the

Church was arguing that it was not getting enough of the 'spoils'. Once the Church and the local council had renegotiated the division of the victims' wealth the persecutions recommenced with great vigour. It is very clear that financial gain was a prime driver for some witchhunts. When, in some areas of Germany, the confiscation of property of a convicted witch was made illegal, witchhunting in those areas came to a virtual halt never to be revived.

The practice of torture was, of course, designed to secure the desired end and perhaps provide the more sadistic with entertainment. As Judge Peter Binsfeld (died 1603) in Germany noted, there were several confessions to the murder of people who later turned out to still be alive.

Favoured techniques for witchfinding included ducking and pricking. Ducking consisted of immersion in water, usually the village pond. The victim was either tied to a ducking stool or secured inside a sack; if they drowned then they were not a witch, if they floated, or did not drown, then they were witches under the protection of the Devil and were condemned to death! The logic was that the witch, having rejected the baptismal water, would be rejected by the water itself and hence would float or the water would not enter his or her body.

Pricking consisted of sticking pointed instruments into the so-called witch's marks or Devil's marks allegedly present on the bodies of his subjects. The witch's mark was anything that looked vaguely like a 'spare' nipple which could be used to suckle a 'familiar'. The Devil's mark was any strange mark which the Devil was said to put on his subjects, more or less in the manner of branding. Since most people have some sort of mark or mole on their bodies it was easy to find some way to justify an accusation. And it no doubt livened the spectacle of the public humiliation of a witch if the woman – preferably young and attractive – was stripped naked in front of the assembled village so that her Devil's mark could be shown to all. If an instrument was pushed into one of these marks it would not bleed, nor would the victim feel pain. Of course many areas of the skin, and many normal childhood scars, become immune to pain, so the test proved little. Add to that the fact that the girl or woman had probably just been stripped naked in front of a group of men, tortured, shaved (to find the marks) and then stood naked in the open sometimes on a cold day. A pin-prick was probably the last thing they would be likely to feel.

In case anyone that 'needed' to be found guilty might have escaped on these tests there were two other techniques that virtually made innocence impossible: one was the declaration that some marks were invisible anyway, so in the unlikely event of not being able to find a mark that was immune to pricking or bleeding it could still be maintained that it was there all the time; the witchfinder would just have to search more thoroughly. Secondly, was the fact now known that some of the 'prickers' who accompanied the witchfinders used hollow tubes with retractable points so that the witch was never pricked at all.

Probably the most famous of witchfinders was Matthew Hopkins, the so-called Witchfinder General, who operated in England in the mid-seventeenth century. He was a demagogue who used his position for his own gratification. He started his dubious career by sending thirty-two people for trial in Chelmsford, Essex, and achieved instant fame. Local authorities would ask for his assistance and he travelled the country with a team of witchfinders seeking out witches across England. He employed the techniques of ducking and pricking and also used more subtle torture to extract his confessions; sleep deprivation, starvation and torture that did not mark the body (torture was not acceptable in England at that time and there is little doubt that Hopkins found that a regrettable omission). In the fourteen months of his 'work' he was responsible for more executions of witches than all other English persecutions in 160 years put together. But finally judges and magistrates came to realise that his 'hit rate' was too good, his methods too dubious and his sadism too obvious. Unable to find work he was forced to retire in 1646 and died a year later of tuberculosis, discredited but with a trail of death behind him hard to equal even in this most ghastly episode of history. Some legends claim Hopkins was himself hanged as a witch.

The Witches of Salem

Although most common in Europe, perhaps the most famous single persecution was in America: in Salem, Massachusetts, in 1692. (The town is now known as Danvers).

It started almost with a game, not dissimilar to a group of youngsters playing with a ouija board, which has happened in virtually every school in the country at some time. In this case a few young Puritan girls in Salem looked into glasses holding the white of an egg and tried to divine their fortunes; who would they marry, would they be rich, the usual interests of young girls playing together.

The girls had acquired a taste for the occult; the Reverend Parris had a black Caribbean slave called Tituba who entertained the girls with stories of black magic and witchcraft on Barbados.

Then one of them – not named, but likely to have been nine-year-old Elizabeth Parris, the daughter of a local preacher – claimed she saw a coffin in the glass which they determined was an omen of death. Hysteria set in with Elizabeth and her eleven-year-old cousin Abigail, indeed in the modern day we would probably recognise it as just that, clinical hysteria. At the time, though, when the girls started having convulsions and fits, and acting strangely – throwing lighted wood around the house which they had lifted from the fires – they were believed to have become demoniacally possessed. This bizarre behaviour spread to their friends: Anne Putnam (aged twelve), Mary Walcott (sixteen), Elizabeth Hubbard (seventeen), Susan Sheldon (eighteen), Elizabeth Booth (eighteen), Mercy Lewis (nineteen) and Mary Warren (twenty).

The condition was similar to one that had been given local prominence just a few years earlier. The local author and preacher, Cotton Mather (1663–1728), son of the preacher Increase Mather, wrote many accounts of witchcraft which set the scene locally. His writings unquestionably influenced the way events unfolded in Salem.

It was Mary Walcott's aunt, Mary Sibley, who first invoked the subject of witchcraft. In order to find out what was happening she asked Tituba and her husband Indian John to bake a witch's cake consisting of meal and the urine of the affected children. This was fed to the family dog who she believed was a familiar of demons. As a result the children were able to name those responsible for their condition: arrest warrants were issued for Sarah Good, Sarah Osborn and Tituba.

The accused were brought before magistrates John Hathorne and Jonathan Corwin. Sarah Good's husband hardly helped; he said she either was a witch or would soon be one and their four-year-old daughter stated that her mother had 'familiars'; three birds. The girls accused Good of coming to them 'spectrally' to torment them. Sarah Osborn was similarly accused. Tituba confessed to knowing the Devil and admitted that he had bidden her to do his will.

Over time the girls, in fits, continued their accusations. Anne Putnam accused Martha Corey, a church-goer and respectable member of the town, as a spectre that tormented them. Corey's conviction seemed certain when she was seen biting her lip during her trial; the girls claimed she bit them spectrally and it was said that she was using her own body rather like a 'voodoo doll'. Over time respectable people, known religious people, four-year-olds, all were accused. It seemed that logic and common sense had gone absent from Salem.

By the end of that summer 141 people had been accused. Ultimately nineteen 'witches' were hanged on Witch's Hill and one man pressed to death. Perhaps Elizabeth Parris had had foresight after all; the omen of death had been right.

The aftermath was a surprising one; an agreement by those involved that they had been wrong. In January 1647, less than five years later, the Lieutenant-Governor, Assembly and Council declared a day of public fasting believing God was still displeased with them. On that day all twelve jurors of the trials signed admissions of error: 'do hereby declare that we justly fear that we were sadly deluded and mistaken ... and do humbly beg forgiveness ...'. The judge of the trials similarly expressed his sorrow. In 1706 Anne Putnam confessed she had also been deluded: '... I desire to lie in the dust, and earnestly beg forgiveness of God, and from all those unto whom I have given offense, whose relations were taken away or accused.'

The common factors in the witchhunts, typifed by Salem, were fear and denunciation. Fear of the Devil's powers, a rise of Communism and denunciation (by a powerful family unit opposing evil) believing that what you hear from the hysterical is true. And it seems that society learns slowly, or never at all. In the modern times we have had 'witchhunts' by social workers in the name of child abuse; whole communities destroyed, children denouncing their parents, in locations such as Cleveland, Orkney, Rochdale and Nottingham.

In America we are even seeing the backlash against this now. Adults who, as children many years ago, believed their therapists who 'discovered' (using so-called 'recovered memory') that they had been abused, rejected their fathers and split their families are now beginning to understand that they never were abused.

The Death of the Witchhunt

Witchhunting ended as the authorities, those with real power, came to realise that it was yielding no positive benefits and was arguably beginning to have the opposite of the desired effect. Such a determination to defeat the forces of Satan seemed to imply that he was powerful indeed, and the religious authorities in particular wanted to demonstrate the opposite. With their approval diminished and fading progressively, so the minor-machos who had played an important part in promoting the hunt lost their authority and their local support. Gradually the death penalty for witchcraft was lifted in one country after another. The last execution was in Switzerland, where it had all started, in 1782. 'Witches' as local healers, as local advisors and counselors, continued to ply their trade and continue to do so in one guise or another to the present day.

Looking back through the history of witchcraft different writers and researchers have recorded various viewpoints, in particular of the days of the witchhunts. Nineteenth-century writers such as Jules Michelet argued that the witches had been keeping alive a nature-loving, pagan religion, which in many cases must have been true. In 1921 Margaret Murray (see page 109) supported this belief and although such a view was rejected until recently it has again come to some prominence with the reconciliation of witchcraft and modern approaches to healing and medicine.

Writers such as Voltaire and Sir Walter Scott regarded the witchhunts as a form of madness that beset religion and the world for a period, and they rounded on the Establishment critically, holding up the witchhunt to show them their follies in much the same way as The Knight of the Mirrors destroyed Don Quixote by showing him his real self.

WITCHCRAFT RESURGENT

The resurgence of a non-demonic, pagan, nature-based understanding of witchcraft came with the work of the English witch Gerald Gardner (see p.104) who, in 1951, wrote of Wicca (derived from the Anglo-Saxon word for a male witch), which he described as witchcraft for the modern world. In a way he was ahead of his time, but certainly more recently Wicca has become established as it appeals to many modern themes: ecological concern and respect for nature; the rise of feminism, including the acceptance of feminine attributes in men; and the New Age search for a more meaningful religion and an alternative to 'establishment' rules and approaches to many aspects of life. As Ronald Hutton, historian and author of The Stations of the Sun: A History of the Ritual Year in Britain, describes '... the figure of the witch has become very prominent as a positive one in wider feminist culture; it is, after all, one of the very few images of independent female power which survives through European history'.

Witchcraft is a combination of pagan worship of nature and of ritual designed to utilise magic for change. It is fascinating to see that many people who would dismiss entirely any empathy or association with witchcraft *per se* actually utilise the same techniques under different names. In particular the overlap between the 'positive mental attitude for change' demanded for business-people in their self-development in modern times. A striking comparison came to us when looking through our own files with writing on witchcraft in mind. Firstly there was an account of the witch Doreen Valiente working with a film crew. She explained to them a simple application of the Craft. 'Today I asked very fervently for the power to provide you with a parking space for your van, and lo and behold, it did. Which is something contrary to the order of the universe, with parking the way it is today!' In short, she believed that by magic she had arranged a parking space ahead of time for a particular purpose.

Secondly there was an event, personally witnessed, relating to a financial advisor who promotes inner change and self-development as part of business training and motivation. He teaches techniques of visualisation. He told us that he could always get a parking place when he wanted one; he would visualise the parking space ahead of time, while travelling to that place, and it would be there when he arrived. At the time his office was in Mayfair, just off of Oxford Street in Central London, where parking is a notorious nightmare and often seems virtually impossible. However, John Spencer witnessed him planning and achieving what he claimed. Twice John was in his car with him when he was driving to his office and on both occasions cars parked within a few yards of his office door pulled away as he turned into the road, leaving available parking spaces in which 'Dave' could park. On the second occasion, to test these claims, John watched traffic movement around that time from the office window to see how frequently traffic moved; one car moved within a few minutes, nothing else moved for nearly an hour. Interestingly, John noticed that on any occasion that he visited the office Dave's car was parked right outside.

Some might say that he is a witch and doesn't know it; but such a claim is unfair. Witchcraft is something a person positively 'signs up for', it is not something one can accidentally 'fall into'. The truth seems to be that witchcraft is an embodiment of techniques that are not unique to its following. They are 'dressed up' within the rituals of witchcraft, but they also exist outside of it. It might not be too unfair to say that witches find method in their rituals, it gives them a framework which works for them, but alternative frameworks (such as self-development for business) work equally well for others. As such, witchcraft as it exists today can be seen as a reflection of modern day approaches taken by a very broad range of people.

Witches see the Goddess, for many their principle object of worship, as an embodiment of the life force, as Mother Nature, the Earth, the Cosmos. She represents the interconnectedness of all life.

An article in *New Society* (December 1964) described modern witchcraft: 'the witches' efforts at self-transcendence should be seen at least as a private exploration of the same region beyond the known which on occasions inspires scientific research, introspection, religious awe'.

Wicca is a highly individual religion. The number of different sects within the Craft may give the impression that no two groups practice the same way. Though practices do vary, often considerably, there are considerable similarities such as the working of magic and a respect for nature. As such most Witches, and most covens, have enough common ground for mutual support and productive networking throughout the witchcraft community.

Critics of witchcraft have referred to it as a cult. By strict definition it is; taking the dictionary definition of 'a system of religious worship especially as expressed in ritual'. However, the evolution of the word cult has tended to focus on those groups which offer almost unquestioning allegiance to one charismatic leader who they believe represents the 'only' path to the 'truth'. They indulge in 'extravagant homage or adoration' according to one definition, thereby sacrificing self-determination. This is clearly not what modern witchcraft is designed for; indeed the highly individualistic nature of the covens and of the practices of certain individuals makes witchcraft less cult-like than 'conventional' religions. There is no overall leader of witchcraft, and it is unlikely that one could emerge except perhaps for a short time and even then only affecting a small percentage of witches. Many are drawn to the religion precisely because it allows them to adapt their need for worship to their own inner belief systems.

Nor do witches have the equivalent of a 'bible'. Such books are generally believed to represent the word of a deity revealed through a prophet or prophets. One dictionary definition refers to a bible as 'a book containing the sacred writings of any religion'. Witchcraft's individuality is based around a folk-religion of personal experience rather than transmitted revelation. Witches create their own personal 'bibles' – their Book of Shadows (see page 150) – but such books are really more the equivalent of a working manual, or record of the 'tools of the trade'. They contain rituals, discoveries, spells, poetry, herb lore and more. Covens may have one such book for all their members. There is no one book or document regarded by all witches as authoritative, as is found in Judaism, Christianity, Islam or other religions. But let us look at how witchcraft itself came to the modern day.

Gerald Gardner

The year of 1951 was a key turning point for witchcraft. It was the time of the repeal of the last of the witchcraft acts. Devotees were now able to openly discuss their religious beliefs without suppression.

Gerald Brosseau Gardner, born in England in 1884, had been initiated into witchcraft in 1939 by Dorothy Clutterbuck ('Old Dorothy') a wealthy woman who belonged to the New Forest Coven in Hampshire, England. Keen to publicise his beliefs, since the practice was still illegal he released material about modern witchcraft in the fictional book *High Magic's Aid*, published in 1949. After the act was repealed he was one of the first to promote the subject widely and openly. He believed that he, himself, was the descendant of a practising seventeenth-century witch.

Although witchcraft always has been, and remains, an individualistic following with no particular 'schools' or 'overall leaders' Gardnerian witchcraft is a major section. Gerald Gardner had been a tea and rubber planter, also a customs officer, in Sri Lanka (then Ceylon) and Malaysia. He came back to England in 1937 where he joined a group of Rosicrucians – the Fellowship of Crotona – before entering into witchcraft. After 'opening up' about his initiation he publicised the fact that it was a very old tradition that had been kept alive by devotees down the ages. It was his opinion that witchcraft was a very ancient practice, going back to the Stone Age, and had been world wide. He created some heated debate with his claims, undoubtedly true to some extent, that most religions around the world encompassed some of this 'old religion'. There is a depiction of a figure that looks uncannily like the 'horned god', thought to be a shaman undertaking a fertility rite, in the prehistoric Trois Frères Caves in France; the possible connection to witchcraft is clear. Gardner made the link between ancient Druid practices and witchcraft; indeed the female 'Druidesses' bear a striking similarity in their characteristics to witches. Norse mythology contains stories of women riding through the air on staffs and being capable of metamorphosis – both common images of witches. An early, pre-Columbus cult in Mexico appears to have had meetings that could be compared to the witches' Sabbath (see page 120). There are many such parallels that Gardner was right to draw. He argued that witches had been active devising spells to keep Hitler from invading England after the fall of France and considered that earlier witches had used similar spells to keep Napoleon on his side of the channel and to stall the fortunes of the Spanish Armada. In the debate that has followed Gardner's death these claims have been rejected by many.

Indeed, there has been debate ever since Gardner brought witchcraft into the open as to how much was his own interpretation and how much was academically provable. The debate itself would seem to be largely academic; since the following of witchcraft is itself essentially unique to the individual the reasons and beliefs that go with it are largely trawled in from a wide variety of origins.

Gardner was influenced by the 'magick' of Aleister Crowley (see page 68) which focused on the ceremonial, the ritual and the application of magic. But Gardner was more devoted to the folk traditions of nature. His non-fiction book *Witchcraft Today* (published in 1954) (and later *The Meaning of Witchcraft* in 1959) was widely sold and widely influential. It described ceremonies and rituals for the 'modern witch' which accounted for those beliefs. Several commentators have pointed out, however, that Gardner paid Crowley to write some of the magic rituals for him, suggesting a stronger influence from Crowley than many of Gardner's followers care to admit to. The nature of their 'business' relationship is debated by witches to this day.

Gardner promoted the idea of witches practising their magic in the nude, believing that they used their own bodies as energy transmitters of a psychic force and that clothing was in effect a form of 'interference'. Some have suggested, perhaps a little cynically, that Gardner devised his own brand of witchcraft to suit his own predilections. Richard Cavendish describes Gardner as being 'interested in magic, Spiritualism, folklore, edged weapons and flagellation'. (*Encyclopedia of the Unexplained*)

Gardner followed Margaret Murray's descriptions of covens organised in groups of thirteen (many have since challenged Murray's claims for the historical accuracy of this and other of her descriptions, see page 109) and also organised the covens into three grades: Priest and Witch of the Great Goddess; Witch Queen or Magus; and High Priestess or High Priest. He described in a 'Book of Shadows' – a kind of handbook for witches – the main rituals to be followed; a mixture of Crowley's magick, masonic symbolism and other influences.

In 1951, witch enthusiast Cecil Williamson established the Museum of Witchcraft at Castletown on the Isle of Man, and Gardner added many of his own items to the collection. He was, in effect, their 'witch in residence'. By very clearly rejecting Satanism – and more important publicly saying so and rejecting it in the name of modern witchcraft – he did a great deal to make the subject respectable. Eventually Gardner purchased the museum, which closed after his death in 1964. The exhibits were mostly sent to Canada.

Gardnerian witchcraft has travelled widely: to the United States, France and Germany in particular. Gardnerian witchcraft was taken to the United States largely by Raymond and Rosemary Buckland who were initiated by Gardner. Since Gardner's death the individual groups have tended to evolve along individual lines with many claimants to being the 'true' linear descendants of Gardnerian following. It is impossible to understate the influence of Gardner on modern witchcraft, but he is by no means the only modern influence. A direct diversion from Gardnerian following is Alexandrian witchcraft.

Alex and Maxine Sanders

Alexandrian witchcraft, or Wicca, was devised by Alex Sanders and his wife Maxine. He was known by the title 'King of the Witches' for a time. He claimed to have been initiated into witchcraft by his grandmother at the age of seven (some accounts say nine) in a house in Manchester. Some, including his own initiates such as Janet and Stewart Farrar, suggest this is not accurate and that he was self-initiated. Others have suggested that he was initiated by a Gardnerian coven in the north of England. They point to the fact that his 'Book of Shadows' is very Gardnerian in concept. The confusion about his early years is probably explained by the suggestion that he was involved in Devil-worship before turning to witchcraft.

The success of Alexandrian witchcraft has been suggested by researcher Francis King as due to it having 'something for everyone – Gardnerian fun and games for some, the ceremonial magic of the Golden Dawn (in modified form) for others, and even the intellectual austerities and the barbarous "angelic language" of Dee's Enochian magic for a select few.'

Alex Sanders died on Beltane (May 1) in 1988.

These two influences are probably the strongest on modern witchcraft following Margaret Murray, though there have been many others, many of whom claim to be 'truest' to the traditions of Wicca. But one witch in particular deserves mention; 'Old' George Pickingill. At the time of his death the local newspaper commented that England had only produced two outstanding magicians, Merlin and Pickingill.

George Pickingill

Pickingill, from Canewdon (where he died in 1909), in Essex, was said to be the head of nine covens, centred in East Anglia and spread around Norfolk, Essex, Sussex, Hertfordshire and Hampshire. It is said that it was one of his covens in which Dorothy Clutterbuck initiated Gerald Gardner. Certainly, Gardner was later initiated into others of Pickingill's covens, and achieved the status of Magister, or High Priest. Many credit Pickingill with being the true father of modern witchcraft. He had a wide circle of contacts within the occult and Masonic societies. He was known, complimentarily, as a 'cunning man'. He used witchcraft rites from the eighteenth century and adapted them to the mood of the times. Pickingill promoted the three grades within the covens, used by Gardner. Each of his covens was headed by a priestess. This was not always popular with many witches who believed that men should lead the covens.

Pickingill was born in Hockley, Essex, in 1816, a farmworker by trade. He stated that he could trace his ancestry back to Julia the Witch of Brandon who died in 1071. He was held in considerable repute locally for his magical powers. He was consulted from much further afield, even the United States. Two of those who consulted him, Hargrave Jennings and W. J. Hughan, were founder members of the Societas Rosicruciana in Anglia which eventually produced the Hermetic Order of the Golden Dawn.

Pickingill certainly impressed these Masons. *The Wiccan* – a newsletter circulated amongst witches and covens – reported:

A small côterie of Master Masons established a lengthy and productive relationship with George Pickingill from the 1850s onwards. These Freemasons entertained Rosicrucian fantasies, and sought personal verification that Masonic Crafters and Rosicrucian Crafters were siblings of the Old Religion. 'Old George' awed these Masonic 'Rosicrucians' with demonstrations of his mastery over various elementals. He was also to fascinate them by expounding 'the inner secrets of Masonry'. None of these learned Master Masons could comprehend how this non-Mason had penetrated their craft mysteries. It was reluctantly conceded that the witch cult may have possessed some secret arcane knowledge.

Pickingill is said to have caused some fear amongst his colleagues by openly campaigning against Christianity and the Establishment. His rejection of Christianity was so marked that he apparently worked alongside Satanists to promote his beliefs. If this is true, in those days he was indeed taking a considerable risk. The penalties for such action were severe. Such a history might well account for why Pickingill's role in modern witchcraft has been somewhat downplayed by witches who do not appreciate the popular, if tabloid, association of their religion with Satanism which they clearly reject. But it appears he did indeed have a major part, and is one of the direct influences on Gardener.

Margaret Murray

Some researchers believe that the roots of modern witchcraft go back no further than the publication of *The Witch-Cult in Western Europe* in 1921 by the Egyptologist Margaret Murray (1863–1963). Dr Murray's publication suggested that the origins were ancient and could be traced back to the cults of the Divine King and the Fertile Mother, what she called a 'Dianic Cult', a worship based on crop fertility. She believed that the late-medieval witchhunts were a genuine fight between Christianity and an organised alternative religion. It was Dr Murray who identified the characteristics of that religion, covens of thirteen members and so on, which have been brought into modern witchcraft. She also argued that witchcraft had been the natural religion of some of the monarchs of England, such as William II, called Rufus.

Most scholars reject her research and in effect argue that modern witchcraft in the shape we see it today was virtually invented by her. Certainly modern witchcraft, through Gardner, follows the patterns she set out to a great degree.

THE WICCAN REDE

The Wiccan Rede is as close as witchcraft gets to having an enshrined law, or code of behaviour. Wicca has very little dogma, very little that is laid down by one person or group that others must follow. All Wiccans however, expressly or implicitly, follow the general moral code indicated in what is known as 'The Wiccan Rede', one version of which is as follows:

Bide ye wiccan laws you must, in perfect love and perfect trust.
Live ye must and let to live, fairly take and fairly give.

Form the circle thrice about to keep unwelcome spirits out.
To bind your spell will every time, let the spell be spake in
rhyme.

Soft of eye and light of touch, speak ye little, listen much.
Deosil go by the waxing moon, chanting out ye baleful tune.

When ye Lady's moon is new, kiss your hand to her times two.
When ye moon rides at her peak, then your heart's desire seek.

Heed the north winds mighty gale, lock the door and trim the
sail.

When the wind comes from the south, love will kiss thee on the mouth.

When the wind blows from the east, expect the new and set the feast.

When the wind blows from the west, Bardic words be at their best!

Nine woods in the cauldron go, burn them fast and burn them slow.

Elder be ye Lady's tree, burn it not or cursed ye'll be.

When the wheel begins to turn, soon ye Beltane fires will burn.

When the wheel hath turned a Yule, light the log the Horned One rules.

Heed ye flower, bush and tree, by the Lady blessed be.

Where the rippling waters go, cast a stone, the truth ye'll know.

When ye have and hold a need, harken not to others' greed.

With a fool no season spend, or be counted as his friend.

Merry meet and merry part, bright the cheeks and warm the heart.

Mind ye threefold law ye should, three times bad and three times good.

When misfortune is enow, wear the star upon thy brow.

True in love ye ever be, lest thy love be false to thee.

Bide ye wiccan laws you must, in perfect love and perfect trust.

These eight words the rede fulfill: An harm none, do what ye will.

A Family Tradition

One modern witch (who requested anonymity) explained in interview not only his initiation into the Craft, but also the surprise he got when he discovered it was a family 'tradition'.

People have many misapprehensions about witchcraft or paganism. In fact it's Wicca, the religion of the wise. In pre-Christian times this land was pagan. Christianity is something that came along and put itself into the place of the pagan places of worship. In my late teens I became interested in witchcraft, the paranormal, the occult; all the allied subjects. I joined a Wiccan group where there were some very good elders, or 'wise ones', around us. I had to go through some tough training before I was allowed to go further.

I went through a gruelling assault course of having to learn how to expand my consciousness, my mind, learning to astrally project, learning to wholly refine my psychic mind, learning tarot cards. All ways of tapping into the cosmic consciousness. I had to learn breathing exercises, fasting, how to put my mind on a more elevated platform, how to be psychically receptive, and so on.

It was all done with a group or coven, it was done with an elder and I was sworn to keep secret what we were doing. I learned certain practices of witchcraft which were very pure: how to heal, how to use candle magic, how to control the candle and look at the flame and control it with your mind. I had to go through all these things before I became competent. I could then go ahead and teach; and I had to teach what I knew.

I was very relaxed about it with my family. But the funny thing about it is I didn't know my mother and father attended covens until I was in my twenties. One day my father saw a pentacle, a pendant I was wearing, and he looked at me, I looked at him. He said, 'Blessed be, son'. And I said, 'Pardon?' He said, 'Blessed be'. And I said, 'How do you know?' He said, 'You've got a pentacle on. Don't you know where we go Thursday night?' I said, 'I had no idea about you'. He was the same, he told me, 'I also had no idea about you'.

Obviously it was bred into our family. My mother took an interest because of my father; my father committed his life to it. It took my mother thirty years to come round to his way of thinking and then she joined in for about five years. So I was lucky enough to come from a family open to the same beliefs. A family that was comfortable about it but also a family that was naturally into it anyway. I am very lucky in that my parents were psychic. My grandmother on my father's side was either a witch, or at least a psychic, so it has kind of come through at least three generations.

Attitudes have relaxed in recent years. In 1994 Ms Susan Leybourne, a white witch, was appointed as a chaplain at Leeds University. Ms Leybourne is a pagan priestess, ordained in Louisiana. She offered guidance on magic and rituals. She was, therefore, placed on a par with the other chaplains from other recognised religions. She stated, 'Witchcraft can play a positive role in people's lives. It emphasises how an individual's needs and ambitions can be influenced by magic and how such beliefs can bring personal rewards, such as academic success'.

In the same year, the town council of Milton Keynes, Buckinghamshire voted to grant permission to the Milton Keynes Wiccan coven to use local land for worship.

Initiation Rituals

The Initiation rituals which derived mostly from Gerald Gardner are three-fold, reflecting the three grades: Priest and Witch of the Great Goddess; Witch Queen or Magus; and High Priestess or High Priest. Rituals will actually vary in detail, sometimes considerably, from coven to coven. The general Gardnerian 'form' was as follows.

For the first grade the initiate is taken, blindfolded, bound and naked, into a circle representing the 'Circle of Power'. The coven leader offers blessings and other ritual phrases, and the initiate receives the five-fold kiss on feet, knees, genitals, breast and lips. They then receive forty lashes from the scourge – usually symbolically, or at least relatively painlessly – but some covens seem to have retained a certain amount of sado-masochism in this part of the ritual. They then take an oath of secrecy:

I, [their name], in the presence of the Mighty Ones do of my own free will and accord most solemnly swear that I will ever keep secret and never reveal the secrets of the Art except it be to a proper person, properly prepared, with a Circle such as this. And that I will never deny the secrets of the Art to such a person if he or she be vouched for by a Brother or Sister of the Art. All this I swear by my hopes of a future life mindful that my measure has been taken and may my magical weapons turn against me if I break this, my solemn oath.

The initiate is then given the implements of the Art; such as the athame (or black-handled blade).

Initiation into the next grade also involves 120 strokes of the lash. This is three times the original forty lashes of the previous grade, in line with the very important 'rule of three' of witches.

> Ever mind the Rule of Three
> Three times what thou givest returns to thee.
> This lesson well, thou must learn,
> Thee only gets what thou dost earn.

Initiation into the third grade involves sexual intercourse in the Circle between the initiate and the leader. Sometimes this is symbolic, sometimes carried out in actuality. Either way it is undertaken in the presence of the whole coven.

These rituals do seem to reflect Gardner's predilections for nudity, voyeurism, and sado-masochism which most commentators attribute to him, at least suggesting that they are more modern in design than is usually promoted.

In more recent times there seems little doubt that witchcraft rituals and beliefs have been openly paraded in the media, but it is probable that some covens have stayed true to the oath, and that most witches have retained some personal rituals that are not revealed. Nevertheless the former secrecy of witchcraft, once a necessity due to the various 'witchcraft acts', has now been lessened to a great degree.

Festivals

There are eight principal festivals in the witchcraft year, known as the Sabbaths. They arise from a time, or from recognition of a time, when the pattern of the changing seasons touched human life more directly, or at least more obviously, than in the present day. In the days when people worked in close harmony with nature just to survive, the pattern of the seasons demanded, and received, powerful recognition. Rituals and festivals evolved to channel these seasonal transformations for the good of the community, seeking good sowing and harvesting, and bountiful herds and hunting.

Witches tend to have adopted the period of the day as an agricultural one, considering the day as beginning at sundown and ending at sundown the following day.

The festivals are set out in what is known as the 'Wheel of the Year', with eight spokes representing the eight major events: the four major agricultural and pastoral festivals, and the four minor solar festivals of the solstices and equinoxes.

Hallowe'en (31 October), the night before All Saints Day; also known as Samhain

Witchcraft tradition, following the ancient Celts, considers this the eve of the New Year. It is one night when the divide between the worlds of life and death are less tangible, allowing the ancestors to walk among the living, welcomed and feasted by their kin. The spirits of the deceased could join in the celebrations before the cold winter began. Celts would honour their ancestors, and hold a feast of remembrance known as the Feast of the Dead. It is not, as some tabloids would have their readers believe, a time of raising the dead, which is not a part of Wicca practice. It is a time when witches seek to develop both divinatory and psychic powers.

The Winter Solstice (21 December); also known as Yule

This is the longest night of the year. Some covens celebrate with a Festival of Light to commemorate the Goddess as Mother giving birth to the Sun God. Others hold the service to depict the victory of the Lord of Light over the Lord of Darkness; it is the point from which the days will lengthen and there will be more light.

Imbolc or Brigid (31 January)

This is the time when the days' lengthening becomes perceptible; frequently candles are lit to bring on the warming of the earth and emphasise the reviving of life. 'Imbolc' is from the Old Irish, meaning 'in the belly'. It is the beginning of new life, of new births of animals. It is also the holiday of the Celtic Fire Goddess Brigid, who rules smithcraft, poetry/inspiration and healing. Brigid's fire is a symbolic representation of healing, visions, and tempering. *Februum* is a Latin word meaning purification – February therefore becomes the month of cleansing. The thaw releases water (Brigid is also a goddess of holy wells) – all that has been held back is let flow at this season.

The festival virtually corresponds with Candlemas in the Christian calendar (on 2 February) which is a blessing with candles commemorating the purification of the Virgin Mary.

The Vernal Equinox (21 March); also known as Ostara

Spring begins to bring richness and life to the countryside. People are thought to feel themselves 'reborn' from the long winter, ready for the warmth of the summer ahead. Day and night are equal in length; but the days will now become longer as time progresses. The Goddess of the Dawn, Ostara, (the basis of the word 'Easter') is the protective deity of this festival. She heralds the sun and the return of life to earth. Witches in the Greek tradition celebrate the return from Hades of Demeter's daughter Persephone; witches in the Celtic tradition see in the blossoms the passing of Olwen, daughter of the giant Ysbaddaden, in whose footprints white flowers bloom.

May Eve (30 April); also known as Walpurgis Night; associated with Beltane

The traditional time of dancing around the maypole, the symbol of fertility. (The word 'may' is derived from a Norse word meaning 'to shoot out new growth'; an expression which symbolises both the 'shoots' of new plant-life and the ejaculation of seed from the phallus – which is represented by the maypole.) The first day of May was the midpoint of a five-day Roman festival to Flora, Goddess of Flowers.

'Beltane' means 'Bel's Fires'; in the Celtic traditions cattle were driven between bonfires to bless them. People would then leap over the fires for luck and purification. The inherent danger of clothing catching fire, plus the desire for the warmth of the fire to purify without obstacle, led some practitioners of this festival to jump the fires naked.

The Summer Solstice (21 June); also known as Litha

The longest day of the year, a time when light and heat is in abundance. It is a time to rejoice and celebrate the fruits of the fields. Some witchcraft traditions choose this time to celebrate the sacred 'marriage' of the Goddess and God.

It also corresponds to the festival of the Chinese Goddess of Light, Li.

August Eve (31 July); also known as Lughnasadh; associated with Lammas

This is the time of the Celtic fire festivals, thanking the Celtic culture-bringer and solar god Lugh. In Ireland, celebration was held in his name and that of his mother, Tailtiu. Lammas (2 August) is the Saxon Feast of Bread, at which the first of the grain harvest is consumed in ritual loaves.

This time is also sacred to the Greek Goddess of the Moon and the hunt, Artemis.

The Autumn Equinox (21 September); also known as Mabon or Harvest Home

The day and night are of equal length again, but from this point on the nights will get longer as the winter approaches. Harvest festivals are held, thanking the Goddess for providing sustenance to see the people through the winter ahead. Harvest festivals are observed in farming countries of which the American 'Thanksgiving' is a version.

Esbats

Magic is most frequently performed at smaller gatherings, called Esbats, which coincide with the phases of the moon. Types of magic practised by the modern witch include psychic healing sessions, the focus and direction of energy to achieve positive results and work towards the individual spiritual development of the coven members.

THE STEREOTYPE OF THE WITCH: ORIGINS

If a child was asked to draw a witch he or she would probably draw an ugly, almost deformed old woman wearing dark loose clothing and a pointed hat, as likely as not flying through the air on a besom, an old fashioned broomstick. It would be hard to find a more perfect depiction of such a witch than the 'Wicked Witch of the West' in *The Wizard of Oz*. Her ugliness, of physique and character, could almost be regarded as a defining feature; indeed in that film Dorothy states her belief that 'witches are old and ugly'. But she is confronting the beautiful Glenda, the 'Witch of the North' who tells her that only bad witches are ugly.

The image is not without its roots, and they are fascinating indeed. Such imagery is depicted in the woodcut of German artist

Hans Baldung Grien (1484/5–1545) dating from 1514 which shows ugly, naked, old women conducting spells while another flies above on a stick, the traditional way of showing the witch travelling to the Sabbat. This was thought to be the place and the time when witches would commune with the Devil.

In order to achieve this temporary power of flight the witch would have to rub an ointment into her skin, and onto her flying stick. The seating across the broom handle is thought to be a reference to the ointment needing to be rubbed onto the genitals, effected by wiping it thickly onto the stick which was then placed between the legs and rubbed onto the body.

If there is a genuine origin to the 'flying on broom handles' it is likely to have arisen from the European tradition of running through fields astride a broom to encourage the grain to grow, and then leaping into the air to show the grain the height to which it should grow. This was a part of the festivals designed to bring about a good harvest to see the local population through the winter ahead. Chinese whispers based on seeing people, usually women, leaping through fields on broomhandles might have led to part of the imagery.

THE SANTA CONNECTION

There is incidentally an odd link with the Santa Claus tradition, the traditions of the shaman, and the use of hallucinogenic drugs. Rogan Taylor, researching for a doctorate in psychology and religion at Lancester University, published, in the *Sunday Times Magazine* of 21 December 1980, an article concerning the uses of hallucinogenic drugs. He referred back to the tundra and steppes of north-eastern Siberia where many shamanic origins can be found. The celebrations of the region have a great deal in common with the witches' festivals which celebrate the seasons (see page 115) though they are led by the shamans. As Taylor described: 'The shamans ensure the spiritual welfare of the tribe. They are masters of the 'three realms' – Heaven, Earth, Hell –

and, through ecstatic trances, they can visit the underworld to defeat the spirits of disease, or fly to the upperworld to consult the gods'.

These tribes were nomadic and depended on the reindeer for travel, food, clothing, tools and ornaments; the reindeer was therefore a central part of their mythology. One of those myths was of the Reindeer-Spirit, and the shaman would be called to bring about reconciliation between the tribe and the Reindeer-Spirit if there was disharmony. To achieve this they would have to travel to the world where the Reindeer-Spirit dwelt and achieved this experience by the use of hallucinogenic drugs, in particular the fly agaric mushroom (*amanita muscaris*). Fly agaric was particularly noted for creating feelings of flying and for spectacular visions. Reindeer also ate fly agaric keenly and those eating the flesh of reindeer might find themselves subject to the same experiences as if they had eaten the mushroom themselves. Taylor believes that the closeness of the reindeer and Man, and the visions and flying sensations associated with fly agaric, are the basis of the modern Santa Claus myth. In particular it may account for the idea of Santa Claus and his team of reindeer flying through the air. He points out also that the colour of fly agaric is red and white, the traditional colours of Santa Claus.

THE SABBAT

The Sabbat is itself the subject of much misinformation and debate. The tradition had it that the witches would congregate periodically, some said nightly between eleven o'clock and one o'clock in the morning – known as the 'witching hours' – in order to work with the Devil. These Sabbats, according to the witchhunters, would be characterised by orgies, overt sexual deviations and of course Devil-worship. The traditional description of the Sabbat would usually include a man dressed as Satan in the form of a horned creature who would receive the 'kiss of shame' or 'backside kiss' on the buttocks. Young children and babies would be sacrificed to the Devil. Witches would marry in inverted ceremonies that were travesties of the Christian marriage service. Ultimately the Sabbat rituals became associated with the Black Mass, an inversion of the Christian Mass.

Most of the 'evidence' for these beliefs was obtained under torture and through leading questions as part of the political and religious suppressions of the witchhunts. There is little evidence of any truth in the stories, though we shall elsewhere look at the phenomenon of Satanism, which is claimed to encompass some elements of these activities.

The Church considered these beliefs unreal, at least for some time. An ecclesiastical regulation known as the Canon Episcopi, quoted by the German monk Regino of Prum around AD 906, stated that there were wicked women who believed that they rode out at night with the pagan goddess Diana. It stated however that they were hallucinating, stimulated by the Devil. As people came to fear the power of the Devil, so the belief that these 'night rides' were happening in actuality took hold. In 1510 the Italian monk Bernard de Como wrote that the Sabbats were real. At the time that Grien was producing his woodcut an Italian lawyer, Andreas Alciatus, insisted that they were not. He believed that they were the product of hallucinogenic drugs.

In the twentieth century this theory was put to the test by Dr Erich-Will Peuckert of Göttingen University who tested the recipe for a 'flying ointment' on himself and a colleague. After applying the ointment to themselves they went into a trance which lasted for twenty hours. When they came out of the trance the men reported flying dreams and taking part in orgies with demons. The Sabbat then, as the Church said, may not have been entirely fictional even if it did not actually take place; witches may have reported their experiences as real, may even have believed that they were indeed transported to some other dimension where the Sabbat took place.

DEVIL WORSHIP AND SATANISM

This is the worship of Satan, the Devil, and is traditionally associated with the occult. It is also associated with witchcraft; but modern witches reject utterly the connection, holding their religion to be one of respect and empathy for nature rather than subservience to any deity, particularly one such as the Devil. Most witches do not even believe Satan exists.

The concept of 'the Devil' is a personification of a spirit of evil and is a creation of Middle Eastern thought fundamental to the religions of that region, including Zoroastrianism, Judaism, Christianity and Islam. Worship of 'Satan' is a practice of profaning Christian symbolism and is thus a Christian heresy rather than a Pagan religion.

The beginnings of Satanism are hard to trace, but a figurine of a goat-headed man has been found in the Indus valley and dated to 3000 BC. Babylonian art includes depictions of goat-headed Baphomet, a figure said to have been worshipped by the Knights Templar. The goat-head is often associated with Satan but such imagery may also represent pagan animal worship or symbolic strength. However, it has come to be a popular image of Satan.

The Devil is the embodiment, the supreme spirit of evil. He is deemed to be the ruler of the kingdom of evil spirits and is in perpetual opposition to God. The word is derived from the Latin 'diabolus' and the Greek 'diabolos', meaning 'slanderous'. In the Greek translation of the Bible, the Septuagint, the expression was used to refer not to human beings, but as a translation of the Hebrew 'ha-satan' ('the satan'), who was a member of the divine court who acted as God's roving spy on earth, gathering intelligence about human beings from his travels. The creation of this being drew from genuine experiences and encounters with agents of ancient Middle Eastern royal secret services who would often act as *agents provocateurs* to encourage sedition which could then be sought out and punished; therefore 'the satan' took on a similar role: an enemy of humankind bent on dividing it from God.

It is not until later Jewish traditions, and therefore also early Christian traditions, that the expression becomes a proper name; Satan is cast into the role not only of the enemy of humanity but of God Himself. He ceases to be God's agent. Almost certainly the origin of this change lies in the influence of Persian dualistic philosophy which promoted the concept of good (*Ormazd*) versus evil (*Ahriman*). In the writings of the Qumran sect, as recorded in the Dead Sea Scrolls, the Devil is described as Belial, the Spirit of Wickedness.

The religious origin of Satanism is a complex one. Judaism did not originally accept the concept of good and evil in conflict. Jews believed only in God. God had commanded them to live by the commandments, those laws designed to bring the Jewish people closer to Him. These commandments include, specifically, not worshipping any other deity. However, this belief mutated following the capture of Jerusalem and the destruction of the First Temple by the Babylonian king Nebuchadnezzar in 587 BC as a specific political/religious act. The religion as it stood would have indicated that God – who was all powerful – had failed the people in allowing them to be defeated. The consequence of that would have been the almost inevitable supplanting of the Jewish faith with that of the victors, which history demonstrates is the common result of conquest. However, prophets such as Jeremiah succeeded in preserving the Jewish faith by teaching that it was not God who had failed the people, but rather that the people had failed God. God was therefore still all-powerful; the defeat of the people could be interpreted as His deliberate act to teach the people to be more devoted to His teachings. Alternatively the defeat could simply be the result of being a flawed people, to be cured by more attentive devotion; the end result was the same 'message'.

While in exile, in the period following the defeat, Judaism became influenced by Zoroastrianism. Zoroastrianism, which developed in Persia, was a primary source of dualist religions. It holds that the Earth is the battleground for the powers of good and the powers of evil. This caused diverse progressions within the Jewish faith. The mainstream developed around the return of the Jews to Israel and the building of the Second Temple. But offshoots of the faith in Egypt had a different history. They prospered as a wealthy class under the Persians and Greeks, but came into conflict with the Romans during their period of supremacy. The Jews would not worship the Roman gods, and the Romans removed many of their privileges. The Jews became an oppressed race and found the world hostile to their religion. From this the concept of Gnosticism began.

Gnosticism

Gnostics hold the view that God, having created the world, has withdrawn and left it in the hands of the forces of evil. Those forces of evil were triggered by an illegitimate desire to know the unknowable – to understand the Supreme Being – and are represented by a deformed, evil god, or demiurge, who created the universe. All that is good in humanity derives from divine elements that fell into this universe from the original 'good' God, or was deliberately sent here by Him to redeem humanity. Gnostics believe that the 'evil' God is the God of the Old Testament. These writings, they argue, represent God's effort to keep humanity in darkness and ignorance, to keep it material only and not spiritual, and to punish it for trying to acquire knowledge.

Now, in the grip of such evil, humanity has only two possible paths: to transcend the world through asceticism (abstinence from all forms of pleasure) or control the world through magic. The general view of Gnosticism is that the good in the soul of humanity must be liberated from a basically flawed and evil world. Either path means acquiring esoteric and arcane knowledge known as *gnosis* (meaning 'revealed knowledge'). Those who attain such knowledge rise above those who do not. This reconciles gnosticism with all beliefs that hold that superiority of spirit comes from acquiring secret knowledge.

This concept produces the basis of Satanism: that the world is in the control of evil, and that a magician might be able to learn how to control those forces.

As the belief in Roman and Greek gods diminished, the destruction of the Second Temple divided Judaism into three paths: Rabbinic Judaism followed the path of one God of good; Gnosticism believed in the supremacy of evil; Christianity, which took a 'middle road' believed that evil abounded in the world but could be defeated not by magic but by faith in Christ.

Gnosticism largely diminished as a mainstream religion; there is one small non-Christian Gnostic sect, the Mandaeans, in Iraq and Iran, but that may be a relatively recent development and not a survivor of the original Gnostic movement. However, aspects of Gnosticism survive in the Cabbala (see page 26), and may be a part of the basis of the alchemy of the Renaissance. It certainly survives in Theosophy, and in twentieth-century philosophies such as Existentialism and Nihilism. The basic tenet of Gnosticism underlies a great many of the moral and religious principles of the modern day; that a good soul within humankind must be liberated from a base, material, evil world.

Rabbinic Tradition

Rabbinic Judaism is, like all forms of Judaism, based on the Hebrew Bible. The Rabbinic movement of the first centuries of the Christian era is the basis of modern Judaism. It is based on the leadership of a rabbi, once a kind of legal counsellor but now basically a pastor. God, it is said, revealed the scripture, known as the Torah, to Moses, part of which was handed down orally and preserved and interpreted by the rabbis. The earliest document of Rabbinic literature, the Mishnah ('that which is learnt or memorised') set out the oral traditions for the first time. Rabbinic study produced the Talmud ('that which is studied'), a commentary on the Mishnah. The Talmud underpins Rabbinic Judaism. Throughout medieval times, Judaism was continually revitalised by mystical and ethical-pietistic movements such as the thirteenth-century Spanish Cabbala.

In some elements of Rabbinic thought, Satan becomes the personification of the 'evil impulse'. This is a Jewish form of the widely accepted, and ancient, belief that human beings can be subjected to malevolent forces distinct from their conscious minds. This is the origin of the belief that humans can be 'possessed' by the Devil or his subservient demons.

Christianity

Christianity has been the most successful survivor of the division of religious paths. It is the central core of Christian teaching about the Devil that Jesus Christ came to Earth to break the grip that the Devil and his minions had on all of humanity. In the Middle Ages the Devil became an important, if not central, theme in art and in folklore, depicted as an evil, impulsive, animal-human hybrid with a tail and horns.

The Islamic concept of the Devil is similar to the Christian one; indeed Islam originally accepted Judaism and Christianity as genuinely inspired by God. In the Koran the Devil is the only angel who refuses to bow to Adam. For that he is cursed by Allah who, however, leaves him free to travel in the Koranic equivalent of the Garden of Eden to subject humans to temptation.

Satanic-like practices have a long history. Early Semitic religions involved ritual sex and child sacrifice. The Phibionites of the third and fourth centuries AD, as described by the Egyptian monk Epiphanius, practised promiscuity and used semen in their sacrament. The rituals of some early Gnostic sects paralleled Black Mass rituals; orgies, reversals of the Christian Mass, use of blood and semen and child sacrifice.

Arguably a major influence in the emergence of Satanism was in the Cathari, often known as the Cathars (see Albigenses page 89). They were ascetics who believed in the dualist theology of conflict between the spiritual world created by God and the material world created by Satan. Their appeal lay in the apparent hypocrisy of the mainstream churches which preached the spiritual but accumulated great wealth. They regarded the orthodox Church as Satanic since it had succumbed to the material world. By the thirteenth century the authorities, both political and ecclesiastical, in France, the stronghold of the Cathari, began to suppress them, a suppression which continued into the Inquisition. Such suppression seemed only to confirm, to many, that Satan had a hold over the world.

By the Middle Ages, Christian teachings had developed a hierarchy of angels, who were associated with God, and fallen angels, or demons, led by the Devil. Satan himself was considered to be Lucifer (light bringer), the original fallen angel. This is the theme of the epic poem by John Milton, *Paradise Lost* (1667). In twelve books Milton relates the story of Satan's expulsion from heaven and his arrival in the Garden of Eden where he brings about the Fall of Adam, written in a context of cosmic drama. Milton sought to: 'justifie the ways of God to men'. It was later followed by *Paradise Regained* (1671), which described salvation through Christ.

Satanism does not regard the Devil as beneficent or ill-treated (though there are one or two modern Satanic cults in England that promote this theme) but generally as a fiend more powerful than the forces of good, which have failed to keep the promises made to the world.

Through the twelfth and thirteenth centuries there were many attacks on heretic groups such as the Waldensians, the Cathari, the Luciferians and of course the Knights Templar. It became a tenet of the accusations that since heretics had turned away from Christ they must have turned towards his antithesis, Satan. Once under torture many of these groups confessed to Satanism, not surprisingly, but the reality is less clear. Certainly many of the attacks on the Knights Templar have dubious foundations: that they worshipped the Devil in the form of a cat, that they worshipped a horned idol Baphomet and anointed him with the fat of slaughtered children, that they copulated with demons, denied Christ and the Virgin Mary, spat at or stamped on crucifixes and partook of ritual sodomy. What is certainly true is that the destruction of the Knights Templar was a political act inspired by greed more than any religious crusade on the part of the French king Philippe IV.

The Church Strikes Back

In the fourteenth century huge social upheaval was caused by a world-wide crop failure and the Black Death which wiped out a third of the population of Europe. Scarcity of produce and labour led the way to increased demands for higher wages; the Church sought to reimpose the pre-plague social order. The economic balance, though, was being established by birth control practices such as abortion and infanticide. The Church held this to be a sin and in effect condemned a majority of the population to a state of damnation; yet such people had little choice in their actions. Faced with a future in hell, many people found the Church no comfort, and turned towards magic to offer them a form of salvation.

The Church effectively responded by reminding people it had magic of its own, a two-edged sword if ever there was one, as it turned out. Curiously enough the spread of Satanism may have been furthered by the activities of disaffected Roman Catholic priests who believed they had magical powers. According to researcher Francis King, by around AD 700 the Roman Catholic Church was promoting a doctrine that the sacrament – the bread and the wine used at Mass – actually became the body and blood of Christ. If that were so then priests were magicians, bringing about the transmutation of matter. Theologians disputed this claim, arguing that the sacrament was representative only, and rejected any suggestion of magic during the Mass. Some less literate clergy appear to have become attracted to the idea that they had supernatural powers, and some turned away from God, but still determined to use the powers they believed they had. King reports that: 'as early as the 7th century, the Council of Toledo [which met in 694] prohibited the performance of Requiem Masses sung, not for souls in purgatory, but for living men with the intention of killing them'.

Such belief amongst less educated clergy persisted into the nineteenth century, and was reported as Breton folklore in *The Golden Bough* (1890) by Sir James Frazer. He called it the 'Mass of St Sécaire'. This may have become known as the Black Mass which was, surprisingly, a perfectly respectable term for the Requiem Mass up to that time. A central ritual of Satanism is the Black Mass. Accounts of it come primarily from literature and legend. Some scholars believe that before the nineteenth century the Black Mass was largely a political invention designed to promote the ruling religions and to provide reason for the suppression of others, particularly witches. R. H. Robbins has argued that 'the black mass, as something that historically occurred, is one of the biggest intellectual frauds imposed on the lay public'. (*Encyclopedia of Witchcraft and Demonology*, 1959)

Black Mass and Satanism

As it is traditionally described, the group seeking to celebrate the Black Mass wears vestments similar to those worn by Christian priests, but adorned with the figure of a goat, representing Satan. Other features of the Black Mass may include the suspension of a cross upside down, parodies and inversions of Christian prayers and creeds, animal sacrifice, mock blessings with filthy water and ritualistic orgies. There is one famous account of using a naked virgin, Florette, as the altar in the Marquis de Sade's *Justine* (1791). In that description Florette is made to strip and lie on a table, and the Black Mass is performed on her buttocks. Julian Franklyn, a modern British author, described a Black Mass:

> ... carried out at midnight in a ruined church with a renegade priest officiating. His assistants must be public prostitutes, and the Holy Eucharist befouled with human excrement. He wears a black surplice cut in three points, and burns black candles. The holy water must have been used to drown an un-baptized, newly-born bastard, and the altar decorated with owls, bats, toads, and creatures of ill-omen. Standing with the left foot forward, the officiating priest reads the Roman Catholic Mass backwards, after which the congregation indulges in all kinds of orgies and excesses. A crucifix is usually trampled and spat upon,

and sexual perversions performed before the altar. (*A Survey of the Occult*)

Franklyn does not claim to have attended such a Black Mass, nor necessarily believe that they were ever anything other than excuses for the sexual excesses.

Over time the descriptions of the Black Mass have become increasingly dramatic and exaggerated, except for the few isolated incidents that are known to have occurred in the early centuries. Christian Masses could be said for all sorts of purposes, for pilgrimages, and to pray for sexual or financial success. However, once priests came to believe they had the power to bring about such gains, a subversive literature designed to teach a selected few the 'techniques' emerged, concentrating on those who had turned towards evil. This is the origin of the document named the *Grimoire of Honorius*, thought to have been circulated since the fifteenth century and finally committed to print in the seventeenth. This document promoted such activities as sacrificing animals after a Mass to encourage demons. What had started with a corrupt clergy had become actual Satanism.

Satanic practices amongst the non-monastic clergy of the Middle Ages appear to have become relatively common; certainly by the sixteenth and seventeenth centuries. Paris was thought to be something of a centre for such activities. It is possible that the French marshal Gilles de Rais (1404–40), who was tried for heresy, Satanism and child murder, was an early adherent. France seems to have adopted Satanism with enthusiasm, and its practitioners are said to have formed something akin to the Mafia to protect the business interests that derived from it. This 'mafia' was uncovered by the Police Commissioner of Paris, Nicolas de la Reynie (1625–1709).

In 1678 la Reynie arrested a forger, Louis de Vanens, who also confessed to being a Satanist. La Reynie's inquiries led him to a fortune teller named La Voisin (real name Catherine Monvoisin, née Deshayes) who was accused of poisoning. In her home he found not only poison but such substances as semen, blood and dirt from graves, all to be used in the manufacture of potions for magical purposes. She confessed to a ghastly catalogue of crimes including the holding of Black Masses designed to kill. La Reynie discovered that she had several priests amongst her côterie, perhaps the most famous being Abbé Guibourg.

Guibourg was said, by la Reynie, to have 'engaged in the practice of poison, sacrilege and every evil business. He has cut the throats and sacrificed uncounted numbers of children on his evil altar ... it is no ordinary man who thinks it is a natural thing to sacrifice infants by slitting their throats and to say Mass upon the bodies of naked women'.

La Reynie's inquiries led him eventually to Madame de Montespan, the mistress of Louis XIV. It was alleged that she had asked for Black Masses to be said in order to ensure she remained in the king's favour. These Black Masses became increasingly adventurous; starting relatively mildly in 1667; by 1673 they included the replacing of the altar by the body of a nude woman, the slitting of a child's throat in sacrifice, prayers to demons and sexual deviations performed with the consecrated host. Body parts from the slaughtered child were later added to the king's food along with love potions. Despite her attempts to keep the king's favour Montespan's star was on the wane by 1679; her response was to have a Black Mass said with a view to killing the king. La Reynie started his programme of arrests before the ceremonies could be completed: 360 people were arrested; 110 were tried. Publicity was severely curtailed as many people close to the king's circle were identified as being involved. Generally the punishment was imprisonment for life. Madame de Montespan was never arrested, but La Voisin went to the stake in 1680.

Satanism seems to have left few traces into the eighteenth century, perhaps driven too far underground by the purges against witchcraft which, at the time, was associated with Satanism by the authorities. Almost inevitably there would have been some practice driven deeply underground, if only evidenced by its re-emergence in the nineteenth century. On the other hand, it is possible that the enthusiasm for the Black Mass in the nineteenth century is derived more from literature than from any genuine tradition being maintained by ritual.

That re-emergence was typified by the activities of Abbé Boullan. Although he seems to have had a promising start as a pious priest he in later life, together with his mistress, a nun named Adèle Chevalier, formed the Society for the Reparation of Souls. It promoted exorcism for possessed nuns using consecrated hosts blended with human excrement. The Society was almost certainly a disguise for a Satanic group, and there is evidence that the pair conducted Black Masses one of which included sacrificing one of their own children. It seems likely that, although he seems to have escaped the attention of the authorities at the time, Boullan ran Satanic groups until his death at the age of seventy. Two Rosicrucians penetrated Boullan's church and learned of its secrets including the invocation of incubi and succubi – sexual demons.

French novelist Joris Karl Huysman (1848–1907) who focused a great deal on spiritual salvation in his works, in his novel Là-Bas (1891) describes what seems to be a 'classical' Black Mass at which it is believed he was present, which seems to suggest that this practice was continuing in Paris through the nineteenth century.

The logic that underpins Satanism might also be said to have derived from the general belief that humankind is either inherently evil or living in an evil world, and also that people are basically sinners who face an inevitable eternity in damnation. If everyone is going to go to hell, then one might as well get on as good terms as possible with its ruler; Satanists might go to hell along with the rest of the population but they will be spared from burning. This was the specific stated philosophy of one modern Satanic cult in South Carolina in modern times.

Satanism today is likely to be a very recent development and largely unconnected with the excesses of previous centuries. The 1960s represented a time of challenge and questioning of values. Within that framework of change celebrity Satanist Anton LaVey created the Church of Satan (1966) and wrote The Satanic Bible

(1969). It was an extension of the 'do your own thing' philosophy of the sixties, and of Crowley's 'do what thou wilt'. As LaVey explained: 'Satanists are encouraged to indulge in the seven deadly sins as they need hurt no-one; they were only invented by the Christian Church to ensure guilt on the part of its followers. Their Christian Church knows that it is impossible for anyone to avoid committing these sins, as they are things which we, being human, most naturally do.' But this call to Satanism was, in that sense, more of a call to hedonism – breaking the Establishment's rules and enjoying yourself while doing it. It was not the Satanism of Black Masses, though there is evidence that that more harmful form of Devil-worship has continued to the modern day.

The question of Satanism in the present day is a vexed one that has stirred up a great deal of controversy. Tabloid newspapers, social workers and some elements of the clergy fear that it is a reality; others have argued it is no more than literary tradition and fear that inspires belief in such activities. It seems unlikely that large Satanic sects exist as an organised 'religion'. However, it is also highly probable that given the widespread publicity of such rituals, and the obvious attractions for some of clandestine sexual activity, that isolated incidents occur. If so, then it is again most probable that it is the sexual activity which is the main feature rather than a deliberate rejection of Christ or the inclusion of the more horrific elements such as child sacrifice.

There is evidence of clandestine Satanic practices in recent times. In 1963 Princess Irene of Greece described a Black Mass that she had herself attended in Paris, at which a cockerel had been sacrificed. In the same year there was evidence of a Black Mass being celebrated in a churchyard in Bedfordshire; graves had been desecrated, bones removed and scattered on the church floor, a Celtic cross had been painted on the church wall, a cock had been sacrificed. In 1964 one Presbyterian minister in Scotland discovered that Black Masses were being conducted in a ruined church; he found a mutilated bible, a broken chalice, and an inverted cross chalked over the altar.

The Demonic Pact

Although it was open to a witch or sorcerer to raise a demon to do his bidding there were several powerful demons who could extract from the witch or sorcerer a pact. This was the most dangerous aspect of the sorcerer's work as it consisted basically of entering the pact and then trying to get out of it when the time came!

The invoked demon, it was believed, would provide the sorcerer with whatever was required for a period usually of twenty years and then the demon would claim the sorcerer's soul for eternity.

A typical pact is included in the grimoire known as the *Red Dragon*, translated in the sixteenth century:

> Emperor Lucifer, master of all the rebellious spirits, I besiege thee be favourable to me in the calling which I make up on my great minister Lucifuge Rofocale, having desire to make a pact with him. I pray thee also, Prince Beelzebub, to protect me in my undertaking. O Count Ashtoreth! Be propitious to me, and cause that this night the Great Lucifuge appear unto me in human form and without any evil smell, and that he grant me, by means of the pact which I shall deliver to him, all the riches of which I have need. O Great Lucifuge, I besiege thee leave thy dwelling, and whatever part of the world it may be, to come and speak with me; if not, I will thereto compel thee by the power of the mighty words of the great Clavicule of Solomon [Keys of Solomon] whereof he may use to force the rebellious spirits to accept his pact. Appear, then, instantly, or I will continually torment thee by the mighty words of the Clavicule.

The sorcerer would then sign the pact in his own blood, spend twenty years making use of the powers of the demon either for occult knowledge or material pleasure, usually lust or wealth, and then have to work out how to get out of the pact when the time came to hand over his immortal soul. The *Red Dragon Grimoire* even allowed for this, advising the sorcerer to declare, after signing the pact, 'Inspire me, oh great God, with all the sentiments necessary for enabling me to escape the claws of the Demon and of all evil spirits!'

Some pacts were written in mirror writing, the logic being that the demons had to reverse ordinary Christian virtues in order to exercise evil power and that the 'reverse writing' represented a symbol for that reversion. Indeed the signature in blood also has similar symbolism representing the giving of human blood to the Devil as the opposite of Christ giving his blood for humanity.

There are very few pacts in existence for obvious reasons; first because for one to be found would almost certainly result in execution, and second because in any case the Devil is said to take it with him to Hell, not leaving it available for future researchers!

One pact does exist however, in the Bibliothèque Nationale in France: that of the priest Urbain Grandier. The fact that it exists, signed by Grandier, suggests that its preservation was deemed necessary by someone, presumably as authority for his execution. For that reason alone we can consider that it was almost certainly extracted under torture, or was fraudulently created to justify Grandier's treatment.

In the seventeenth century in Loudun, in the Ursuline convent there, seventeen nuns and their students were allegedly possessed by demons. The possessed nuns writhed in contortions and blasphemed, and it was said that they had been possessed by demons. (Other priests visiting the convent were less certain; what they regarded as the expected signs of possession were missing: extraordinary strength, levitation and 'speaking in tongues'. But the event undoubtedly became a political battleground when it came to involve Cardinal Richelieu (1585–1642) the ruler of France in all but name at the time.) Grandier was eventually tortured and burnt at the stake for his alleged responsibility in bringing this possession onto the nuns.

'His' pact reads as follows:

Grandier's Vow
My Lord and Master, I own you for my God; I promise to serve

you while I live, and from this hour I renounce all other gods and Jesus Christ and Mary and all the Saints of Heaven and the Catholic, Apostolic, and Roman Church, and all the goodwill thereof and the prayers which might be made for me. I promise to adore you and do you homage at least three times a day and to do the most evil that I can to lead into evil as many persons as shall be possible to me, and heartily I renounce the Chrism, Baptism, and all the merits of Jesus Christ; and, in case I should desire to change, I give you my body and soul, and my life as holding it from you, having dedicated it for ever without any will to repent.

Signed: [in blood] Urbain Grandier.

NECROMANCY

We are familiar with the claims of mediums that they can contact the dead and enquire of them information. Such practices are usually regarded as innocent, even a parlour-room diversion. What is not generally acknowledged is that the practitioner is performing necromancy; a form of divination which is generally associated with black magic.

Necromancy is the art of conjuring up the dead, or the spirits of the dead, for the purpose of prognostication. The basis is that the dead, having entered the realm of the divine, now know everything that has ever happened and ever will happen. As such they can be a source of information about the future. Some magicians might also use the dead for magical or other purposes; to cast spells, to discover where a person's weaknesses are in order to more specifically bind them with a spell or to locate hidden artefacts or treasures. The most extreme form of the art is to raise the dead in order that they may be used as a weapon against the living.

It is a form of divination, as described by Francis Barrett in 1801 in *The Magus*, acquiring its name: 'because it works on the bodies of the dead, and gives answers by the ghosts and apparitions of the dead, and subterraneous spirits, alluring them into the carcasses of the dead by certain hellish charms, and infernal invocations, and by deadly sacrifices and wicked oblations'.

Most modern analysts, however, acknowledge that the methods and purpose of spiritualist mediums and psychic researchers probably do not constitute true necromancy which is, in its 'usual' form, ceremonial and cloaked in ritual. The more magical intent of traditional necromancers is also at odds with modern mediumship. Nevertheless the connection cannot be ignored.

It is an ancient belief, and one that is clearly described in the Bible in the story of the 'Medium (or Witch) of Endor' in the Old Testament. The Medium (or Witch) of Endor called up the spirit of the prophet Samuel. After Saul had 'put the mediums and the wizards out of the land' he sought help from God who apparently ignored him and so he turned to a medium. 'And when Saul inquired of the Lord, the Lord did not answer him, either by dreams, or by Urim, or by prophets. Then Saul said to his servants, "Seek out for me a woman who is a medium, that I may go to her and enquire of her." And his servants said to him, 'Behold, there is a medium at Endor.'

Saul travelled to the woman in disguise (bearing in mind that he had been the one who had turned out the mediums), and visited her at night. He convinced her that he was not 'setting her up', but remained in disguise, and persuaded her to 'bring up Samuel for me.' She did and got a shock when she discovered who her client was!

'When the woman saw Samuel, she cried out with a loud voice; and the woman said to Saul, "Why have you deceived me? You are Saul." The King said to her, "Have no fear; what do you see?" And the woman said to Saul, "I see a god coming up out of the earth." He said to her, "What is his appearance?" And she said, "An old man is coming up; and he is wrapped in a robe." And Saul knew that it was Samuel, and he bowed with his face to the ground, and did obeisance.'

This is quoted from the Revised Standard Version of the Bible which states in its introduction: 'Words that have changed in meaning, and are therefore misleading, have been replaced by the language of today'. It is interesting that earlier versions of the Bible refer to the woman not as a medium but as a witch.

The Oracles (see Section Three) sometimes used necromancy to gain information for their clients.

In *Bellum Civile*, often known as the *Pharsalia*, an epic of the Roman civil war, the Roman poet Marcus Annaeus Lucanus (AD 39–65) describes what the writer Robert Graves (1895–1985) has described as a 'a horror-comic witch' who practices necromancy. Although a fictional epic it demonstrates that the practice was recognised at the time. The witch lives in Thessaly, in a tomb, where she eats the flesh of the dead. She forces the dead to speak by animating them using a mixture of menstrual blood, the intestines of a lynx and the froth of a mad dog. Her magic is completed with animal-like screams calling on the powers of the underworld.

Other ancient writers also described the process. Aeschylus, in *The Persians* described the raising of Darius. Homer in *The Odyssey* describes a mass raising of the dead.

A well-known necromancer was Edward Kelley (1555–95), colleague of Queen Elizabeth I's court magician, John Dee. They are the subject of a classic print depicting necromancy: both standing in a powerful magical circle in a graveyard, in the moonlight, where the bones have obviously been disturbed from their grave and, standing up from the grave, the whitened figure of the summoned spirit.

It is not uncommon for necromancy rituals to take place in graveyards as the most dramatic of ceremonies involves corpses, or fragments of corpses, being used in the service. The rituals may include meditation upon death itself, wearing the clothes of the deceased being sought to be raised, eating the flesh of a dog (a dog being the guardian of the underworld in mythology) and performing services similar to parts of the Black Mass. It was a medieval myth that necromancers ate the flesh of the dead, a prevalent belief about the necromancers of Seville, Toledo, and Salamanca in Spain.

Typical of the type of ritual chant would be: 'By the virtue of the Holy Resurrection, and the torments of the damned, I conjure and exorcise thee, Spirit of [stating the deceased's name] deceased, to answer my liege demands, being obedient to these Sacred ceremonies, on pain of everlasting torment and distress'.

The service either restores the dead to animation by forcing the spirit back into the corpse, or raises an apparition of the decreased. It is said that only those that have died a natural death can be easily raised. To raise the body of a suicide victim is supposed to involve a good deal more magical power and ritual.

Once the necromancer has completed his task the corpse should be destroyed, either by burning or burial in quicklime, to prevent the spirit of the decreased becoming troubled and walking the earth, seeking out the necromancer.

Zombies

Although not necromancy, because nothing is being divined, an allied belief in raising the dead by witchcraft is the creating of zombies in Vodoun (see page 141). In Vodoun, commonly referred to as 'voodoo', the priest, or *bokor*, can revive a dead body if it has not started to decompose. The awakened body is known as a zombie; it can walk, eat, hear and speak, but it is deprived of memory. It acts like an automaton, demonstrating no obvious ability to think for itself. Such a zombie is under the control of the *bokor* who uses it as a slave. Although sometimes used as weapons against the living, the most common claim of Vodoun is that zombies are a form of cheap labour, used as workers in the fields. They may work directly for the *bokor*, or be sold by him to other farmers.

The Haitians (Haiti is the principal location of modern day Vodoun) have a great fear of the zombie, but their greater terror is reserved for the fear of themselves or a relative becoming one. It is traditional to place huge and heavy stones on graves to prevent the *bokor* claiming the corpse. Relatives are 'posted' to keep watch over graves until it is likely that the corpse has started to decompose. Another 'technique' used to prevent the deceased being claimed as a zombie is to mutilate it so that it cannot function properly even if raised from the grave. More obscure methods to prevent zombies are sometimes employed; for example, relatives will scatter thousands of tiny seeds or beads and lengths of string around the grave in the belief that the corpse, if raised, will then become so fascinated with the problem of trying to thread them into a chain that it will not hear, or attend, the call of the *bokor*.

The *bokor* needs to be watchful over his zombies. If they eat meat, or salt, then it is believed that the zombie will become alert to his condition and return to the grave.

Alfred Metraux, a French anthropologist, studied the phenomenon of zombies but was sceptical of the evidence. In particular he discovered that one figure claiming to be a zombie was in fact a mentally retarded woman who at the time was most certainly still alive. But he found some evidence impressive. One case concerned a woman who had been buried in a coffin that was manifestly too small for her; her neck had had to be twisted to fit into the coffin. During the burial ceremony an accident had caused the corpse's foot to be badly burned. In life, she had spurned a would-be lover, but it was reported that years later her zombie was identified, performing menial tasks for the same man. The deceased's brother was able to identify her, noting the badly twisted neck and burned foot.

There may be a pharmacological basis for the zombie. The *bokor* may be employing drugs rather than magic to 'create' the zombies; perhaps to further their own reputation. Wade Davis is an ethnobiologist who studied the phenomenon. He believed poisons found in the puffer fish, and in a particular toad, might be responsible for producing a death-like coma. While modern doctors would be able to analyse the condition, those of more primitive cultures, in an atmosphere of superstition and a strong belief in zombies, might believe the comatose person to be dead. After an appropriate period of time the *bokor* would administer the antidote to the poison, seemingly bringing the dead back to life. The side effects of the drugs would include brain dysfunction and loss of memory, and the 'zombie' would act in a 'robot-like' drugged state. Perhaps without clear mental faculties the 'zombie' would be dependant on the *bokor* for assistance; furthering the *bokor*'s claim to be controlling the 'corpse'.

'Zombification' is recognised in Haitian law. Article 249 of Haiti's Criminal Code makes the practice illegal. 'Also shall be qualified as attempted murder the employment which may be made against any person of substances which, without causing actual death, produce a lethargic coma more or less prolonged. If, after the administering of such substances, the person has been buried, the act shall be considered murder no matter what result follows'.

It may seem that zombies are a subject of either science fiction or horror in the modern day, having no place in reality. But in fact the superstitions of Haiti run deep and zombies form a part of its most modern politics and culture. The Duvalier dictators of Haiti, 'Papa Doc' François and 'Baby Doc' Jean-Claude, both used the myth of the zombie in their roles as dictators. Pap Doc made it well known that he was a powerful *bokor*; emphasised by his naming his personal 'army' the 'Tontons Macoutes' – after the powerful voodoo sorcerers. Even in 1994 the Haitians used the myth of the zombies in an attempt to frighten off US marines who were preparing to invade the island. As the *Daily Mail* reported at the time: 'Battalions of "zombies" have been formed in Haiti – to halt the threat of an American invasion. The military junta claims to have created a force of men once dead, but brought back to half-life to serve voodoo priests.'

VODOUN

The witchcraft and the use of magic and ritual generally examined in this section is not a mainstream belief system or branch of religion in the West although it is becoming an increasingly popular one in the modern day. It is still a minority group form of worship and following, conducted largely in secret or if not actually concealed, then with privacy and respect for the privacy of others.

However, it is important to remember that such practices are not secret the world over. Having considered the phenomenon of zombies, it is perhaps useful to examine the religion in which zombies arise: Haitian Vodoun. Vodoun, popularly known as 'voodoo', in practised by virtually all – 97 percent at one estimate – of the population of Haiti and is in very public acceptance.

Vodoun is based on the cults from West Africa and has parallels or offshoots in other parts of the West Indies and in Brazil. It almost certainly originated in an area of Africa now part of Nigeria. Its export across the world, particularly into the French and Spanish colonies in the Caribbean, was the product of the slave trade. Maya Deren, who studied Haitian Vodoun in the 1940s commented that the slaves: 'brought with them their particular traditions, their language, their gods, their rituals, their dances, their drum beats, the memory of their homelands and the names of their towns and rivers. *Bokono* [magicians] and *vodu-no* [priests] trained in Africa, taught the following generations, born in slavery, the names and characteristics of the gods and the sacrifices required'. It is almost inevitable that the first slave ships must have transported learned priests of Vodoun who were able to keep the religion intact in the New World and not allow it to collapse. This fact, plus the needs of a people uprooted and cast away from their homeland, probably contributed to the importance of Vodoun amongst the early slaves. It is believed to have fifty million followers across the world and has become the basis of some magic on mainland North America, where the following has a hold. For example, in Harlem in New York there are many shops and market stalls selling the components of Vodoun rituals.

It was suppressed by the white slave-owners on pain of death. Practitioners, and those found with fetishes (objects that invoke magic or are held to contain a spirit and which create a bond between humans and the supernatural), were subject to imprisonment, hanging or being flayed alive. White slave-owners, to save the souls of the black slaves, had them baptised into

Catholicism, and Vodoun gradually incorporated elements of the Catholic faith into its rituals and beliefs. Tribal gods began to acquire the names of Catholic saints and fetishes were often replaced with the instruments of Catholic worship, such as statues and candles.

The central feature of Vodoun practice is the willing, indeed invited, possession of the practitioner by gods or spirits, known as *loa* who 'ride' – 'overshadow' is a term used in the practice – the possessed during the ceremonies, while the invitee is in a trance state. Although it tends to have become a tourist attraction on Haiti and plays up to its own rather dramatic image – usually including animal sacrifice of some sort – it is as profound in its structures as any following around the world. It does involve animal sacrifice which contributes towards its reputation, particularly in an era of ecological concern and animal rights. During the initiation of the servants of the *loa*, for example, chickens and other animals are torn apart while still alive.

The preparatory Vodoun rituals include the drawing of sigils (signs), called *vevers*. These are symbolic images rather akin to amulets and talismans (magical symbols of protection and power) and many researchers have commented on the similarity between the *vevers* of Vodoun and the demon-sigils depicted in Western grimoires. The *vever* represents the *loa* to be called upon.

It is deeply symbolic religion and virtually everything in Haiti has a double meaning; the road is both the route to a place and the route to a new spirituality, illness is partly a retribution for wrongdoing, and so on. This is a reflection of 'dual significance'; an awareness of the visible and the invisible. The Vodoun concept of the soul, in particular, is one of two spirits; the good big angel (*gros-bon-ange*) and the good little angel (*ti-bon-ange*). The former is the intellect and personality, the latter is effectively conscience. On death the souls are released from the mortal body but must be rehoused, usually in clay jars. If they are not then they will haunt the relatives for neglecting their needs. These ancestors gradually acquire the attributes of local gods; once the relatives of a deceased person are themselves dead, then all that is left is the clay pot that preserves his soul, which then begins to be transfigured into a god.

The pantheon of gods in Vodoun are divided into two classes; the ancient gods that were worshipped in Africa and the gods that have come into being from the death of important people. They are regarded as 'living' gods to their worshippers; they drink, argue, make love, can be jealous and spiteful and seeking of revenge. Vodoun does not revere the gods at a distance, nor does it regard them with piety. Religious devotion is not measured in solemn terms; Vodoun worshippers live with their gods in the true sense. The gods are their companions, mentors yes, but also local gossips! Above all these gods is one supreme deity known as Gran Met but this god is regarded as so far above humanity as to be unreachable, and the worship is through the *loas* who interface with humanity.

Worship is either public or private, but not secretive. Domestic worship usually takes place in a private area set aside for the purpose, rather akin to a family chapel, and available to members of families who worship their family deities. Public worship has arisen due to the move from rural to urban living and is conducted in *humfos* (Vodoun sanctuaries). These are more akin to churches and provide for a congregation of people bound rather by geographical proximity than by family ties. The *humfos* are basically buildings set aside for worship and ritual dancing and are presided over by a priest who is very much a local leader of the community as a whole.

Vodoun services are energetic exercises and for that reason are usually conducted on Saturday nights allowing for a period of recovery the next day. The congregation gets together in the *humfo* in a casual, friendly and informal gathering with plenty of gaiety. There will be salutes to the gods – many of whose clay jars are present – and to the Holy Trinity. Then the *vever* to summon a particular god is inscribed into the sand and consecrated. There follows a time of singing and dancing to bring the gods and the people closer together. The wild frenzy of some of the dancing and the power of the rhythmic drumbeats may assist in putting some of the worshippers into trance, an essential part of Vodoun. The gods then take possession of the humans at their invitation and they manifest the classic signs of possession: convulsions, trembling, fear. Others will watch over the possessed and protect them from undue harm if their thrashing about becomes too dangerous or extreme. The god is then deemed to be 'riding' the person. The possessed person becomes the god 'for real' and articles said to belong to the god are brought for the god's use. The possessed person then becomes a physical manifestation of the god who is deemed truly present amongst the worshippers. The lack of solemnity becomes apparent, even 'serious' deities will be welcomed into the *humfo* with ribald jokes and gaiety. '[The gods have] a fine repertoire of obscene songs . . . In some *humfo* a huge wooden phallus is kept on the altar in case such an attribute is suddenly required by the god. The possessed masquerade with it, dance obscene dances ...' (Alfred Metraux)

Such gods include the *Guede* – the gods of Death – including Nibo, Baron Saturday, Baron Cemetery, Baron Cross and others. In addition to being gods of death they are the gods of obscenity and licentiousness. Those possessed by them dress as corpses for the ritual dances, strap imitation penises to their loins, tell bawdy stories, sing bawdy songs and enact rape scenes with female worshippers or dance the *banda* – the most sexually explicit of ritual dances.

Other gods include an Earth-force depicted as a snake-god, Damballah. Worshippers possessed by Damballah never speak but only hiss, and they wriggle along the ground or climb trees.

When the possession ends, the person usually has no recollection of what was said or done during the time, rather in the manner of the spirit mediums who channel from the spirits of the deceased.

This might be regarded as akin to 'white magic' inasmuch as the services are not intended to create harm to anyone. But Vodoun has a 'black magic' side that is the aspect most commented on by observers. Rituals can be used to kill, and the role of the priest easily becomes overlaid with the role of magician. Magic as such is actually illegal in Haiti, though thought to be widely practised. Sympathetic magic is probably the best known version of Vodoun 'black magic'; a wax doll representative of the victim is harmed in some way so as to produce the same effect on the real person. Rituals exist to kill, to gain wealth, to condemn enemies to periods of bad fortune and so on. There are also rituals to raise the dead as zombies (see page 139).

In Vodoun it is believed that the spirit of a dead person can be sent to possess another as a curse placed by a sorcerer. To remove these spirits the subject needs the services of a more powerful sorcerer. Felicitas D. Goodman in her book *How About Demons?* (1988) describes a man called Antoine's exorcism, sought by his family because following such a curse he was now ill and wasting away. The priestess Lorgina, after deciding that the man was possessed by three 'dead', had Antoine's body prepared as if it were a corpse. She then performed a ritual which included the use of a hen and rooster that were then buried alive as a sacrifice, fire and water, and prayers to 'God the Father, God the Son and God the Holy Ghost, in the name of Mary, in the name of Jesus and all the Saints and all the dead'. During the ritual, the priestess called for help from her personal *loas* and also the *loas* of the possessed man. The ritual included the symbolic death and rebirth 'complete with reducing him to a corpse, burying him, and then having him be born from the depths of the ditch-womb, and finally giving him his first bath and making him drink like a new born infant'. It is reminiscent of 'New Age' rebirthing.

There are many parallels between the history of witchcraft and the history of Vodoun. Proponents of modern witchcraft are at great pains to point out that they are not workers of black magic but pagans who are following a nature religion. Many admit that witchcraft in the past might have contained elements of a more grim nature, and certainly it was viewed that way in some former periods of time. Vodoun also has a past that certainly did contain black magic elements, and it is strongly promoted as such today. Yet in modern times Vodoun is attracting a white, middle class following in major American cities despite the high cost of the practice (materials have to be imported from Haiti for the most part). And those modern converts are arguing a quite different character for their religion than the traditional image. American Anna Branche, after holidaying in Haiti, became a voodoo priestess and states: 'it is an earth religion ... we need to go back to our roots, our primitive and natural beginnings ... people are searching, searching for our salvation, our sanity, our purpose, our mission on this planet'. She stresses the spiritual and the healing nature of Vodoun. As is becoming common in the last few decades, it is another religion seeking to be relevant to an age where awareness of the world as a whole is becoming a widespread phenomenon.

White witch Lois Bourne, from England, visited Jamaica where she met with an *Obeama*, a practitioner of *Obeah* which is Jamaica's version of Vodoun. Lois states of the practices in her book *Dancing with Witches* (1998): 'According to some writers it has been distorted; human sacrifices, vampires, dripping blood and devil worship did not originate in or belong to Voodoo, which is presented as a life-affirming practice that encourages its participants to better understand the natural processes of life and their own spiritual natures.'

THE TOOLS AND WORKINGS OF MAGIC

Magic is an art which requires adherence to certain principles, and a conscious direction of will toward the desired end. Witches believe that the power of magic is such that it releases energy which returns to the witch three-fold, i.e. three times more 'powerfully'. Therefore, witches are very conscientious in their use of magic. Magic is generally divided into two main categories: white – positive, or good – magic and black – demonic, or evil – magic. White magic is used for healing and to combat the forces of black magic. Black magic is used for harm or killing, or to attract undue wealth or other gain.

Magicians, in the same manner as any other trade or profession, have a range of specialist tools at their disposal which are used to work their art. As to the use of the tool: '... magic is black or white according to the intention of the operator ...', according to Doreen Valiente, in '*Witchcraft for Tomorrow*'.

Magical practices can themselves be subdivided. The first of these divisions is called sympathetic magic, which is derived from symbolism and wish-fulfilment. The desired outcome is brought about by imitation or the use of associated objects. This is the basis of harming enemies by sticking pins in waxen images. It probably originated from the ancient hunters first 'imagining' their prey captured and killed as part of the pre-hunting ceremonies to give them good fortune. An extension of this would have been the belief that by eating the animal an individual could acquire their attributes: the strength of a bear, the speed of a fox. The second main division of magical practice is the use of charms and spells and calling on supernatural entities for assistance.

We will now look in more detail at these practices and the 'tools' of the trade.

The Altar

The witchcraft altar traditionally displays the tools of the practice of the religion, and of magic making; the four ancient elements represented by the chalice (water), salt (earth), and the censer (air and fire). The penacle or pantacle, a kind of ritual bowl also representing earth, is used to hold 'mooncakes' (the witchcraft version of consecrated bread) and ritual wine. There is an altar candle, also a white-handled knife (a utilitarian instrument), the very important *athame* (or black-handled knife), the magical wand, the scourge (used for self-purification), and the sword (used for initiation). The *athame* is charged with the energy of the owner and is used as a pointer to define space (such as casting a sacred circle) and as a conductor of the owner's will and energy.

Grimoires

The magical mythologies of ancient times are preserved in books known as grimoires. They describe, often with illustrations, the demons and their seals. An ancient grimoire is the *Lemegeton* also known as *The Lesser Key of Solomon the King*. Another one is called *The Greater Key of Solomon the King*. These describe secret seals of the seventy-two demons known to King Solomon. The seals, effectively a magical imprint or signature, contain the power of the demon and those who knew how to draw the image could evoke the demon. These keys which many believe were written by Solomon himself were thought able to utilise the occult powers. Solomon was the ruler of Israel in the tenth century BC and regarded as one with the powers of the Magi and certainly with the ability to evoke and control demons and spirits. It was said that he evoked such spirits to assist in building the temple in Jerusalem which bears his name. According to legend the keys should have remained where they were, concealed beneath King Solomon's throne, but on his death demons encouraged Solomon's courtiers to seek out the keys and once they were exposed to the world they created all manner of mayhem.

The two keys of Solomon were said to be the basis of the *Grimorium Verum* printed in 1517 and believed by many to be a more authoritative source of ritual than any other black magic account.

The Grimoire of Honorius is – falsely – credited to Pope Honorius III who ascended to the Papacy in 1216. It instructs priests in the art of demonology with many formulas and benedictions and makes the invocation and control of demons a part of the priest's job. It states: 'Only the Ruling Pontificate has possessed the virtue and power to command the spirits and invoke them. Now His Holiness, Honorius III, having become mellowed by his pastoral duties, has kindly decided to transmit the methods and ability of invoking and controlling spirits, to his brothers in Jesus Christ, the revered ones.' It is, the Grimoire states, based on the fact that when Jesus was on Earth he exercised power over demons. The reasoning for opening up demonology to the priests was as follows: 'We feel that while exorcising those who are possessed, [the priests] might become overcome at the frightful appearance of the rebellious Angels who were thrown into the Pit for their sins, so they may not be well enough versed in the things that they should know and use; and we desire that those who have been redeemed by the Blood of Jesus Christ should not be tortured by sorcery or possessed by a demon, and so we have added to this Bull [edict] the unchangeable manner whereby they may be invoked.'

The Book of Shadows

It seems to have been Aleister Crowley (see page 68) who first created the concept of the 'Book of Shadows'. This tool of witchcraft is a manual of the rituals and tools at the disposal of the coven. Traditionally it is handwritten by the witch.

The Book of Spirits

Every magician had, in addition to a Grimoire and a Book of Shadows, a Book of Spirits (*Liber Spirituum*). This had to be hand-created by the magician himself, listing the spirits that he might wish to conjure up, and the incantation that would summon that spirit. Once successfully invoked it could then more easily be invoked in the future. The *Grimoire of Honorius* also prepares the conjuration needed to consecrate the Book of Spirits.

Pentagram

Eliphas Lévi describes the pentagram as 'the allegorical star of the Magi'. The ratio of the lines which make up the pentagram are held to be in sacred proportion, the divine proportion as Leonardo da Vinci called it. The pentagram, the five-pointed star, can be displayed in two ways – firstly, with one point upward and two downward. It symbolises the human form. The upper point represents the head and the other four points the extremities of the hands and feet. The pentagram in this configuration is often shown as with a dot at the centre as it is displayed in Egyptian hieroglyphics. The dot represents the sexual parts. Where the pentagram is said to represent the etheric body, the invisible body made of the stuff of the stars, then the dot represents the powerful force of *Kundalini* (see pages 25 and 162). In Egyptian hieroglyphics the pentagram is the *sba* – star, the combination of God, time and spiritual essence. It is also the sign of the microcosm, i.e. of humanity as a symbol of the entire cosmos (the macrocosm). The five points also being thought to represent the four elements of earth, air, fire and water plus the fifth element which was the combination of them all.

The pentagram can be inverted, however, with one point downwards and two points up. It is in this configuration that it is used to call up the forces of evil. In this configuration the points of the pentagram represent the goat's head, the two horns, the beard and the ears. In the Order of the Golden Dawn (see page 66) the upturned pentagram was used for any 'absolute necessity for working or conversing with a Spirit of an evil nature.'

The pentagram is a 'unicursive figure', which means that it can be drawn with a single stroke of a writing instrument; the instrument not having to leave the paper. Each line in the pentagram is therefore dependent on the others. The lines are connected to one another. No one line is more important than another line. This is the essence of the 'strength' of the image. Rudolf Koch described it in *The Book of Signs*:

> The pentagram, a five-pointed star (can be) drawn with one stroke of the pen ... The pentagram has had several different significations at different times in the history of man ... The Pythagoreans called it the pentalpha (because it looked like five capital 'A's' interconnected), and the Celtic priests (called it) the witch's foot. It is also known as Solomon's Seal, known in the Middle Ages as the goblin's cross ... It also represented the five

senses; ... Amongst the Druids it was called the sign of the
Godhead, ... This sign was also popularly believed to be a
protection against demons, and, by analogy, a symbol of safety.
It is believed, too, to be the emblem of happy homecoming,
whence its employment as an amulet.

The pentagram has meant many things to many different people.
During periods in the Middle Ages, the pentagram was used by
the Catholic Church as a symbol of truth.

The Circle of Power

Another shape which has great meaning for those practising
the occult is the circle. It is the simplest shape, has no beginning
and no end, is a symbol of unity and oneness and has been used
as the protective shape in magic probably since the beginning of
time. Various cultures have drawn circles around the sick to
protect them from attack by demons. Magicians use it to protect
them while they are conjuring up demons. This is known as a
conjuration circle. If a magician draws the circle correctly and
remains safely within it the demons cannot attack. The circle
must always be drawn in a clockwise manner if it is designed for
use in white magic and anti-clockwise for black magic.

Gerald Gardner (see page 104) promoted the basic difference
between the uses of the circle by black and white magicians. He
believed that black magicians used the power of the circle to keep
out evil spirits and protect the black magicians from their power,
having called them up in the first place to use them for their own
evil ends. The white witch, Gardner proposed, used the circle not
to keep outside influences out, but rather to keep magic and
psychic energy contained and to focus the power.

Some witches emphasise the value of a circle of protection
when using Ouija, which they believe is a powerful instrument,
but one much abused by being trivialised as a 'party game'.

For witches, the circle, which may just be drawn in the earth,
also symbolises a rejection of special buildings such as churches.

Witches believe that all the Earth is sacred and in touch with the Goddess, therefore any place, indoors or out, may be 'consecrated' for ritual use. Outdoor spaces tend to be used from Ostara to Lughnasadh, indoor spaces from Samhain to Imbolc.

Within the sacred circle, two main activities occur: celebration, and the practice of magic. Celebration is most important at the major seasonal holy days, the Sabbats. At these times, the myths of the particular festival are enacted in ritual drama, celebrated by dance and in singing, and often with feasting and revelry.

Wish-fulfilment and Curse Magic

Well known, if not well understood, is the claim of magicians to be able to curse. It is a claim and a belief that goes right back to the earliest times, and certainly as early as our history of witchcraft can be traced back.

Curse magic is referred to in Egyptian papyri, it is in the oral traditions of shamans of non-technological cultures such as aborigines and there are some who believe that it is represented in the cave painting of our earliest ancestors. Cave pictures of, say, the hunting of animals for food often contain images of arrows aimed at or hitting the animals. It may be that the pictures are just images of the hunt itself. But there is a school of thought that the images are 'wish-fulfilling'; that the images were of what the hunters sought to happen, creating the magic that would make it come to pass. Certainly such magic is well documented, and is a large part of curse magic.

Originally it is probable that curse magic consisted of a verbal curse delivered by a practitioner, the power and timbre of the voice being important to the effectiveness of the curse. But very quickly the written curse was believed to have the same powers; in days of high illiteracy, indeed when few except clerics could write, the writer was believed to be almost magical for that talent alone. At one point the authorities actively decried reading as almost diabolical, no doubt because it threatened to put knowledge of the occult into the hands of 'the masses'. Over time the written curse was thought to be more powerful than the spoken one, presumably because the written one existed for longer than the spoken word.

The Romans, in order to make their curses of even longer duration, carved them on lead. Part of their reasoning may have been astrological; lead is associated with dark, brooding, serious Saturn. The curses were often nailed to trees, to shrines and so on. Nailing may have been designed to demonstrate the permanence of the curse. Welsh curses were inscribed on slate, a commonly available material in Wales. Some commentators have suggested that this may not have been the only reason for using such material; it also has a similar appearance to lead, invoking the image of the Roman curses.

Curses are also held to be 'binding', i.e. they bind the person to the fate demanded by the curse for a time, or for ever. Such binding also forms a part of curse magic known as 'ligature magic'. Some magicians specialised in 'tying up' a curse in a ligature, or leather strap. The ligature was knotted, the knot retaining the curse and binding it to the victim. Such a curse could only be released if the physical ligature was found and therefore it was hidden in obscure places; under floorboards, in chimneys, inside the trunks of trees, thrown into rivers where it became buried in the sediment. Today, as a result of that, many such ligatures have been found in relatively good condition, preserved in various ways by their concealment from the environment.

Guazzo, an Italian monk of the seventeenth century, described a ligature curse used to prevent a woman and her husband copulating, and thus preventing them producing offspring. They were still in love – an even worse part of the torture – but they could not come together without great distress. In order to try to break the curse the woman was tied down so that her husband could not be fought off. Nonetheless: '... when he came in, never was seen such terrible fury. No wild beast was ever so fierce or so filled with madness and rage as that woman. She foamed at the mouth, gnashed her teeth and rolled her eyes, whilst her whole body seemed to be shaken and possessed with demons. The women who were present said that when they touched her belly, which was twisting under the ropes, it appeared to be stuffed full, and all her skin was covered with weals as if she had been beaten.' Given the recognition through witchcraft and eastern philosophy of sex magic and the power of sexual union, we might speculate that the couple who were victims of the curse were being prevented from more than just a pleasurable act or the ability to procreate; it may have been the intention of the one placing the curse to render them less spiritually powerful.

The origin of ligature magic may have come from the nautical practice of 'capturing the wind'. A magician could tie up the wind in knots and the knotted ligatures were taken aboard a ship to be untied, and the wind released, if the ship were becalmed. It was only a short step to believing that the power of the curse could be as contained as the wind itself.

Apart from spoken or written words a good deal of curse magic arises from imagery; classically the wax image of the 'target' person who is to be cursed. By emulating on the wax image what was sought to happen in real life to the victim it was believed that the reality could be made to come true.

'Boning' is an aborigine curse designed to kill. A bone, around six inches long, would be imbued with a killing curse and then pointed at the victim. The curse was believed to fly out of the bone and into the victim. In the book in this series, *Powers of the Mind* (1998), we describe the release of a curse placed in this way, the victim only recovering from debilitating illness after being told that the curse had been 'a mistake' and was therefore lifted.

Graham James is an English white witch, and practitioner of white magic, but as he explains, he has to be well versed in the processes of black magic as part of his work is to combat such curses. He explained the workings of curse-making to us. 'To produce curses a black magician will work upon the Dark side of the Moon, during the Waning Moon phase which is from the last quarter to before the New Moon, a time traditionally when the

Moon is sleeping and should not be disturbed, while she recharges ready for the next waxing part of the cycle. This is the time used to cast a spell or curse using black magic to bring havoc, ill-will, misfortune, back luck or even poor health to another person or family.'

Graham described some of the processes involved. 'The materials used will depend upon the tradition or type of black magic spell used. For maximum effect a subject-link from the intended victim is used, typically hair, nail clippings or a photograph. Graham described what a black magician would do to produce a curse: 'The name and, if known, the date of birth of the victim is carved on candles or doll effigies and the materials anointed with specially prepared oils. The words of the curse are also inscribed upon these personalised items of evil. The doll effigy or black male/female candle will have the hair and photo attached to it, or the nail clippings mixed with graveyard dirt stuffed inside or attached to the effigy. The appropriate sacred words of the rite are used as the ritual is secretly performed. The effects, if performed correctly, can be devastating to the victim.'

Why in a modern society would such practices be evoked, we asked. Graham's view was that the same reasons had existed since time began. 'The most common reasons for this distasteful practice would be hatred, spite or petty jealousy; the strongest negative human emotions.' Graham has dealt with many people who have been cursed by a former relationship partner as a result of a love affair ending, or being caught having an affair. 'They can pay a black magician to carry out this distasteful deed or the person may purchase a readily available DIY book of black magick and perform the rituals themselves.' For anyone thinking of trying it Graham has very clear words of warning. 'This is a very dangerous practice for the uninitiated novice or beginner. All magic returns to the practitioner three-fold and black magic will seriously harm an unprotected person. As a white witch I often have to deal with the casualties of [people's] own misdirected spells and protect them by banishing and neutralising the curses they have brought on themselves.'

Graham offered the following signs and symptoms of curses:

- Sudden and continual ill-health or prolonged headaches, especially in an otherwise normally healthy person.

- Depression for no apparent reason, especially in a non depressive person.

- A long period of bad luck and missed opportunities; financial downfalls and losses.

- Sudden accident-proneness of self or a close family member.

- Haunting nightmares, seeing apparitions and strange entities; insomnia and night time anxieties.

- Unexplained sudden fears, phobias and panic attacks, especially in a normal mentally stable person.

- Unexpected family or marital problems which are out of the ordinary and out of character with the normal family environment.

- Loss of appetite or sudden loss of sexual desires; also virility problems.

However, Graham cautions against becoming hysterical when recognising these symptoms. Cursing is still a 'poor second' to 'natural' ailments and problems in modern life. All of the above can, and usually do have normal origins. The first stop for someone suffering from these is the doctor, not the magician.

Graham has dealt with many people who have come to him believing that they have suffered the loss of homes, families, businesses, jobs, money, health, sanity and more as a result of being cursed. He suggests that if a person believes this to be the case they should contact a reputable white witch, and even get second opinions if in doubt. He believes his profession suffers from the same problems all professions have to deal with; there are good practitioners, poor ones, many that think they are better than they are, and a few charlatans that give the business a bad name.

He points out that many people would prefer to seek out their local clergy and completely agrees with that choice; the individual must feel comfortable with the procedures. The Church itself of course is a good deal less tolerant of witchcraft, even in the present day. However, we have spoken to at least one Canon who recognises that cursing in primitive societies – where he worked as a missionary – was a very real part of the lives of the people and needed to be dealt with in a way that was appropriate to their culture and belief systems.

Graham provided us with an example of a curse from his own files.

The subject was an Afro-Caribbean woman who had broken up with her partner of over twenty years and had lost her home and many possessions. Although she retained custody of the children the court had ordered her removal from the family home. Her appeal also failed. Although she and her children were still in the family house along with the estranged ex-partner, their deadline was quickly approaching. She believed that her husband had been working black magic upon her and the children, to produce the court decisions he desired. Graham asked her to seek out the evidence for this accusation, and advised her on what, and where, such evidence might be found. A few days later she returned, having found 'black magic' materials and a book hidden behind the ex-partner's wardrobe in his room. The book was one of magic and the appropriate curses had been highlighted. Given that Graham now had the spells and materials used to hand he was, he believes, able to defeat the curse. 'I requested a photograph, full name and date of birth of her ex-partner. I also had the advantage of his personal handwriting in the book. To have such ammunition to work with gives blissfully quick results and a high degree of accuracy.' Graham also sent back the curse three-fold onto the practitioner as a punishment. 'I protected and exorcised my client and restored her life to normal. Before my work had been completed, my client reported some strange behaviour from her ex-partner: he was mumbling all the time and reading the Bible continually, he was totally uncommunicative and appeared nervous and scared. His previously threatening and abusive behaviour ceased, and his callous attitude and confidence were removed. I knew at that stage that all my efforts were paying off and success was imminent, even though I had not completed all the work, But for thoroughness, a professional witch will see a lunar cycle through for completion and not quit, lest the spell returns. The secret of success in magic is arcane knowledge, serious commitment, dedication and persistence. After working through the lunar cycle, I produced a spellpouch, which was an extension of my altar workings, for the client to carry around and use to ensure ongoing success. The spellpouch was for protection, psychic self-defence, hex-breaking, exorcism, banishing evil, health-drawing, peace, harmony and to restore courage, strength, confidence and lifeflow. All of these petitions are compatible with each other and easily charged and consecrated into one spellpouch. I gave the spellpouch to my client, she had already informed me that she was feeling much better and that her ex-partner had left the home and continued to act strangely. I received a call from my client a couple of weeks later, and she told me that her solicitor had informed her that to his surprise the High Court had reopened her appeal.'

We also examined many files from Graham's work, with literally hundreds of letters from people thanking him for similar successes and turnarounds in their lives. Needless to say many people would accept neither Graham's, nor his client's, view of what happened. Some would put the events down to coincidence, the change in attitude and health in the woman down to nothing more than a change of outlook on life. The fact that a person – any person but in this case a witch – took a caring interest in the client might have been enough to let her 'heal herself'. In that we see both a reconciliation to holistic healing and a return to the earliest days of the 'medicine man' or 'witch doctor' who was the central figure and healer of the tribe. Even if all magic is just a totem to allow others to do what is natural, the fact is that for some, in some way, it works.

Talismans and Amulets

One activity of witchcraft is the production of what might loosely be called 'charms'. These are usually devices to protect an individual from illness, harm or bad fortune. They can also be used to bring about specific good fortune; for example, success in business, in finance, or in matters of the heart.

Technically the talisman is a personalised charm which contains a seal and something personal: the name or address, typically, of the client. An amulet usually contains a symbol, often of ancient derivation. The witch will prepare the talisman or amulet at his or her altar and imbue it with a spell to bring the necessary effect. The 'charm' is then carried or worn by the individual for whom it was prepared.

A most popular use of magic is in the production of love charms.

Love Charms

These are designed to make a person fall in love with another, or to encourage sexual attraction.

The general form of such charms is to take something belonging to the person who is desired to be brought under the spell, or to impose on them something from the person generating the charm. The latter might involve slipping something from the body of the charm-caster into the drink of the intended 'victim', not infrequently secretions from the genitals.

Alternatively, love potions might be created; made of herbs, sometimes honey or wine made from elderberry. The concept is not dissimilar to the concept of aphrodisiac potions. One apocryphal tale claims that one such potion was far too successful. Applied by a Welsh man to his intended the result was: '... pitiful to see her following him. She would run through pools, over hedges, up hill and down dale only to catch sight of him. At last he got tired of her and wished to undo the spell, but he could not. The girl died, worn out with mental anguish.'

Sex as a Form of Transformational Magic

When asked why there seemed to be a lot of sex in witchcraft, one witch blandly replied that there was a lot of sex in life. Certainly there is, and it would be surprising if sex were not a focus of witchcraft and magic, in various forms.

There is much similarity between the sexuality of witchcraft and the sexual expressions of worship which arise in the East, particularly in Hindu beliefs. Indeed, it is a Tantric expression that the universe is the product of sexual union between Shiva and Shakti. This union is symbolised by the images of the *Lingam* – the male sexual organ – and the *Yoni* – the female counterpart. In China the male and female qualities of the universal life force are known as yin and yang, the cosmic union of which is the basis of the divination system known as the *I Ching* (see page 173).

This brings about the belief that sexual union can be an act of worship, representing the original union that created the universe. Many witches believe that this basic belief which is expressed in the East is the same as the one adopted by witches in the West. The Tantric 'chakrapuja' – a circle of worship – has been likened to the witches' Sabbat; an image strengthened by the stories of Krishna, the Hindu god, dancing in circles in the moonlight with the cow-girls of Brindaban. In the Middle East a cult known as the Beni Udhra believed in a form of sex magic akin to that of Buddhist Tantras.

In both the East and the West there has been a certain suppression of the sex act as a form of worship, possibly due to the base motives attributed to exponents. In the East, while following the teachings of Krishna, there is some rejection of the erotic themes no doubt in part due to the influence of the West, and in the West sex-magic promoted by witches is either regarded as immoral or the subject of ribald, tabloid humour.

Nudity is a feature of many witch rituals though it should be emphasised that the purpose is not to be nude, but rather to be – as it is sometimes called – skyclad, i.e. clad in the clothing of the heavens only. It is not a distinction likely to gain intelligent comment from tabloid accounts of witches dancing naked in the moonlight. Yet there are parallels in Eastern philosophy also: Krishna sought to remove the chains of ignorance and artificiality from men and women and symbolised this by removing the clothes of the bathing milkmaid Gopi, forcing her to come to him unclothed, the symbol of her artificialness divested.

Common to many of these beliefs is that of 'cool sex'; the deliberate prolonging of the act of sex rather than the flurry of passion. In these teachings the avoidance of climax and the indefinite prolonging of the union is the central aim. The belief is that the energy so created and retained within the couple becomes 'higher state' energy. In effect, sex is used to create something of an 'altered state of consciousness'. The French language has long recognised this, their expression for climax is 'petite morte'; 'the little death'.

As Valiente states: 'The techniques by which control is maintained are regarded as among the most important secrets of sexual magic'. Those techniques are akin to yoga; controlled breathing and meditative concentration. Climax is averted by such control and concentration without losing the erection and thus maintaining the act of union.

The Tantras of both Buddhism and Hinduism contain reference to the 'subtle body'; the network of energy channels around the body linked by the energy centres known as the *chakras*. Coiled up at the base of the 'spine' in the subtle body is the energy known as *Kundalini*, depicted as positioned in the subtle body where the sexual organs are in the physical body. The controlled release of *Kundalini* is a 'goal' of yoga, and it is clearly linked to sex magic. It is held to be a powerful force, one capable of damaging the mind and body if released unexpectedly or without proper training. It has even been suggested as a cause of spontaneous human combustion. The energy, channelled properly, has been held to grant prolonged youthfulness, longer life and a more permanent spiritual awareness. Cool sex and celibacy would appear to be opposite ends of the spectrum, but in reality they both represent a channelling of sexual energy.

In 'Alchemy' (see page 21) we describe the Language of the

Birds; the occult, hidden language that was used to impart knowledge to the initiated without revealing the same knowledge to those not thought worthy, or prepared enough, to receive it. Many who have studied the alchemical texts believe that the core of alchemy is sex magic; that the Language of the Birds is describing sexual union for magical purposes.

It will be remembered that the description of the 'Philosophers' Stone' sought by alchemists was given as: 'It is a stone and it is not a stone, it exists everywhere in nature but is ignored or despised, it is unknown and yet known to everyone, it is made of fire and water, it is a fluid without weight, it comes from God but does not come from God.'

- 'A stone and not a stone'; is this a reference to the egg within the female that, if fertilised, becomes the bringer of life?

- 'it exists everywhere in nature but is ignored or despised' could be a reference to love and the act of sex.

- 'it is unknown and yet known to everyone' could be a similar reference; sex and sexual union are universal, yet philosophers would argue that no-one fully understands the true nature of love.

- 'it is made of fire and water, it is a fluid without weight'; not an obvious combination if taken literally but a clear reference to love if taken astrologically. Valiente describes the vessels used in alchemy as representing the male and female organs, the athanor – the furnace, and the curcurbite – the gourd. The furnace is referred to as male – a reference to the 'purest male element, fire', the gourd representing the vessel in which alchemical change takes place. It is in the female body that the alchemy that changes semen and egg into living matter takes place. Valiente describes the semen as 'the blood of the red lion' from Leo, the sign of fire, and the female lubricative fluids as 'the gluten of the white eagle', the symbol of Scorpio representing the female element of water.

- 'it comes from God but does not come from God'. 'God is love' and that many pray to God for His love demonstrates the belief that love is God-given to the world, but each act of love also comes from each person.

The fluids from the two sexes, mingled during sexual union, produce 'first matter'. Combined with the power of the mind heightened by sexually enhanced altered states of consciousness this produces the elixir – perhaps the alchemists' 'elixir of life'. In the *Karpuradistotram Tantra* it is prescribed that the male should drink the combined fluids directly from the female vagina.

It is almost certainly this elixir – this sexually united mix of fluids – that Aleister Crowley referred to in *Magick in Theory and Practice* (1929): 'The highest form of the Eucharist [note: the Christian sacrament of the body and blood of Christ] is that in which the Element consecrated is One. It is one substance and not two, not living and not dead, neither liquid nor solid, neither hot nor cold, neither male or female. ...'

The 'youth revolution' we have come to call 'the Sixties' focused a great deal on changing attitudes to sex. Under the banners of sexual liberation the revolution advocated liberal attitudes towards sexual freedom, embodied by the term 'permissiveness'. Permissiveness allowed for sexual openness, sexual experimentation and so on. 'Anything goes' was another expression from the hippie communities which basically meant do anything as long as it did not infringe on the rights of others to 'do their own thing'. They are surely instinctive versions of Crowley's 'do what thou wilt shall be the whole of the law', (though it is doubtful that Crowley would have shared the sixties movements of female liberation and sexual equality). Nor was it merely a liberation of sex as an act, nor the admission that it frequently took place outside of marriage (as it always had, of course) that characterised the sixties. A variety of sexual acts was positively encouraged and became a norm; indeed the march of sexual experimentation has been clear. At the simplest level was the appreciation of sex outdoors, most obviously promoted during music festivals such as 'Woodstock'; such an act allows for sex to be a part of communing with the wider nature, feeling the wind and smelling the flowers and so on. In the nineties, magazines for people of all ages are highly descriptive in their advice on sexual experimentation, virtually teaching a variety of sexual practices that is almost limitless.

But all of this movement towards sexual experimentation brings us back to the variety of sex acts revered in witchcraft and Eastern philosophy. The *Kama Sutra*, for example, is well-known as a repository of creative sexual positions, but is perhaps less popularly recognised as the spiritual book it is; the sexual unions described are there to bring a heightened state to the couple involved, not merely sexual pleasure for its own sake. It can hardly be a coincidence that the sixties and sexual liberation closely followed on from a flowering of Eastern philosophy (publicly embodied by The Beatles embracing the teachings of the Mahareshi Mahesh Yogi) and indeed from the repeal of the Witchcraft Acts that first allowed witches freedom of worship and, inevitably, to describe their beliefs publicly.

In the recent decade there has even been a clear movement towards cool sex. Couples have been encouraged to make the act of sex a joint worship of each other rather than just a frantic tumble between the sheets. The techniques used for ritual in witchcraft and the East have been utilised in sex manuals for married couples to make sexual union with one partner for life 'more interesting'. And the advent of AIDS has created a need to consider forms of 'non-sex' sex, many of which can add to the prolonging and pleasure of either non-sexual contact, or as foreplay for the sex act if it does take place.

In reaching out for variety in sex, and in seeking deeper meaning to sex, modern day couples are – probably without realising it, and perhaps at a level unknown even to themselves – rediscovering the magical qualities that philosophies of centuries ago promoted. Sex, performed with spirituality and an enlightened frame of mind, could be the magic alchemists concealed with their hidden language; the true magic of transformation of the spirit of humankind.

3

DIVINERS OF THE GODS' INTENT

Divination simply means trying to access the divine intentions of the gods. Divination takes many forms, and has been in use probably since the dawn of time.

DIVINATION IN ANCIENT GREECE AND ROME

An early form of divination used by the Greeks, Etruscans and Romans was extispicy, telling the future by examining the entrails of sacrificial animals. It is probable that it dates back to the earliest humans.

Generally the two main organs used in extispicy are the liver and the intestines. The liver was believed to be the seat of the soul. It was also believed to be a mirror which could reflect the divine light from the gods. (The origin of this belief could derive from the fact that the liver of a freshly slaughtered lamb will give a perfect reflection for some fifteen minutes or so until it dulls). Since the gods knew the future, the logic of ancient diviners was that by looking at the reflection of their divine rays the future could be foretold. It was the Babylonians who apportioned the lamb's liver into fifty-five separate areas, each giving an indication of some future event if strange markings were found in those areas. The Greeks tended to examine the liver as a whole and were particularly looking for the main shapes they expected to see. For example, if the head protrusion was missing it foretold very bad things indeed. It has been said that it was absent in divinations that took place just before the deaths of both Julius Caesar and Alexander the Great.

Regarding the intestines, these were often laid out to form a spiral and this was similar to both the Greek labyrinths and the various spiral-shaped marks that have been found on sacred stones for millennia; it also mimicked the orbital motion of the heavenly bodies. The Etruscans, in particular, made the connection between the celestial bodies and the intestines of sacrificed animals.

Oracles

The Greeks also used oracles as a form of divination. An oracle is the advice or prophecy given by a deity to an enquirer; it also refers to the location at which people consulted their deities. Probably the most famous is the Oracle at Delphi though there were several scattered around the Aegean Sea. Interestingly the original purpose of the oracle sites seems to have been less for divination and more for mapping of the Earth's surface. The oracles were located at key points of latitude. For example, three main oracle sites in the 'west' (Dodona, Delphi and Delos in Greece) were located at precisely the same latitudinal positions as three 'eastern' sites (Metsamor, Sardis and Miletus in Turkey). These layouts are believed by some to be evidence of worship of the Mother Earth or Earth spirit.

The traditional story of the Oracle at Delphi seems to have been a piece of early disinformation designed to keep the actual site a secret and perhaps the workings more mystic. It was said that the Sibyl, the seer or prophet, sat on a tripod over a gorge from which smells arose which would send her into a trance. The smells were supposedly from the corpse of a mythical Python. In the trance the Sibyl would answer questions and predict the future. Resident poets would record her predictions for the future. However, excavation at Delphi showed that there was no such gorge in the earth at the given location, and that the actual site of the Oracle at Delphi was some two miles away in a small cavern. It has been suggested that either the site was a secret to all but a few or that the story of the strange smell was there to cover up the fact that the Sibyl was using hallucinogenic drugs.

There is some evidence that the Oracle of Apollo at Calophon (in modern Turkey) used drugs as did the Oracle at Branchidae slightly further to the south. Some theorise that the Greek oracles may have been based on Egyptian practices. For example, the historian Herodotus (c. 485–25 BC) writes that Dodona was founded from Egyptian Thebes and that the Oracle at Delos was founded by an Egyptian ('The son of Cecrops') who later became king of Athens in 1558 BC. Although not particularly associated with the oracles at either Delphi or Dodona, it is very clear that the Greeks would also drug those who came to consult the oracles. Pausanias, the Greek geographer and historian, describes this in his *Itinerary*. The subject was first made to fast and then drugged and then slid down into underground vaults amidst a mass of snakes. Now in a state of terror and suggestibility the subject would hear a prophetic message. If the subject appeared to be sceptical it is thought that occasionally a person was murdered to prevent their spreading the story of a failure of prophecy.

In Book 6 of Virgil's *Aeneid* there is a description of the descent into Hades which includes rowing across the river Styx. It was only in 1967 that the evidence was produced that this description might have related to visiting an oracle. An English engineer, Robert Paget, excavated the Baian Oracle near the cave of the Sibyl of Cumae in Italy. In this astonishing underground cave network, carved a fifth of a mile into the rock, is an artificial river, presumably representing the Styx, across which those seeking to consult the oracle were rowed in a small boat. It is presumed that those visiting the oracle were led to believe that they were genuinely journeying to the Underworld and perhaps with the additional use of drugs they were very inclined to believe so. The complex had been sealed up during the reign of the Emperor Augustus (63 BC–AD 14).

Scholars believe that the enigmatic and ambiguous utterings of the oracles assisted in stimulating creative thought and as such they played their role in establishing the Greeks as free revolutionary thinkers. Such ambiguity could be dangerous, however. Croesus, the king of Lydia, asked the oracle what would be the result of his declaring war on the Persians and he was told that he would destroy a great empire. Encouraged by this pronouncement he went to war and did indeed destroy a great empire – his own!

The Oracle at Delphi has been studied not just as a site of occult divination but as an intelligence centre and it is apparent that many factors contributed to its reputation as a highly successful predictor of the future. It was located centrally and was very popular; therefore the priests working there had a good inflow of information from people from all over that part of the Mediterranean and beyond, including leading political and religious figures, farmers, soldiers and sailors. In effect the oracle was a clearing house for information and the priests were running an intelligence-gathering network. The pronouncements of the oracle were therefore based on a certain amount of information that probably was not readily available to most people. It has been suggested that a network of carrier pigeons was used to keep Delphi informed of the latest events which could then be offered as prophecy since the information would reach Delphi probably long before any human had done so. It would not, however, be fair to suggest that this amounted to a fraud. It was, in effect, a political design to concentrate wealth and political power for the good of the empire.

There was probably a good deal of psychology at play. Most people consulting the oracle were not looking for guidance but rather for support for their plans which they intended to undertake anyway (King Croesus almost certainly comes into that category). No doubt this reinforcement actually did help certain people to feel more confident and do a better job thus making the prediction come true. Where that was not the case the pronouncements were usually made sufficiently ambiguously to give the oracle a 'get-out clause'.

Although oracles ceased to be used by the Greeks and Romans, who moved into astrology for divination, the technique certainly did not die out and indeed has been used to the present day. The Dalai Lama was warned by an oracle of the Chinese invasion in 1959 and was able to escape Lhasa in time. Even in exile the Dalai Lama has maintained contacts with an oracle. The Azande people of Sudan consult oracles before travelling or planting crops.

METHODS OF DIVINATION

The list of methods of divination since earliest times is almost literally endless; divining from shapes in clouds, in flames, in tealeaves, etc. In this section we will look at the main forms of divination that have become famous throughout the world.

I Ching

The *Ta Chuan* or Great Commentary is a treatise written by an unknown scholar or group of scholars to explain the multi-layered meanings of the Chinese divination system known as the *I Ching*. In it is written:

> With the help of the fundamental principles of the *I Ching* it is possible to arrive at a complete realisation of man's innate capacities. This unfolding rests on the fact that man has innate capacities that resemble Heaven and Earth, that he is a microcosm. Now, since the laws of Heaven and Earth are reproduced in the *I Ching* man is provided with the means of shaping his own nature, so that his inborn potentialities for good can be taken into account: wisdom and action, or intellect and will. If intellect and will are correctly centred, the emotional life takes on harmony.

The German poet and novelist Hermann Hesse (1877–1962) stated simply: 'The *I Ching* can transform life'.

Unlike many techniques of divination, such as the Tarot and casting the Runes (see pages 199 and 191), the *I Ching* is not merely a set of symbols designed to release inner thinking or act as a sort of Rorschach test, providing a random pattern to enable the diviner to create their own interpretation. Although interpretation of the *I Ching* is still required, this system of divination comes with written script offering interpretation of the sixty-four possible patterns that can emerge. In addition to being a system of divination these Chinese texts are a system of philosophy adopted by the two principal religions of China, Taoism and Confucianism. Indeed Confucius once said that if he had extra years he would devote fifty of them to studying the *I Ching*.

The basis of the *I Ching* is in the yin and the yang which are the two components of *T'ai* and *Chi* – the ultimate cause, the basis of everything. T'ai Chi is a self-contradictory essence described, for example, by John Blofeld in his work on the *I Ching, The Book of Change* published in 1968 as: 'The Never-Changing, the Ever-Changing, the One, the All. Nothing lies outside it; there is nothing which does not contain all of it. All things come from it; nothing comes from it. All things return to it; nothing goes into or returns to it. It is all things; it is no thing.'

The main characteristic of T'ai Chi is change. (*I Ching* means 'The Book of Changes'). Yin is the female, the negative and the passive (depicted in the *I Ching* by the broken line) and yang signifies the male, the positive and the active (signified by the unbroken line). Yang is light and yin is dark. Change is therefore the moving balance between proportions of yin and yang. Yang literally means the sunny, south side of a hill. Yin literally means the shaded, north side of a hill.

The origins of the *I Ching* are lost in time but it is thought to be 4,000–4,500 years old. One myth of the discovery of the *I Ching* is attributed to the alleged first emperor of China of 4,500 years ago, Pao Hsi. It has been said that the patterns were discovered when using scapulomancy, the very early system of divination in China; this involved burning either a cow's shoulder-blade or a tortoiseshell and interpreting the patterns of cracks. Other legends claim that the eight trigrams (see below) of the *I Ching* were discovered on the back of a sacred tortoise. In one commentary on the *I Ching* it is said:

> In ancient times, when Pao Hsi ruled all things under heaven, he looked at them, contemplated the bright patterns of the sky, then looked down and considered the shapes on the Earth. He noted the decorative markings on birds and beasts, and the appropriate qualities of their territory. Close at hand, he studied his own body and also observed distant things. From all this he devised the eight trigrams, in order to unveil the Heavenly processes in nature and to understand the character of everything.

The Eight Trigrams

It has also been suggested that the *I Ching* developed through stages. If so it is probable that the original *I Ching* simply had the unbroken line of yang and the broken line of yin which would provide simple yes or no answers to questions. By pairing these, four combinations would be possible which were known as:

Greater Yang ———————   Greater Yin —— ——

Lesser Yang —— ——   Lesser Yin ———————

Then in order to increase the possibilities a third line was added which creates eight possible trigrams and these are the basis of the modern *I Ching*. The eight trigrams and their characteristics are:

1. NAME: *Ch'ien*

INTERPRETED NAME: The creative

DIAGRAM: ———————
———————
———————

ATTRIBUTE: Strength

IMAGE: Heaven
FAMILY RELATIONSHIP: Father
PART OF THE HUMAN BODY: The head
COMPASS DIRECTION: North West
ELEMENT: Metal
SEASON: Autumn moving into Winter
FEATURE IN NATURE: Heaven
DESCRIPTION: Represents creative originality, change for the better, variation to achieve harmony. Represents vitality, strength and good fortune.

2. NAME: *K'un*
INTERPRETED NAME: The receptive

DIAGRAM:

ATTRIBUTE: Devoted and yielding
FAMILY RELATIONSHIP: Mother
PART OF THE HUMAN BODY: The belly
COMPASS DIRECTION: South West
ELEMENT: Earth
SEASON: Summer moving into Autumn
FEATURE IN NATURE: Earth
DESCRIPTION: In all things it represents the opposite of *Ch'ien*.

3. NAME: *Chen*
INTERPRETED NAME: The arousing

DIAGRAM:

ATTRIBUTE: Enticing movement
FAMILY RELATIONSHIP: Eldest son
PART OF THE HUMAN BODY: The foot
COMPASS DIRECTION: East

ELEMENT: Wood
SEASON: Spring
FEATURE IN NATURE: Thunder
DESCRIPTION: Represents movement and development, apprehension and alterations.

4. NAME: *Sun*
INTERPRETED NAME: The gentle

DIAGRAM:

ATTRIBUTE: Penetrating
FAMILY RELATIONSHIP: Eldest daughter
PART OF THE HUMAN BODY: Thighs
COMPASS DIRECTION: South East
ELEMENT: Wood
SEASON: Spring moving into Summer
FEATURE IN NATURE: Wind or wood
DESCRIPTION: Represents pliability, influence, the growth of vegetation.

5. NAME: *K'an*
INTERPRETED NAME: The abysmal

DIAGRAM:

ATTRIBUTE: Dangerous
FAMILY RELATIONSHIP: Second son (or middle son)
PART OF THE HUMAN BODY: The ear
COMPASS DIRECTION: North
ELEMENT: Water
SEASON: Winter
FEATURE IN NATURE: The Moon
DESCRIPTION: Represents inner strength, thought and concentration.

6. NAME: *Li*

INTERPRETED NAME: The clinging

DIAGRAM:

ATTRIBUTE: Light giving
FAMILY RELATIONSHIP: Second daughter (or middle daughter)
PART OF THE HUMAN BODY: The eye
COMPASS DIRECTION: South
ELEMENT: Fire
SEASON: Summer
FEATURE IN NATURE: The Sun
DESCRIPTION: Represents firmness and beauty.

7. NAME: *Ken*

INTERPRETED NAME: Keeping still

DIAGRAM:

ATTRIBUTE: Resting
FAMILY RELATIONSHIP: Third son (or youngest son)
PART OF THE HUMAN BODY: The hand
COMPASS DIRECTION: North East
ELEMENT: Wood
SEASON: Winter moving into Spring
FEATURE IN NATURE: Mountain
DESCRIPTION: As a mountain this represents a blockage to progress or a time of rest during progression.

8. NAME: *Tui*

INTERPRETED NAME: The joyous

DIAGRAM:

ATTRIBUTE: Joyful

FAMILY RELATIONSHIP: Third daughter (or youngest daughter)

PART OF THE HUMAN BODY: The mouth

COMPASS DIRECTION: West

ELEMENT: Water or Metal

SEASON: Autumn

FEATURE IN NATURE: The lake

DESCRIPTION: Represents happiness at achievement and progress, also satisfaction.

These eight trigrams were further developed to the present level of complexity of sixty-four hexagrams by combining each of the trigrams with another in turn. This was developed in the Second century BC by a powerful feudal overlord called Wên. Having incurred the wrath of the Emperor Chou Hsin he was imprisoned and sentenced to death but later released after pressure from his friends. When the Emperor was overthrown, Wên's son became the new ruler and founded the Chou Dynasty. It was during his year in prison that Wên examined the trigrams to create the sixty-four hexagrams. He also wrote the explanatory texts which go with them. Wên's son, following his father's death, added his own commentaries to these and it is probable that during the fifth century BC Confucius also studied the hexagrams, adding further commentaries. In 213 BC the Emperor Hwang-Ti had all books and literature in China destroyed in order to eradicate the past. This included Confucius' commentaries on the *I Ching* but several copies survived and have therefore come down into the modern day.

The Sixty-Four Hexagrams

1. *Ch'ien*
CREATIVITY

2. *K'un*
RECEPTIVITY

3. *Chun*
BIRTH PAINS OR
DIFFICULTIES AT
COMMENCEMENT

4. *Meng*
INEXPERIENCE
OR YOUTH

5. *Hsu*
CONTEMPLATION
ON NOURISHMENT

6. *Sung*
CONFLICT

7. *Shih*
THE ARMY

8. *Pi*
UNITY

9. *Hsiao Ch'u*
RESTRAINT

10. *Lu*
TREADING

11. *T'ai*
PEACE

12. *P'i*
STAGNATION
AND DISCORD

13. *T'ung Jen*
SOCIAL HARMONY

14. *Ta Yu*
WEALTH

15. *Ch'ien*
MODESTY

16. *Yu*
CONFIDENCE AND
ENTHUSIASM

17. *Sui*

FOLLOWING

18. *Ku*

DECAY OR
REPARATION

19. *Lin*

MOVING AHEAD
OR CONDUCT

20. *Kuan*

CONTEMPLATION
AND
CONSOLIDATION

21. *Shih Ho*

BITING THROUGH

22. *Pi*

ADORNMENT OR
GRACE

23. *Po*

SHEDDING

24. *Fu*

RETURN

25. *Wu Wang*

SIMPLICITY AND
INTEGRITY

26. *Ta Ch'u*

RESTRAINED
POWER

27. *I*

NOURISHMENT

28. *Ta Kuo*

EXCESS

29. *K'an*

THE DANGEROUS
AND DEEP CHASM

30. *Li*

FIRE OR
BRILLIANCE

31. *Hsien*

MUTUAL
ATTRACTION,
STIMULATION

32. *Heng*

CONTINUANCE

33. *Tun*
RETREAT

34. *Ta Chuang*
POWER AND
STRENGTH

35. *Chin*
PROGRESS

36. *Ming 1*
ADVANCING
DARKNESS

37. *Chia Jen*
THE FAMILY

38. *K'uei*
OPPOSITES,
DISUNITY

39. *Chien*
OBSTRUCTION,
FAULTY

40. *Hsieh*
LIBERATION

41. *Sun*
DECREASE

42. *I*
INCREASE

43. *Kuai*
DETERMINATION

44. *Kou*
SUDDEN
ENCOUNTERS,
TEMPTATION

45. *Ts'ui*
COLLECTING
TOGETHER,
HARMONY

46. *Sheng*
ASCENDING

47. *K'un*
RESTRICTION,
OPPRESSION

48. *Ching*
THE WELL

49. *Ko*
REVOLUTION

50. *Ting*
THE CAULDRON

51. *Chen*
THE THUNDER
CLAP

52. *Ken*
REMAINING STILL

53. *Chien*
ADVANCE
GRADUALLY,
PROGRESSIVE
DEVELOPMENT

54. *Kuei Mei*
THE MARRYING
MAIDEN

55. *Feng*
PROSPERITY,
FULLNESS

56. *Lu*
THE TRAVELLING
STRANGER

57. *Sun*
THE
PENETRATING
WIND

58. *Tui*
JOYOUSNESS

59. *Huan*
DISPERSION

60. *Chieh*
LIMITATION

61. *Chung Fu*
TRUTH

62. *Hsiao Kuo*
SMALL SUCCESSES

63. *Chi Chi*
COMPLETION
ACHIEVED

64. *Wei Chi*
BEFORE
COMPLETION

One last level of complexity is given by considering the so called 'nuclear' trigrams. These are the two sets of three lines which are formed at the join of the two original trigrams. So for example in the following hexagram, *K'un*, which appears thus:

```
———— ————  1
————————   2
————————   3
———— ————  4
————————   5
———— ————  6
```

We see that it is composed of the top trigram:

```
———— ————  1
————————   2
————————   3
```

of *Tui*
and the lower trigram:

```
———— ————  4
———— ————  5
———— ————  6
```

which is *K'an*
But we also see that the links formed by lines 2, 3 and 4 and 3, 4 and 5 are themselves trigrams:
in this case

```
————————   2
————————   3
———— ————  4
```

which is *Sun*
and

```
————————   3
———— ————  4
————————   5
```

which is *Li*.

In fact, the ultimate complexity is then given by each of the sixty-four hexagrams being reinterpreted by 'moving lines' offering a total 4,096 possible resolutions to any question. Moving lines may be read as their opposite, i.e. a moving unbroken line (transforming yang) becomes a broken line (yin) and vice versa thus creating the multitude of possible hexagrams from each initial question.

In the third century AD the scholar Wang Pi described the *I Ching* not just as the occult device that it had hitherto been but as a philosophical system which could bring wisdom to all aspects of modern life and it is this aspect which is honoured in the present time. The book used to be required reading for senior ranks of the Japanese military and indeed Japanese military tactics were largely based on the writings of the *I Ching*.

In the West the *I Ching* made its first appearance in 1882 in a translation by the English writer James Legge. Legge, however, took rather a crude hatchet to the *I Ching* somewhat missing the elegance and eloquence of its purpose. It was a German who lived in China, Richard Wilhelm, who published a translation in the 1920s that effectively brought the *I Ching* to the Western world. He was assisted by a Chinese aid, Lau Nai Süan. Wilhelm was a friend of Jung and there is little doubt that Jung's own attachment to the *I Ching* increased its prominence in the West. In *Memories, Dreams, Reflections* (1963) Jung describes:

Even before meeting [Wilhelm] I had been interested in oriental philosophy, and around 1920 had begun experimenting with the *I Ching*. One summer in Bollingen I resolved to make an all-out attack on the riddle of this book. Instead of traditional stalks of yarrow, required by the classical method, I cut myself a bunch of reed. I would sit for hours on the ground beneath the 100-year-old pear tree, the *I Ching* beside me, practising the technique by referring the resultant oracles to one another in an interplay of questions and answers. All sorts of undeniably remarkable results emerged – meaningful connections with my own thought processes which I could not explain to myself ... When I often used to carry out the experiments with my patients, it became quite clear that a significant number of answers did indeed hit the mark. I remember, for example, the case of a young man with a strong mother complex. He wanted to marry and had made the acquaintance of a seemingly suitable girl. However, he felt uncertain, fearing that under the influence of his complex he might once more find himself in the power of an overwhelming mother. I conducted the experiment with him. The text of his hexagram read: 'The maiden is powerful. One should not marry such a maiden.'

Jung believed that there was a huge network of relationships between people, events and things and concluded that the *I Ching* was an instrument which enabled the conscious mind to tap into that network. He developed his concept of synchronicity as an explanation of why the *I Ching* produced such accurate information and guidance and stated in his 1949 foreword to the translation by Wilhelm: '... The hexagram was understood to be an indicator of the essential situation prevailing in the moment of its origin. This assumption involves a certain curious principle that I have termed synchronicity, a concept that formulates a point of view diametrically opposed to that of causality. Since the latter is a merely statistical truth and not absolute, it is a sort of working hypothesis of how events evolved out of one another, whereas synchronicity takes the coincidence of events in space and time as meaning something more than mere chance. ...'

The *I Ching* was no doubt given a further boost in the West by its adoption by Aleister Crowley. In *Magick* (1973) Crowley comments:

> It is in some ways the most perfect hieroglyph ever constructed. It is austere and sublime, yet withal so adaptable to every possible emergency that its figures may be interpreted to suit all classes of questions. One may resolve the most obscure spiritual difficulties no less than the most mundane dilemmas; and the symbol which opens the gates of the most exalted palaces of initiation is equally effective when employed to advise one in the ordinary business of life ... The intelligences which direct it show no inclination to evade the question or to mislead the querent. A further advantage is that the actual apparatus is simple. Also the system is easy to manipulate, and five minutes is sufficient to obtain a fairly detailed answer to any but the most obscure questions.

Casting the Hexagram

There are two main ways to cast the hexagram, that is, to

determine the lines which form the hexagram patterns: yarrow stalks or tossing coins. Purists believe that the use of coins shows less devotion than the use of the traditional yarrow stalks but the coins have the advantage of being somewhat simpler to use. It is important when casting hexagrams in the *I Ching* that the mind be focused on the question of the problem at hand and therefore there is something to be said for the argument that the more complex the ritual the more it aids the questioner in focusing their mind.

Tossing Coins

Traditionally *I Ching* users prefer to use the original Chinese coins, which were round with square central holes and were once ordinary currency in China but are now used mainly for the *I Ching*. One side of the coin is the yang side and has a value of three and the other side of the coin is the yin side with a value of two. (You can use any two-sided coins as long as you assign the relevant value to each side.) Three coins are tossed and there is therefore the possibility of producing a total number of either six, seven, eight or nine depending on the fall of the coins. Six presents a moving yin line and nine a moving yang line. Seven represents a non-moving yang line and eight a non-moving yin line. Each throw of three coins represents one line of the hexagram and therefore the coins are tossed six times to produce the full six lines of the hexagram. The first throw of the coins represents the bottom line and the hexagram builds upwards from the base. To demonstrate how this might work:

Throw 1 produces 3 + 2 + 3 = 8 = non-moving yin line

———   ———

Throw 2 produces 2 + 2 + 2 = 6 = moving yin line

———   ———   often designated with an x to show it is a moving yin line

Throw 3 produces $2 + 3 + 2 = 7$ = non-moving yang line
_____

Throw 4 produces $3 + 3 + 3 = 9$ = moving yang line
_____ often designated with a zero to show that it is a
moving yang line

Throw 5 produces $3 + 2 + 3 = 8$ = non-moving yin line
____ ____

Throw 6 produces $2 + 3 + 2 = 7$ = non-moving yang line
_____

The result of this is the following hexagram:

≡≡ == ()
≡≡ == X

This produces hexagram No 56 *Lu*, the travelling stranger.

However, it is the moving lines which are important for
divination and so for example in this case there is moving line six
in the second place (counting up from the bottom) and moving
line nine in the fourth place. Moving line six in the second place
according to the text suggests: 'The traveller occupies his lodging
house carrying with him his means of livelihood and provided
with trustworthy servants – good fortune.' Nine in the fourth
place states: 'A traveller is in a resting place, but he has not got
his proper position. He has the means of livelihood and the axe,
but he is apprehensive.'

It is now necessary to redraft the hexagrams changing the
moving lines to their opposites and this will produce the
following:

This is now hexagram 18, *Ku*, arresting decay. This is a non-moving hexagram and is interpreted using the appropriate passage, in this case: 'Ku indicates great progress and success – advantage in efforts like that of crossing the great stream. He should weigh well the events of three days before the turning point and those to be done three days after.'

Overall hexagrams 56 and 18 appropriately interpreted seem to suggest that progress and changes are taking place. The questioner must be cautious as he is entering an area in which circumstances are not yet certain. The indicated outcome is likely to be favourable, negative factors will be arrested.

Use of Yarrow Stalks

Yarrow stalks are a second method. They are available to everybody, as yarrow (*Achillea millefolium*) grows wild. Sometimes, bamboo stalks are used. The diviner begins with fifty stalks of yarrow, removes one leaving forty-nine (the square number seven of seven, which is regarded as 'magical' in divination). The forty-nine are divided into two random piles. Then four stalks are removed from one pile and then the other until three, two, one or no stalks are left in each of the piles. The remaining stalks are then counted and this produces the numbers which indicate either the moving or unmoving yang lines or moving or unmoving yin lines. The whole procedure is done five more times to produce the lines of the hexagrams, built from the bottom up.

Because there are texts which accompany the sixty-four hexagrams it is impossible to go further in a book of this nature into the matter of interpretation as all of the texts would be needed. However, for those who are interested there are several excellent books and also sets of *I Ching* cards available which also offer practical guidance on getting the best from this particular form of divination.

The Runes

The Runes are an alphabet that originally belonged to the Norse and Germanic people of approximately 1,500 years ago. However, the 'letters' of the 'alphabet' contain secrets which allow for divination. Indeed the word *rune* means 'secret' or 'hidden'. It derives from the German word *raunen* which means 'to whisper'. The earliest rune alphabet and indeed the one most commonly known is the Elder Futhark (so called because futhark represents the first six runes (*Feoh, Ur, Thorn, Ansur, Rad* and *Ken.*)

The power of the runes in divination is that each pictogram which represents an aspect of interpretation has increasingly deep levels of meaning.

The Elder Futhark contains twenty-four letters. There are futharks with as few as sixteen runes and as many as thirty-three. In addition to the standard twenty-four characters there is sometimes a twenty-fifth rune known as a *Wyrd* (fate) which is blank. This is the symbol for both destiny and karma but is only a recent addition to the runes; many people believing that its meaning is already implied in other runes.

The runes are not used only for divination but can also be used to seek a desired outcome. The use of rune script is not to predict or see into the future but rather to create it.

The desired runic texts are written on paper or cut into wood and are carried by the person day and night. When the rune script has worked its magic then it should be reverently and respectfully burned. It is also considered polite to thank the runes for their efforts in assisting you. Translating that into a modern psychological explanation, the ritual of preparing the rune script which requires focus and quietness of mind probably allows the mind to begin the process of working out its best and most favourable course of action in order to reach the desired future.

Rather in the nature of the witch's talismans and amulets, individual runes can be carried to protect against danger or to attract successes or love. Runes tied together are called bind-runes and are carried like jewellery either to attract the good or ward off the bad.

Runic symbols have been found on rock carvings which date back as far as 8000 years BC and are widespread through

Scandinavia. The power of runes is indicated by their images being carved on swords to make warriors stronger in battle and to inflict greater pain and death on enemies. Magicians would inscribe runes on their tools and 'activate' them by sprinkling them with blood. When Norse explorers took their culture abroad, the runes and Christian symbolism coexisted for a while but over time the individual religions rejected the amalgam. Even in the late nineteenth century priests in the remoter areas of Scandinavia were expected to be able to read, write and interpret runes. On the other hand the Catholic Church made strong efforts to stamp out their use.

Characteristics of the Runes

The twenty-four letters of the Elder Futhark are divided into three groups of eight, called 'aetts'. The three aetts are: Frey's Aett, Hagal's Aett and Tyr's Aett. We will now look at the twenty-four runes and their implied meaning.

Frey's Aett

Feoh: At its simplest level this rune indicates cattle. However, in a nomadic primitive society cattle represented the accumulation of wealth and there is therefore the deeper meaning of wealth implied by the runes. Cattle being transportable or moveable the implication is of transferable or moveable wealth and therefore in more modern days of money and possessions. At its third and deepest level it represents wealth in the sense of wealth of energy, wealth of emotion, wealth of spiritual riches. It is notable that *Feoh* belongs in Frey's Aett, Frey being the god of fertility which for a primitive society was perhaps its greatest riches of all.

Ur: The *Ur* represents the bison. The bison is essentially a beast of strength and courage. The rune also indicates, at a slightly deeper level, the untamed and uncontrollable power of freedom. At a deeper level it represnts spiritual and inner strength, robust health and sexual potency.

Thorn: The *Thorn* is a weapon of attack and a device of protection which can surround the person and ward off enemies. It represents energy and excess including violent anger and sexual lust. This is an ambiguous rune which can indicate good luck or can indicate that the good luck is about to change.

Ansur (or *Ansuz*): This is the rune of prophecy and of revelation and symbolises wisdom and reason. It usually indicates good advice.

Rad: the direct meaning of *Rad* is travel or wheel. However, it can also mean a journey either physical or spiritual or emotional, i.e. something of long duration which requires fortitude, planning and the determination to see it through.

Ken: This rune means light as in the light which illuminates the path ahead. It has a deeper meaning in the light of knowledge which illuminates the dark of uncertainty or of ignorance. It is almost certainly associated with the Scottish word 'ken' meaning knowledge or understanding. At its deepest level *Ken* represents the light of creativity and the creation of new ideas.

Gifu: *Gifu* is a gift, something given from one person to another. It implies a deeper meaning in that the receipt of a gift places the recipient in a position of obligation to the giver and perhaps a further deeper meaning in that it creates a bond between the two. At a deeper level *Gifu* implies the bond of love or affection.

Wyn: *Wyn* is the rune of reward. It symbolises victory and the feeling of satisfaction and happiness, perhaps even of achievement. At the spiritual level the rune symbolises closeness to God. At its deepest level *Wyn* represents companionship and sharing on the basis that joy is meant to be and is best enjoyed shared.

Hagal's Aett

ᚺ *Hagal:* This rune stands for hail; it represents disruption, difficulty, delay, limitation, illness. Implied within this rune is also the suggestion that the onset of these attributes is sudden and unexpected.

ᚾ *Nyd:* This rune represents need or hardship and at a slightly deeper level adversity. It is also a rune of persistence and patience and implies that every experience however adverse is always a learning experience which has value.

ᛁ *Is:* Quite simply this rune indicates ice. However, at a slightly deeper level it is a reflection that ice is graceful, elegant and beautiful but also deceitful in that what looks like it will support you may not. Ice can be a blockage. At the deeper level it represents possible delay to plans. Emotionally it represents the cooling of the heat of passion or affection but may also represent cooling off of anger.

ᛃ *Ger: Ger* means harvest and represents the autumn gathering of the crops. However, it also represents the whole cyclical year of crop growth and therefore the cycle of change and growth. At the deeper level it represents cause and effect showing that what is sown results in what is reaped. It is therefore at its deepest level the symbol of natural justice, i.e. you are appropriately rewarded for your actions, good or bad.

ᛇ *Eoh:* This is the rune of the yew tree and symbolises death and rebirth. The yew tree is an evergreen which therefore never dies, representing either rebirth in Norse Valhalla or through reincarnation. At the deeper level *Eoh* represents continuity and persistence.

Peorth: This the 'dice shaker' cup which implies gains of skill and random luck. It is held to indicate a need for a person to make the best of their opportunities. It also represents the revelation of hidden secrets and also of pregnancy and birth (the hidden baby within). At a deeper level *Peorth* represents moderation in the enjoyment of food, drink and sexual exploration.

Eolh: Eolh represents the antlers of the elk. Symbolically it is a hand warding off danger. It is therefore the rune of protection and of success in a quest. Because the rune represents either the antlers or the hand stretched upwards there is the suggestion of reaching up into the realm of the gods.

Sigel: This is the power of the sun and represents victory of good over evil, light over darkness, clarity over obscurity. It is a victory symbol.

Tyr's Aett

Tyr: Tyr is the Norse god of war or fair play and regulation. It represents determination, fortitude and male sexuality.

Beorc: Beorc is the birch tree and represents the family and the family unit and the enjoyment of the cycle of sexuality, birth and growth. This may be of people, of ideas, of new ventures. At its deepest level it represents regeneration, purification and renewal.

Ehwaz: This represents a horse, and at its simplest level is a means of transport or movement. However, the horse is also a symbol of strength and speed and at its deepest level *Ehwaz* represents spiritual advances. Because the horse and rider must have a relationship from which both can benefit *Ehwaz* is also the rune of partnership, faithfulness, loyalty and progress.

Man: This rune represents the human individual and is held to show the paradox between humanity as a family together and the fact that we journey into death alone. The rune represents all that is thought to be special to humanity: intelligence, speech, the ability to plan and manipulate our environment and the implication of advanced mental abilities.

Lagu: Lagu is water, which means different things in different ways. Water is the most vital substance in life. It indicates danger (from flooding or from seafaring) yet it also represents the challenge of a journey and the risk of shipwreck. At a slightly deeper level *Lagu* demonstrates the fluidity of life. It generally represents the so-called feminine qualities of intuition, psychic awareness and access to the unconscious mind. It also embodies the impulsiveness of sexual lust.

Ing: Ing represents conclusion or completion. Ing like Frey was a fertility god and the conclusion can represent orgasm or birth, each conclusions of a build-up. It is a positive rune representing strength, security, success, health and sexuality. At a deeper level it represents spiritual aspiration and attainment.

Daeg: Daeg represents day and therefore light. It is the light of dawn and the light of the midsummer sun. It also represents the divine light of spirituality and therefore of growth, change and development.

Odel: Odel represents the wealth attributed to property and indeed the land itself. Because this is inherited from one generation to another it is also the symbol of inherited traits or characteristics, those elements of self which are passed on from one generation to another. At a deeper level it therefore represents an accumulation or growth over time.

Reading the runes consists first of casting them. As in most forms of divination this is done either to acquire the answer to a question or to seek guidance as to the proper direction forward. Those choosing the runes as a form of divination might remember that Odin the Norse god of wisdom and divination gained his knowledge of the runes by hanging upside down from Yggdvasil, the world tree for nine days and nights impaled on a spear. Norse thinking might be the original of the expression 'no pain, no gain': the Norse gods are apt to seek a sacrifice from you as the price of your gain from their wisdom!

Casting the Runes

Casting the runes consists of taking a number of runes from a bag or selecting them at random from a spread face down on a table. It is implied by either method that your hand is psychically guided to the appropriate rune in order that it can impart its knowledge to you. If the runes, as other forms of divination, are a way of connecting the conscious mind to its unconscious pool of resource then the implication is that it is the unconscious mind which selects the appropriate runes. When the runes selected have been laid out in the appropriate rune cast pattern they should be turned over, like the Tarot, sideways and not top to bottom as sixteen of the twenty-four runes can arrive reversed and in doing so are showing the client their negative or opposite attibutes, of which he or she must be careful to take account. There are many types of readings of which the following are examples:

A Three Rune Reading/Six Rune Reading

The first rune represents the position where the client is at the present time either emotionally or in business or in whatever situation is being considered. The second rune represents the way forward and the third rune the consequences of the action.

For slightly deeper readings a six rune cast may be used which is the same as the three rune above but each position is represented by two runes rather than one. The interaction and symbolism of the two runes in each position offer deeper insight.

A Cross Reading

In a cross reading, five runes are laid out in a shape of a cross, the centre rune representing the present position, the rune to the 'west' representing the history which has brought us to that position, the rune to the 'east' representing the future. The rune to the 'north' represents those factors which will help and progress the client towards the future he or she desires and the rune to the 'south' represents those factors that will disturb or hinder the path towards the desired future.

The Peorth Reading

This rune cast is laid out in the shape of Peorth the dice cup, and is a complex pattern representing not only the past, present and the future but the client's physical, emotional and spiritual state. The runes show the path from the past to the present and into the future but are also represented by three triangles, the uppermost triangle representing the spiritual, the lowermost triangle the physical and the central triangle the emotional. There are key nodal points in the rune cast, two central runes bridging the spiritual and emotional, and the emotional and physical.

The Tarot

One aspect of the Tarot's mystery relates to the obscurity of its origins. Perhaps the most popular theory is that the Tarot playing cards were invented by a painter, Jacquemin Gringonneur in 1392 as a present for Charles VI of France (1368–1422) to provide the king with entertainment during his periods of depression and madness. It was Père Ménestrier who in the seventeenth century uncovered a document by Charles Poupart, the Treasurer to Charles VI which stated: 'To Jacquemin Gringonneur, painter, for three packs of cards in gold and divers colours of several designs, to be laid before our said lord the King for his diversion. ... LVI Sous of Paris.' However, our research indicates that while Gringonneur might well have produced these cards he did not invent them and there were packs of cards, which were almost certainly early Tarot cards, in use in Germany over sixty years earlier and similar cards in existence in Belgium, Italy and Spain before Charles VI ascended the throne.

In the mid-eighteenth century the French clergyman Antoine Court de Gébelin applied his expertise as both archaeologist and egyptologist to suggest that the Tarot were derived from the ancient Egyptian myths in the *Book of Thoth*. This theory was picked up and furthered by a fortune teller, Etteilla, and by the philosopher D'Odoucet. In fact the theory is not valid given the state of egyptological knowledge at the time and the fact that the Rosetta Stone had yet to be discovered.

Another alleged origin is that it was the Tarot of the gypsies, or Bohemians but in fact it is known that the Tarot was in existence well before their appearance in Europe. Eliphas Lévi attempted to reconcile the Tarot with the Cabbala and indeed the Hebrew alphabet, neither link of which was valid. Lévi had high hopes for the Tarot, stating of it in book form: 'An imprisoned person with no other book than the Tarot, if he knew how to use it, could in a few years acquire universal knowledge, and would be able to speak on all subjects with unequalled learning and inexhaustible eloquence.' Even the origin of the name 'Tarot' is uncertain. De Gébelin believed that it originated with a combination of the Egyptian words *tar* (meaning road) and *ro* (meaning royal) and therefore that Tarot referred to 'the royal road to wisdom'. It has also been suggested that 'Tarot' is a French derivative of the Italian word *tarocchi* which means trumps or triumph. Or is the word linked to the Taro, a river in northern Italy or the French word *tarottée* which describes the thatched design on many card sets?

However uncertain the origin we do know that in 1910 Arthur Edward Waite, an English occultist, published a version of the Tarot deck, the Rider–Waite pack, which is the basis of most modern packs. The pictures had been designed by an artist colleague, Pamela Coleman Smith. Waite's proposition was that the Tarot dated back only to the fourteenth century but used symbols which were much older in origin. It was his belief that his work brought the symbols back into their original context, drawing from the Cabbala and Hermeticism, which was favoured by the Hermetic Order of the Golden Dawn (see page 66) which numbered Waite amongst its members.

The Tarot Cards

The Tarot is a deck of seventy-eight cards depicting the symbolic pictures. It is probably the most famous deck of cards used in cartomancy (divination by use of cards). It has been said that in the last fifty years the Tarot has been the most popular form of occult divination. Through various interpretations – and there have been well over 200 different designs of Tarot in the past quarter century – the imagery and original symbolism has probably been diluted and in some cases lost to time.

The seventy-eight cards of the Tarot are divided into two separate groups: the Major Arcana and the Minor Arcana.

The Major Arcana

The Major Arcana is made up of twenty-two cards depicting ancient symbolism. No single book, let alone a single section of a book such as this, could encompass all the possible combinations of imagery nor apply to them every likely symbolism or indication which they give. However, the types of symbolism that apply to each card of the Major Arcana might be approximately as given in the following descriptions. Each card is deemed to have positive and negative attributes which are generally held to deflect the duality of all interpretations: every positive carries with it certain negatives and vice versa.

1. THE JUGGLER OR MAGICIAN
Typical imagery:
Often depicted as a jester or conjurer performing tricks.

The positive side
The positive attributes of this card indicate new beginnings and new opportunities. There may be indications of choices of actions in the future and therefore this card might indicate a need for inner contemplation about the course of action being sought. The opportunity to use the skills and talents may arise. Generally this card is held to reflect the material or business world rather than the spiritual or relationship world.

The negative side
One negative aspect of the card is that it is warning the client not to miss opportunities that are soon to arise. It is also suggesting that business opportunities should be examined cautiously to detect less favourable or less honest propositions being maintained. The juggler and the magician can both represent tomfoolery and trickery.

General
If this card does arise, and if in a prominent position in the spread, then it is wise to take heed of it. If it shows in the upright position then it is probably indicating that it is wise to venture into the business opportunities that are opening up before the client.

2. THE LADY POPE (OR HIGH PRIESTESS)
Typical imagery:
Usually depicted as a woman wearing a papal head-dress.

The positive side
This card represents the intuitive and common sense. By the same token it is also an acknowledgement of the secret knowledge and life's mysteries. This card can represent scholarship and learning and might indicate the imminent arrival of a guide or teacher

who will be of use to the client. Such a guide or teacher would probably be a woman; perhaps in the modern world a professional or qualified person. Another, presumably positive, aspect of the card is that when it arises in a reading it suggests that the client does not have all the facts that will be needed and indicates that there is something yet to be learned or understood about a forthcoming proposition.

The negative side

The negative side of the intuitive and emotional qualities are uncontrolled emotion and carelessness. The card may indicate selfishness or impatience. In another context it may represent sexual tension. The card may indicate a choice between emotional opportunities, for example that the client may have to choose between the emotional needs of a family and the emotional needs of the self.

General

If this card arises in a prominent position then it suggests that the client should trust their own intuition or the intuition of a valued friend or colleague. In a reverse position it may indicate the dangers of over-emotion and lack of caution.

3. THE EMPRESS

Typical imagery:

A woman seated on a regal throne and holding the badges of office such as a sceptre.

The positive side

The Empress is of course a woman and this card represents femininity, female sexuality and the maternal drive. It is a card of satisfaction, comfort and warmth. The card also represents the fertility and abundance of the Earth itself and might therefore indicate positive moves in basic values and possessions but ones with an association with nature. It may suggest a move to, or a future in, the country rather than the town. It is a card of ownership of 'things' rather than emotions. It could indicate an abundance of material goods.

The negative side

This card might indicate possessiveness or jealousy which has become destructive in its extreme or at a lesser level that the person has become too self indulgent. The card arising in a reversed way might indicate loss of fertility, temporary or otherwise, the loss of contact with nature or with the country and with the loss of possessions, even financial loss.

General

At its simplest this card turning up in a prominent position indicates the possibility of pregnancy or the birth of a close relation. If the card arises in a reading for a man it will indicate the arrival of a loving woman or perhaps a change in someone close – a wife previously 'cold' becoming 'warm'. The card might indicate marriage, material satisfaction or impending abundance.

4. THE EMPEROR

Typical imagery:

Normally depicted as a mature male leader, often enthroned.

The positive side

Overtly masculine, this card is representative of authority and a strong personal presence. This card indicates the arrival of a person in the client's life who will be dominant, or at the very least difficult to ignore. This card also represents a strong ability to influence events from a position of power or a strong financial base. The client finding this card in their reading is guided towards using their logic and reasoning rather than the emotional side of the brain.

The negative side

If the card is reversed then the person is not as strong, upright and honest as the client would like to believe. A reversed card might indicate immaturity, lack of reliance.

General

This card in a positive position indicates that a person of strong leadership may be about to enter the person's life. In a negative position it may indicate either someone who cannot be relied on or, where a man is the client, a diminution in their own strength or leadership powers, perhaps due to a future onset of ill-health.

5. THE POPE (OR HIEROPHANT)
Typical imagery:
An image of the Pope wearing the papal crown and sometimes giving blessings to those kneeling before him.

The positive side
This is a card of spiritual guidance and of kindness. The card may represent a spiritual or religious teacher in the life of the client. In a business sense it might be someone at work who will develop those characteristics in the client. However, generally this card represents situations and circumstances and as such generally represents lines of conventional response. If the client is questioning then this card indicates that the conventional answer is probably the right one or that traditional paths should be followed.

The negative side
This card indicates that a person might be non-assertive and putting other people's needs ahead of their own. Non-assertiveness leads people to make excuses for others and to allow them more rights than we allow ourselves.

General
The general impression suggested by this card is that there are helpful people surrounding the client who will offer useful guidance. If this card arises when the client is suffering delays, perhaps in business matters, this indicates that the delays will soon end. If this card arises reversed then the client should follow a path of non-traditional action or non-conformity.

6. THE LOVERS (OR THE MARRIAGE)
Typical imagery:
Sometimes depicted as a man and a woman locked in embrace or as a man and a woman in the process of the marriage ceremony.

The positive side

This card denotes love and passion or perhaps just friendship and a peaceful relationship. The card could answer questions about the workplace in which case it would refer to relationships with business colleagues. The card is also a card of choice; a choice between two career paths, to possibility between two people and so on. It arises when the matter of choice is significant and important.

The negative side

If the card appears reversed then it may indicate a forthcoming separation or parting of the ways between either lovers or business associates. It may indicate an impending mistake or error.

General

If the card arises where there has been a separation between people this card indicates that there will probably be a reunion. If the card appears reversed then it is highly likely that it is indicating the client is about to make a bad mistake and will remain unsatisfied in their desires be they relating to love, friendship or business.

7. THE CHARIOT

Typical imagery:

Usually a horse drawn chariot and often being driven by a royal servant.

The positive side

The chariot indicates effort and productive hard work. It may indicate that the results of such effort already undertaken are about to be forthcoming or that such effort is due in the near future. It is a card of chaos and struggle. It might relate to a forthcoming choice where the proper choice will result in hard work or to a forthcoming problem that will take a great deal of effort and patience to resolve; but it is a card of success.

The negative side

The negative aspect of this card is that the struggle may not lead to quite as productive an outcome as would be hoped for. It will depend on other cards arriving with this card in the reading to determine quite how that will have to be interpreted. If the card is reversed it will indicate a time of frustrating struggle perhaps with intangible outcome.

General

When this card arises it indicates productive useful activity under way or to be undertaken shortly. If the card arises in connection with travel then it is a good omen. It may also indicate that useful and purposeful travel is on the horizon.

8. JUSTICE

Typical imagery:

A figure, usually female, holding both the sword of justice and the balancing scales.

The positive side

The card represents balance, equilibrium, fair play and of course justice itself. It is a good omen card in its positive aspect and if arriving in a reading when there are legal matters to hand it suggests the outcome will be good for the client. The card does not only relate to legal affairs but to all matters of natural justice and honesty.

The negative side

In its negative aspect this card is a warning of unfairness which will perturb the client, perhaps even an unfair or unreasonable accusation or setback.

General

If the card arises in a positive aspect then any legal matters are likely to be resolved for the client's good; if the card arises in the negative position the outcome is likely to be poor or disappointing. If this card arises in a reversed position it could typically indicate a person who will be passed over in their career perhaps by somebody who has succeeded through politics rather than on merit which the person passed over would find unfair.

9. THE HERMIT (OR THE SAGE)

Typical imagery:

An old and wise figure, sometimes depicted carrying the lantern of new light.

The positive side

The card reflects a need for re-evaluation of long-term goals. It also indicates that the client should be circumspect and conservative in forthcoming matters. The image of the hermit is very specific in that it indicates a certain self-denial and self-reflection that will be needed before the client can reassess their own position correctly.

The negative side

The negative aspect of this card is that the client is so wrapped up in themselves that they turn away from their friends and family. It may also indicate that the client is turning away from himself or herself, perhaps failing to act maturely in a situation.

General

This card arising almost always indicates that the client must be patient and take time to think through a problem. If the card arises during a period of illness then it may indicate a time of convalescence ahead. This card in a reversed position could indicate bereavement or rejection by a partner or lover.

10. THE WHEEL OF FORTUNE

Typical imagery:

Often depicting a cat and a demon chasing each other endlessly around the wheel.

The positive side

The Wheel of Fortune indicates change. The wheel is itself a very significant symbol which indicates that change is constant and goes on forever, also that there is no starting point or ending point but rather a continuous cycle. As an autoscope (see page 217) this card is the equivalent of 'the bottle half full or the bottle half empty'. Optimists see change as opportunity; pessimists see change as potential struggle and gloom.

The negative side

If the card arrives reversed then it may be an indication that forthcoming change may not be beneficial or may bring difficulties. However, this card more than any other shows the duality of every event; even in its negative aspect there are those who will rise to the challenge, struggle through and emerge victorious.

General

This card does not indicate anything by itself. It is a card of change and it depends where in a reading it arises as to what that change is likely to be.

11. STRENGTH

Typical imagery:

Sometimes depicted as a woman forcing open the jaws of a lion.

The positive side

The card indicates the likelihood of overcoming obstacles. It may show a need for determination and perseverance. In its positive aspect it indicates that success is on the horizon. It is a card of inner strength and inner courage. In its positive aspect it indicates a person guided positively by their conscience and able to overcome petty behaviour in others.

The negative side

If the card arises reversed it may indicate a defeat on the horizon though perhaps of the battle rather than the war. The card is also a warning that lack of inner strength and conviction may lead to the client becoming underhanded and the worse for it.

General

If this card arises during a period of illness it indicates recovery and return to full health. If the card arises during a period of depression or lack of vitality it signifies a return to a positive outlook. If the card arises reversed then it indicates impending ill-health, depression or lack of vitality.

12. THE HANGED MAN (OR THE HANGING MAN)

Typical imagery:

Usually depicting a man suspended upside down by a cord around his foot.

The positive side

This card relates to attitude and would typically show a change in direction, perhaps a halt in progress and a turning point in life. It might typically show someone who is moving away from materialism and into the spiritual though it carries with it the concept of sacrifice or opportunity lost: for every choice taken something else must be given up.

The negative side

If the card arises reversed it may indicate that the client is failing to acknowledge future change or even attempting to ignore it.

General

If this card arises during the fragmentation of a relationship whether it is of love or business then it will suggest a period of isolation and 'life on hold' to be followed by a change which in the long run is for the best. If the card arises when parents are questioning their family values it may indicate that their offspring are soon to leave home to build their own lives, resulting in, for a while, the parents feeling lonely and unsure to be followed by a new and different life ahead. If the card arises when the client is questioning their career path it may indicate a period of unemployment or redundancy which will be disturbing for a time but which will in the long run be positive for the client's career outcomes. If the card arises reversed it may indicate that the client must accept the need for change. The card reversed may indicate that the client has been trying to force a situation in a desired direction, perhaps a love life gone astray or a business relationship that is not working and they must step back and allow a more natural course to unfold.

13. DEATH (SOMETIMES UNTITLED BUT USUALLY REFERRED TO AS 'THE DEATH CARD')

Typical imagery:

The image of a skeleton or of time wielding a scythe.

The positive side

Contrary to popular belief this is not a card of death in that it predicts the death of the client or those around him or her but rather it is a card of permanent change, i.e. the death of one situation leading to a new life.

The negative side

If the card arises reversed it is an indication that there will be suffering in the permanent change ahead. Even then that is not a suggestion that there could not be a good outcome long into the future.

General

In its negative aspect this card may indicate that a person has reached the end of their career growth or is afraid to make the necessary changes to go further.

14. TEMPERANCE

Typical imagery:

Sometimes depicts a woman pouring liquid from one container to another.

The positive side

This card represents a time of tranquillity ahead. The person who receives this card in their reading is about to find that they will cope better than they have done with situations and they will find peace and relaxation more easily available to them. This is a card of moderation and an indication that if a person has been suffering or living to excess then a rebalance is about to adjust their lives. Although the expression 'resting on one's laurels' generally has negative connotations this card is an indication that it is time to do so at least for a period.

The negative side

If the card arises reversed then it is likely that the client will fail to see the opportunity for peace and tranquillity ahead and will struggle unnecessarily.

General

If the card arises when there have been struggles and strife then a period of peace and tranquillity is now soon to follow. If the card arises reversed it is an indication that the client must take time to seek out the tranquillity and perhaps cut back their excesses.

15. THE DEVIL

Typical imagery:

A wide variety of demonic images are used to depict this figure.

The positive side

It may seem impossible to offer a positive aspect to a card like The Devil but the positive aspect is perhaps most easily seen in the expression 'Devil's advocate'. In other words this card at least at one level asks us to look at The Devil within to examine whether we are leading ourselves down wrong paths into danger or into trouble, perhaps even enslaving ourselves in an inappropriate way,

The negative side

Arising reversed may in this case be a good sign as it indicates that the devilish influences that we have allowed ourselves to be enslaved by are about to leave us.

General

If this card arises in a positive aspect when we are about to engage in, say, a large mortgage or a new career path it may be an indication that at heart we know that we are making a millstone for our own necks and that we should think again. This card is a warning not to behave stupidly, particularly towards ourselves. The Devil enslaves people. This card is a warning not to enslave ourselves with inappropriate desires, longings, acquisitions, emotions and so on. This card reversed is a warning not to become involved with bad or evil people. It is a reminder to the client to follow their own conscience.

16. THE HOUSE OF GOD (OR THE HOSPITAL, OR THE LIGHTNING
    STRUCK TOWER)
Typical imagery:
A structure, often shown struck by lightning.
This is a card of destruction and indicates loss, disaster, perhaps a
destruction of security. In a situation it may indicate that
positively held beliefs we have about people are about to be
shattered by a truth that we will find difficult to believe or accept.

The positive side
Not a terribly positive card. The best that can be said for it is
'forewarned is forearmed' and the client must be ready to accept
the loss and carry on beyond.

The negative side
If this card arises reversed indicating the negative it probably
indicates that the impending loss is happening already rather
than soon to arise. It could even indicate sudden disaster or
catastrophe.

General
If this card arises during questioning of finances it could indicate
something as serious as potential bankruptcy. The client must
be ready for the forthcoming struggle to rebuild their financial
security.

17. THE STAR
Typical imagery:
A star or a sky full of stars.

The positive side
The star is the symbol of hope and of bright outcomes ahead. It
depends where this card arises in a reading as to what situation it
relates to but it always indicates a sign of hope and good fortune
ahead. It is also a card of surprise in that it may indicate that
something the client thought insignificant, something even as
simple as a long weekend of work may turn out to have a much
more than expected outcome and always positive. It is a card of
new horizons and may indicate unexpected travel or travel with
particularly good outcomes.

The negative side

If the star is found in a reversed position it may be an indication that the person has been seeking far wider horizons and that a time of contraction is called for. Even when negative this is still a relatively positive card with positive outcomes ahead.

General

If the card arises when the client is going through a bad time then it indicates that good times are on the horizon. If the client has been ill then full health is just around the corner.

18. THE MOON

Typical imagery:

Sometimes depicted as astrologers pointing up at the crescent moon in the sky.

The positive side

This card is the card of confusion and illusion and arises when there is uncertainty. It may indicate out of control emotions and in a loving relationship withholding or insincerity in the parties. If the card arises during questions of career or finance then it indicates susceptibility to fraud or trickery. At its simplest level it is a card of minor upsets, disturbed plans, irritations and aggravations. The card indicates that the client should use their imagination and artistic side of their brain and may even indicate that the client is about to or should develop their psychic side. It is not a card of logical reason.

The negative side

If the card arises reversed it may only indicate that the confusion and irritation which goes with the card has not yet arisen and is coming up over the horizon, that uncertainty being one further irritation to add to the list.

General

The arrival of this card indicates that it is best to let things drift for a while rather than try to force outcomes. The card indicates that natural forces must be allowed to come into equilibrium without intervention.

19. THE SUN

Typical imagery:

A bright full sun beaming down on people below.

The positive side

A card of happiness, gaiety and joy. Wherever this card arises in a reading it indicates that there will be success, pleasantness and a feeling of uplift. Business will expand or thrive, relationships will enter a period of laughter, friendships a period of ease.

The negative side

If the card arises reversed it indicates an opportunity for happiness ahead but one which may be missed. In its negative aspect it may indicate that the happiness and gaiety are still a long way off although they are there in the future. In its negative side it may indicate a forthcoming illness, a lack of relationship success or causes of disagreements.

20. JUDGEMENT

Typical imagery:

A heavenly figure above looking down on those below.

The positive side

It is important where this card arises in a reading as it indicates that a particular period or situation is about to come to an end. The card indicates a time of looking back over the shoulder and of evaluating 'where we are now and how we got here'. It can be a card of reward and, in a business sense, promotion. It indicates that something is coming to an end but in a sensible, expected and fair way which will not be a shock to the client. It is a card of youth and rejuvenation since inevitably every ending must also be a beginning.

The negative side

If the card arises reversed it is still an indication of an ending but one in which the client will not be particularly satisfied. For many people it is a card which indicates that although they have now taken and finished with an opportunity they realise they could have done better or made more of themselves. It is a 'moral' card and might indicate to the client that they could have treated someone else better than they have.

General
If the card arises during legal disputes the client is likely to win.

21. THE WORLD
Typical imagery:
A woman encased in a circle.

The positive side
This card is the card of 'the big picture' and may allow the client to review the end of, or large change in, situations. It may indicate long term or permanent travel, i.e. perhaps moving to another country and may indicate a whole new life ahead.

The negative side
If the card arises reversed it suggests the client cannot accept endings or change. At its most negative this card suggests that a person has evaluated their life and ended up jealous of others or unfulfilled.

General
Positive or negative this is a card which indicates that determination is necessary and that the client should keep trying and move on.

1. THE FOOL
Typical imagery:
The traditional image of the jester, or joker, or Court Fool.

The positive side
This card represents the dangers and risk inherent in beginning a new future. Although sometimes shown as the first card in the Major Arcana this aspect shows why it is often shown as the last card, i.e. it follows from The World and is the new life into which the major change is allowing the client to step. It is a card of doors opening, of opportunities arising and of the likelihood of joy and fun ahead. It is also a card which warns the client to be

restrained and not to go to excess in the future.

The negative side

If the card arises reversed it is an indication that the client may be about to act irrationally, stupidly or obsessively with the inevitable difficulties that would arise. Ignoring the warnings of The Fool could leave the client looking foolish or could even, at the extreme, result in disaster.

In fact, The Fool is a card with no number and is sometimes played either at position 21, therefore making The World 22, or placed at the very beginning and therefore displacing each other card by one number.

The Minor Arcana

The Minor Arcana is similar to a standard deck of cards and consists of four suits, each of fourteen cards consisting of Ace, 2, 3, 4, 5, 6, 7, 8, 9, 10, Knave, Knight, Queen and King. The fifty-two cards of standard playing decks omit the Knight and this figure is sometimes omitted from some Tarot decks, therefore leaving fifty-two in the Minor Arcana rather than the traditional fifty-six.

The four suits are: Sceptres, Cups, Swords and Pentacles though these also have an evolution. Up to the end of the eighteenth century the four suits were Money (representing trade and commerce), Cups (representing the sacred vessels of the priesthood, and perhaps The Holy Grail), Swords (representing the warrior or soldier) and Wands (representing agriculture as it was first depicted as the staff of the peasant). The Cups and Swords have remained to the present day, the Wands are the Sceptres but Money has been replaced by the Pentacles perhaps indicating a change from materialism to spirituality. In the present day even standard packs of cards in some countries, such as Spain, use some of these images on playing cards.

Some clairvoyants use both the Major and Minor Arcana in divination but it is also common to use only the twenty-two cards of the Major Arcana.

Each of the cards and their placements in the spreads have detailed meanings according to most Tarot readers, but this book is not the place to go further into such detail. There are a number of books available dedicated to the detail of readings. Some outline of the principles is, however, set out below.

Reading the Cards

To use the Tarot the cartomancer will typically ask the client to shuffle the deck, cut the cards perhaps a number of times and then lay them out. The cartomancer will then divine the answer to specific questions, predict the future and so on. The combination of images provides either answers or guidance according to the interpretation of the reader.

The Spreads

The cards are spread on the table and 'stirred' before being reassembled into a pack. The pack is then placed on the table and the cards dealt. It is recommended that the cards are turned over from side to side rather than from top to bottom. The reason for this is that to do otherwise would possibly reverse all the cards and therefore their intended meanings. Below are some examples of spreads using the Major Arcana only:

A Six Card Spread

Six cards either from the top of the deck or at random are set out either in a line or in two lines of three. These six of the Major Arcana will indicate the broad areas which will either answer questions, or give direction or indication of the future. To continue, the cards can be reshuffled and the new six cards laid out to continue the tale that is unfolding or alternatively to 'zoom in' on the specific areas in which the client has particular need or interest.

A Consequence Spread

The client chooses a card, called the Significator which represents the client him or herself for a specific reading on a specific topic. This is placed in the centre of the spread. The second card is placed atop of this and represents the question. A third card placed above represents the cause of whatever problem is being analysed. A fourth card placed to the left represents the past. A fifth card placed to the right represents the future. A sixth card placed bottom left is the indication of future action. A seventh card placed to the bottom right indicates the circumstances surrounding the client and the eighth card placed 'due south' represents the consequences of the course of action.

The 'Year Ahead' Spread

The cards are laid out rather as in for 'clock patience' with cards in the position of one o'clock, two o'clock, three o'clock and so on. Each position represents a month and will give an indication of the most significant aspects in that month that will relate to the client.

Questions and Answers Spread

This spread is used to answer a specific question. The client is asked to frame that question specifically and clearly and to focus on it.

The first card chosen becomes the significator. The client then chooses two cards which will indicate the area of the question, perhaps the cause of a problem, for example. The client then chooses three further cards which represent the answers to the problem and lastly, a final card representing the final consequence.

There are many other, and some more complicated, spreads used by different cartomancers.

The Tarot is probably one of the most effective autoscopes, a word used by Jung in this context. By this he meant that the patterns and combinations of the ancient symbols would provide a link between the creative and intuitive human mind and the archetypes in the unconscious. As such therefore the Tarot allows for the reader to assess their own unconscious mind and bring forward the images to the conscious analytical mind, thus providing answers 'from within' to questions and needs.

The most famous Tarot reader was arguably Mlle Marie-Anne-Adelaide Lenormande who was born in France in 1772. She was a noted clairvoyant but it was her skill with the Tarot cards which gave her the opportunity of becoming a consultant to the Empress Joséphine. She accurately forecast marriages, births, travel, failure and death for leading figures in revolutionary France including the writer Madame de Staël and the painter Jaques-Louis David. Lenormande's talents created great wealth for her and it was in her nature to be extremely generous. When she died in 1843 a huge number of people attended her funeral. Her death, however, has an element of pathos about it. She had predicted the dire consequences of a visit by a raven and when she apparently saw one fly into her bedroom she suffered a stroke, dying shortly afterwards. Her death was in fact earlier than she herself had predicted. Unfortunately her failing sight had caused her to mis-identify the bird that had flown into her bedroom; it was not a raven but a pigeon.

4

PREDICTION AND PROPHECY

If Mlle Lenormande was ultimately a little unsuccessful in her predictive skills there are those who seem to have fired the world's imagination as psychic 'seers'. Most famous amongst those must be Nostradamus, whose work we shall now examine. To show that such skills have not been altogether lost in the modern world, we will also look at the work of a modern psychic, Jeane Dixon.

NOSTRADAMUS: DOCTOR AND DIVINER

Unquestionably the most famous set of predictions are those given by Nostradamus. He was born Michel de Nostredame in 1503, at St Rémy de Provence, in France, the eldest of five sons. His parents were Jewish and converted to Catholicism when he was aged nine, which gave Nostradamus a background in both the Cabbala and the Bible. He was educated largely by his maternal grandfather. From an early age he had visions which he credited as being given by God, a glimpse into the divine world.

Many commentators have reported that his family was descended from notable doctors at the Court of Anjou though, in fact, his family came from Avignon. His grandfather, Pierre, was a Jewish grain dealer who had married a non-Jew. Nostradamus's father, Jacques, married the daughter of an ex-doctor cum tax collector, Reynière de St Rémy.

In 1522 Nostradamus began studying medicine at Montpellier University but was widely educated in Hebrew, Latin, Greek, mathematics, astronomy and the then allied discipline of astrology. As a physician he worked treating victims of the plague in southern France but incurred the wrath of fellow physicians by refusing to use conventional treatment such as bleeding, introducing instead medications of his own invention. The recipes of some of those medicines have not survived through the ages, yet some remedies are found in his book *Excellent et Très-Utile Opuscule* published in 1572 after his death. Nostradamus married in 1534 and had two children but just a few years later his life was devastated by the death of all of his family from the bubonic plague. In addition, he was hounded by the Inquisition (see page 89) because of his association with the physician, philosopher and astrologer Julius-César Scaliger (1484–1558). The Inquisition wanted to talk to him about his association with Scaliger because of Scaliger's relations with a Huguenot teacher, Philibert Sarazin. Many believe that Scaliger regarded Nostradamus highly and almost certainly introduced him to the psychic and to prophecy. It appears that for around six years Nostradamus wandered around Europe, studying the occult and developing his psychic side and his visions; he evidently stayed in Venice and Sicily, though his full whereabouts over that time are not known.

Later Nostradamus married a wealthy widow, Anne Ponsart Gemelle, and together they had six children. He settled down in Salon en Craux de Provence. From around 1550 he delved deeply into his psychic side and recorded many prophetic visions. He believed they came from a divine presence; they were often accompanied by a disembodied voice. He furthered his visions by scrying (crystal gazing), using a bowl of water on a brass stand. He appears to have entered into a trance-like state while scrying. (This method of prediction is thought to have been derived from the Fourth-century text *De Mysteriis Egyptorum* (Concerning the Mysteries of Egypt) by the neo-Platonist philosopher Iamblichus.

Quatrains and Centuries

In order to record his visions for future ages, but in order not to incur the wrath of the Inquisition, Nostradamus used the deeply subtle language of the occult known as the Language of the Birds (see page 232) to hide the true meanings of his prophecies. He set out his prophecies in quatrains, poems of four lines each which were known as 'The Centuries' because they were divided up into ten groups of one hundred. Each group did not specifically relate to a given period; the quatrains are randomly distributed. According to his calculations his prophecies extended to the year 3797.

He published the prophecies first in 1555 under the title *Les Propheties de M. Michel Nostradamus*. An expanded edition was published in 1568, the first publication of his prophecies in complete form. He became an instant success and was widely praised as a prophet by such notables as Catherine de Medici. The year after the publication of *Les Propheties* he was summoned by the queen to attend her at Paris. She believed that one of his quatrains predicted the death of her husband, Henri II, in a forthcoming duel. (Such a duel did take place in 1559; the quatrain in question is detailed below.) Nostradamus apparently managed to satisfy the queen with his explanation of the quatrain and he was asked to draw up horoscopes of all the royal children.

The quatrains are difficult to translate because of the language in which they are written. Even at face value they include anagrams, Hebrew, Latin, Portuguese, Greek, French, Provençal and further the subtlety and multi-layered meaning of the Language of the Birds.

From 1551 onwards Nostradamus published annual almanacs and prognostications, predicting local weather, agriculture and local events but his reputation suffered as many people published forged versions using his name to increase their value.

Because of the power and prominence of the Inquisition, Nostradamus took great pains to ensure that he always praised the Church, observed its practices to the letter and publicly denounced magic and sorcery, though it is evident that he was an initiate. Having the favour and protection of the queen also helped and it appears that he had a skill for survival, knowing when to keep a low profile. In one gesture, no doubt designed to protect his own existence, he burned his own library of books, declaring that he had found they contained ancient magical texts that were dangerous and should be destroyed.

Just before the end of his life Nostradamus was visited by the queen and her second son, Charles IX and he was given the high accolade of being appointed Médecin du Roi (court physician).

In 1566 he died and was buried in an upright coffin in the Church of the Cordeliers in Salon. His grave was opened in 1791 by French soldiers and his remains reburied in the nearby church of St Laurent. A plaque donated by his wife Anne can still be seen at the location.

The Predictions

The degree of subtlety of the predictions issued by Nostradamus have been the subject of controversy since their publication in 1568 and over 400 years of constant attention have not yet resolved the true meaning of the quatrains.

Some interpreters of Nostradamus' work believe that the quatrains have predicted accurate details of the French Revolution, the flight of Louis XVI to Varennes, the Napoleonic wars, the British Monarchy from Elizabeth I onwards including the execution of Charlies I and the abdication of Edward VIII, the American Wars of Independence and the American Civil War, the First World War, the Second World War, the rise and the fall of Hitler, the assassinations of Abraham Lincoln and the Kennedy brothers, the prominence of the Ayatollah Khomeini and the rise and fall of Mikhail Gorbachev. They believed that he has predicted air travel, space travel, the lunar missions, the inventions of submarines, gas masks and the atomic bomb.

Some interpretations have undoubtedly been incorrect such as one which predicted the rise of the Prince and Princess of Wales to become King and Queen of England on 2 May 1992.

The interpreter's job is not easy because the so called

'Centuries' are not laid out chronologically and therefore any quatrain can be held to apply to any date, in most cases with no particular indications from the author. Nostradamus himself admitted the obscurity of the quatrains was deliberate, no doubt partly to protect himself from persecution but also because it was his belief that the majority of people were not ready for his prophecies. This would be in line with most recent theories that he was an Initiate. He himself stated: 'But now I am willing for the general good to enlarge myself in dark and abstruse sentences, so that my predictions will not wholly offend present sensibility. The whole work is therefore written in a nebulous rather than a plainly prophetic form. ...' Not everyone has been charmed by Nostradamus' obscurity. The sixteenth-century sceptic William Fulke commented that Nostradamus' writings were 'in such dark wrinkles of obscurity that no man would pick out of them either sense or understanding'.

Let us take some of the more famous quatrains and see how these have been interpreted by analysts.

The first of the quatrains which analysts argue came true just four years after its publication is I.35 (using the usual convention for numbering Nostradamus' quatrains, the first number referring to the Century and the second number to the quatrain contained within that Century.

> Le Lyon jeune le vieux surmontera
> En champ bellique par singulier duelle,
> Dans cage d'or les yeux luy crevera
> Deux playes une, pour mourir mort cruelle.

> The young Lion will surmount the old
> On a warlike field in a strange duel,
> He will split his eyes in the golden cage
> Two wounds one, to die a cruel death.

Most analysts agree that this is a reference to the death of Henri II and indeed it was this quatrain which came to the attention of his wife, Catherine de Medici and which initially caused

Nostradamus some discomfort when questioned. The fact is that in 1559, on 30 June, Henri II took part in a jousting tournament with Gabriel, Comte de Montgomery. Henri was killed when Montgomery's broken lance pierced his face visor. It is said that the lance pierced Henri's brain, some say through his eye. Henri was older than Montgomery and therefore 'the young lion did surmount the old'. They were in a duel on a warlike field; it was a strange duel as it was a tournament duel rather than a genuine combat and the field could be described as 'warlike' as it was the scene of the tournament rather than a real battle. The cage would be the face visor and quite possibly the lance did split his eyes. The cruel death would also seem be correct; Henri took ten days to die in agony.

The next quatrain for which the prediction is generally agreed upon is II.51 which is held to predict the Great Fire of London.

Le sang du juste à Londres fera faute,
Bruslez par foudres de vingt trois les six,
La dame antique cherra de place haute.
De mesme secte plusieurs seront occis.

The blood of the just in London will be demanded,
Burned by lightning in the year of 23 the sixes,
The ancient lady will fall from a high place.
Of the same sect several will be killed.

The simple translation of this is as follows: the first line indicates that many died. The second line tells us they died by fire in the year 1666. In the third line 'the ancient lady's fall' has been deemed to be the destruction of St Paul's Cathedral and in the fourth, the death of those of 'the same sect' would refer to Protestantism.

However, hardly any of this seems to make any real sense. 'Death in London' would seem to be indicated by the first line. But the Great Fire of London was not started by anything resembling lightning. The date 1666 is a convenient contrivance that cannot be arrived at by the quatrain. The best 'shot' is to take the numbers 20 × 3 = 60 plus 6 = 66 and refer to the year '66 but it is very clear that any number of years could be created from the clues in the quatrain and that 1666 is far from obvious. St Paul's Cathedral as the 'falling lady' also seems extremely stretched. There are no real grounds for referring to St Paul's as a lady and there are no obvious other 'ladies' that are candidates. As for the question of further deaths in the sect there is really no obvious translation of this either that relates to the Great Fire of London. It seems that the imagery of lightning in London is the only given clue that leads us to this interpretation of the quatrain.

David Ovason in *The Secrets of Nostradamus* (1997) (later reprinted as *The Nostradamus Code*) suggests a more convoluted translation but one that at least fits the original a little better. He believes the blood of the just and the references to the sect to be the execution of thirteen Catholics in 1556. Nostradamus as a Catholic might well have believed this to be 'unjust'. The trials of the Catholics have taken place in the old Lady Chapel and it might be that the fire is regarded as a retribution from God for which the lightning bolt would become symbolic. All in all, however, it is easy to imagine that the quatrain could be used to 'predict' any number of London incidents.

Quatrain VIII.37 is alleged to prophesy the execution of Charles I of England.

> La forteresse auprès de la Tamise
> Cherra par lors, le Roya dedans serré,
> Auprès du pont sera veu en chemise
> Un devant mort, puis dans le fort barré.

> The fortress near the Thames
> Where the King will be kept aside,
> Near the bridge he will wear a shirt
> One before dead, locked in the fort.

Charles I was captured in 1647 and imprisoned in Windsor Castle, a fortress by the Thames. He must have crossed London

Bridge to reach Whitehall where, dressed in a white shirt, he stepped to the scaffold for execution. After death he was taken back to the same fortress in which he had been imprisoned, Windsor, where he was buried.

It is the twentieth century and future predictions which of course have been the focus of most attention and we shall look at these now.

The most commonly quoted of the 'modern' quatrains is the so called Hitler quatrain, II.24.

> Bestes farouches de faim fleuvres tanner,
> Plus part de camp encontre Hister sera,
> En cage de fer le grand sera trainner,
> Quand Rin enfant Germain observera.

> Beasts, wild with hunger, will swim across rivers,
> The greater part of the battlefield will be against Hitler,
> He will drag the leader in an iron cage,
> When the German child observes no law.

Other translations of the fourth line include: 'When the German child will see the Rhine.' In order to interpret this as a premonition of the rise of Hitler it is important to rename Hister Hitler (see Metathesis, page 237) which many analysts do, including Oxford scholar Erika Cheetham. However, David Ovason rejects that translation believing Hister to refer to the River Hister 'the Latin name for the lower part of the Danube'. If the quatrain relates to Hitler then it has been argued that the iron cage is a reference to his Berlin bunker. Another analyst, de Fontbrune, believes that the reference to the cage actually relates to Mussolini and is the van in which the partisans dragged away the Italian leader to his execution. Ovason points out that the popularity of the prophecy as one referring to Hitler was promoted by the Führer himself and was used by Goebbels during the war as propaganda to announce that the stars themselves had foretold the rise of a Great Leader. Removing Hitler from the quatrain probably also removes it from the twentieth century, indeed it becomes far less meaningful.

One interesting quatrain also much quoted is I.64.

> De nuict soleil penseront avoir veu,
> Quand le pourceau demy homme on verra,
> Bruit, chant, bataille au Ciel battre apperceu,
> Et bestes brutes à parler on orra.

> By night they will think they have seen the sun,
> When they see the half pig man,
> Noise, screams, warfare in the Sky are seen,
> The brutish beasts will be heard to speak.

Generally speaking there is agreement about what this is believed to predict: twentieth-century aerial warfare. The first line, the reference to the sun seen at night, has been taken to be either the light of bombs exploding or of searchlights. The battle in the sky refers of course to aerial dogfights. The half pig man is an interesting translation which has been held to be either the appearance of a fighter pilot wearing an oxygen mask or of a civilian or pilot wearing a gas mask. Reference to the brutish beasts being heard to speak is held to refer to the half pig man speaking through his mask.

Another quatrain on which there seems to be some general agreement is X.22 which is held to refer to the abdication of Edward VIII in 1936.

> Pour ne vouloir consentir au divorce,
> Qui puis après sera cogneu indigne,
> Le Roy des Isles sera chassé par force,
> Mis à son lieu qui de Roy n'aura signe.

> For not wishing to consent to the divorce,
> Which afterwards will be recognised as unworthy,
> The King of Isles will be driven out by force,
> One is put in his place who will have no mark of kingship.

Although this one seems to highlight the situation relating to Edward VIII it is not actually as close a fit as it looks; and some more recent books on Nostradamus' predictions have suggested that it relates to the divorce of the Prince and Princess of Wales. Taking the more generally accepted interpretation there are some aspects which seem to fit. The 'King of Isles' would seem reasonably enough to be a British king, for which Edward VIII qualified and it is true that he was driven out by force. He believed until his abdication that he would be able to win over Parliament and the people and get them to accept Wallis Simpson. When he failed to do so part of the terms of his abdication included his living outside of Britain. It is probably a bit unfair to say that the one who took his place had no mark of kingship; all in all his brother George V did as good a job as any of the monarchs. However, it is true to say that he made it clear he had never wanted the job nor expected to have it and as such he had probably not been as properly trained for it as had his older brother.

It is the first two lines which give problems. If we assume that the quatrain refers directly to Edward VIII then there was no question of him consenting to a divorce; it was his marriage that was in question. Perhaps the quatrain was designed to refer to someone else, perhaps one of the Parliamentary leaders, indeed possibly the prime minister of the time, who was responsible for putting pressure on the king to abdicate. That might mean that that person has brought about the King of the Isles being driven out by force and his replacement by one with no mark of kingship because he had not consented to the divorce. The quatrain would also seem to indicate that not consenting to divorce will afterwards be viewed as unworthy though the general analysis seems to have been Edward VIII would not have been a particularly dynamic king. So that seems again to be rather stretching a point. Perhaps the reference to 'the divorce' could be taken to be a slightly obscure use of the word meaning 'divorced person' in which case the person we are referring to, perhaps the prime minister, could be said to have not consented to Mrs Simpson herself (she was a divorcee).

It is quatrain X.72 that is undoubtedly the most famous Nostradamus verse even over and above that of the 'Hitler quatrain'. Since it seems to predict either the end of the world or an awesome extraterrestrial invasion in July of 1999 it is currently popular because of its proximity in time and made more significant by the millenarianism which has, obviously, gained apace in the last decade of the twentieth century. The quatrain is as follows:

> L'an mil neuf cens nonante neuf sept mois
> Du ciel viendra un grand Roy d'effrayeur
> Resusciter le grand Roy d'Angoulmois.
> Avant apres Mars regner par bon heur.

> The year 1999 and seven months
> From the sky will come the great King of Terror
> To return to life the King of Angoulmois
> before and after war to reign by good fortune.

'Angoulmois' has been held to refer to the Mongolian King and at least one interpretation of this quatrain is that in July of 1999 a huge war will commence with an invasion from the sky like the Mongolians of old (or possibly linked to the area that was Mongolia). Many analysts have stated that this prophesies the end of the world though in his own writings Nostradamus makes it quite clear that this is not the case.

David Ovason challenges this interpretation believing that this quatrain must be interpreted with the degrees of meaning inherent in the Language of the Birds (Ovason uses the alternate term Green Language). The key to his interpretation is the word Angoulmois which he believes 'is a Green Language construct, which breaks into three units: ANG OUL MOIS'. In a rather lengthy piece of reasoning Ovason concludes that it is a reference to the Archangel Michael. Ovason concludes that:

'Nostradamus seems to suggest that in the year 1999, or 2087, some great entity – possibly harmful to humanity, and certainly

231

being a terror – will descend to the Earth. The effect of his evident evil will be to polarise our civilisation. While many will be persuaded to follow this terrible being, others will find themselves charged with a renewed spirituality – with a feeling for the work of Michael, the archangelic governor of our times. As a result of this, there will be warfare and great social upheavals. As we have seen, however, there is sufficient ambiguity in the verse to suggest that the great king may not be terrible at all. Were we to take into account the fact that Nostradamus was working within the esoteric tradition, then we might see his prediction as a long term confirmation of the event which has been widely anticipated in modern esoteric literature – the entry of the Christ into the spiritual realm contiguous to the physical plane.'

The Language of the Birds

In our description of the writings of Nostradamus we mention the belief by many analysts, and recently the writer David Ovason, that Nostradamus was an Initiate whose quatrains were written in the Language of the Birds (sometimes known as the Green Language).

The Language of the Birds is an especially structured language designed to allow communication between Initiates but which maintains obscurity to the non-initiated who either will not be able to understand the meaning of the phrases at all or can only understand at an unimportant surface level of meaning, while the true and important meanings remain hidden.

The phrase 'Language of the Birds' is likely to be a reference to the origin of the occult Secret Language, possibly to the thirteenth-century Norse epic *Volsunga Saga* in which Sigurd slays the dragon. While roasting its heart he burns his fingers and quickly sucks on them to ease the pain. In doing so he drinks dragon's blood and is initiated into the occult world. He finds that he can understand the language of the birds and from the birds learns of the treasure of the dragon and falls in love with Brunhild.

Fulcanelli, the early twentieth-century French alchemist referred to the Language of the Birds as 'the language which teaches the mystery of things and unveils the most hidden truths'. David Ovason offers another origin for the term.

'It is said that when spiritual beings finally decided to take physical bodies, some descended too quickly to the Earth. They were unprepared for the hardness of the Earth, and were not able to accept its challenges. However, since they had dipped themselves into the Earth stream, they were compelled to remain in physical bodies, in incarnate form. Unable to dwell intimately with the Earth, they found it more comfortable to live some way from its surface. They grew wings, and took to flying in the air, building their nests in the trees. These creatures – who eventually became the birds – remained highly spiritual, however, and watched in astonishment as those who followed them took bodies which could manipulate the Earth while they could relate to it only as thieves and beggars. The Language of the Birds ... remains the most spiritual of languages'.

The Language of the Birds is also known as the Green Language, a term which is perhaps more commonly used nowadays because of its implied connection to 'green' ecology. There is in fact no such connection intended for the language. Indeed the origin of the term is uncertain. Ovason offers a clever possible origin for the term. He points out that the French for Green Language is *Langue Vert*. In French *ouvert* means open and therefore by using an aphesis (see below) and converting *ouvert* to *vert* it then means the opposite, i.e. closed, and therefore has the hidden meaning of 'closed language'. The definition therefore becomes itself one which has used the hidden language to hide its own meaning.

Charles Walker in *The Encyclopedia of Secret Knowledge* (1995) gives a good example of the hidden meanings used in the Language of the Birds. He refers to the thirteenth-century occultist Michael Scot (see page 37) who 'insisted that honey falls from the air into flowers, whence it is collected by the bees', to take to the hives. Although not actually the process by which honey is formed we might assume that this could be a description of the actual process that happens in nature. Whether it was once believed to be or not is irrelevant. Scot would have intended a deeper meaning. As Walker says, 'Bee is an ancient symbol for the human soul, while honey is the thing which feeds the soul.' In this imagery the beehive relates to the human body and the bee to the soul which sometimes, but not always, inhabits the body. But there can be deeper meanings still as Walker again expands: 'This hive represents not only the industry of the bees, but also the "body corporate" – the idea or impulse which unites human souls in one spiritual undertaking'. At a deeper level of meaning, therefore, 'the arcane symbolism of the hive relates to the fact that when groups of people meet and work together with clearly defined and awesome aims, they are bathed in the warmth of the spiritual world.' Walker goes on to analyse Scot's intended meaning.

When Scot tells us that honey falls from the skies, his arcane theme is quite simple: he is saying that all things fall from the air, from the invisible realm of the spiritual. All things are the gift of the gods – man, woman, nature, ideas are loaned to the Earth, yet have their origins on high. In Scot's view, the bees that collect the sky-given 'honey' are the occultists, who try to make sense of this perpetual manna, in the hope that they can strengthen their wings, destined to carry them back into that invisible creative realm.

Walker then takes us still further to show how deep and how meaningful the Language of the Birds can be. Walker likens the bee, for which the Latin name is *apis*, to the sacred bull that was worshipped in ancient Egypt and which has the same Latin name. Both Greek and Roman religion linked the bee and the bull together. As Walker explains:

The word *apis* refers to a duality of nature – to the creature of flight, and to the heavy creature of Earth, the sacrificial bull. This duality made the bee a useful symbol for the Initiate, who, as we have seen, was the inhabitant of two worlds: The Initiated human was free to wing through the astral realms, but remained also a dweller on the lower physical plane, in the familiar human body ... Since the bees are Initiate souls, the hive becomes, by extension, not merely a symbol of the physical body on ordinary men ... It is the place wherein dwells the Initiate soul, or the place where the Initiates work together. It is ... the Mystery School itself.

Techniques used in Constructing the Language of the Birds

Secondary anagrams

As any unraveller of crosswords will know an anagram is a rearrangement of the letters in a word. Within the Language of the Birds anagrams are constructed not merely to hide the true meaning of the word in question, though that is partly the intention, but also to produce an underlying meaning as well.

Anastrophe

This is the reversing of the word either reversing its letters or its phonetics.

Antonomasia

Either the substitution of a summarising, descriptive word to represent somebody or some place's proper name or the use of a proper name to represent the more general concept. Nostradamus typically used the name 'la Dame' to refer to important women such as Marie-Antoinette and Catherine de Medici. The true meaning of the substituted word can only be taken from the context in which it is set.

Aphesis

The omission of a letter or syllable at the beginning of a word. Combining aphesis and anagram is one example of where unravelling the true meaning of the Language of the Birds can be complex indeed.

Apocope

Similar to aphesis but the omission is from the ending of a word.

Arcane association

Using oblique or specialist language to describe an event. For example Nostradamus in quatrain X.67 refers to 'cancer in boeuf'. The specialist knows cancer to be a reference to the moon and therefore the astrological phrase, 'Moon in Taurus', can be understood.

Archaising

Describing new places, people or concepts using old names, typically substituting Greek and Latin names and phrases for more modern words. In the famous quatrain II.24 Nostradamus refers to Hister, probably the River Hister which is now the Danube.

Epenthesis

Adding a letter or syllable to the middle of the word.

Homonyms

Words which have the same sound and/or spelling but have a different meaning. For example, the ancient word for France is Gaul but the use of the term may also refer to the French leader Charles de Gaulle.

Hyphaeresis

The omission of a letter from a word.

Metathesis

Exchanging the consonant sounds within a word to produce different words.

Metonym

A word in which the person's qualities are used to identify that person, i.e. a defining characteristic. The word *boîteux* is thought to have been used by Nostradamus to refer to the Duke of Bordeaux. The word means lame, and the Duke of Bordeaux was lamed in an accident.

Paragoge

The addition of a letter or syllable to the end of a word.

Protothesis

The adding of a letter or syllable to the beginning of a word.

Syncope

This is simply abbreviation.

Synecdoche

A technique where a lesser part of the whole is used to denote the whole. For example, a capital city such as London might be used to denote the whole of England or Britain.

Occult Blinds

Much of the object of the Language of the Birds is to create what is known as an 'occult blind', or deflection. The idea behind the occult blind is that the reader is given an image which is apparently sufficiently coherent and meaningful to allow the reader to believe that they have understood the meaning of what is being proposed and therefore let them pass on to the next phrase or text having completely missed the hidden meanings which are only there to be understood by the Initiated. In our example of the bees, hives and honey it may be that if it was sufficiently described the reader might believe that they are understanding quite simply the process of honey-making by bees without being taken into the deeper meaning. Alternatively the phrases might be constructed in such a way as to lead the reader into the interpretation of those phrases as meaning the human body and the human soul but without revealing that it also relates to Initiates working in the Mystery School. Ovason offers us the example of 'the silent fox'. The word *renard* means fox as used by Nostradamus in quatrain VIII.41, 'esleu sera Renard ne sonnant mot'. (The fox will be elected, not saying a word). Ovason points out that *renard* comes from an Old High German word meaning strong in rule and has migrated to include cunning and wiliness. When appearing in the phrase drawn up in the Language of the Birds the word *renard* may mean all of these qualities. However, *renard* also breaks down phonetically into 'reign' and 'art'. Reign may refer to king, art to skill or dexterity and therefore the word may also be used as an occult blind to refer to someone skilled in kingship.

Ovason uses the Language of the Birds to demolish the belief that the 'eye of the sea' referred to the periscopes of U-boats. The phrase in question is 'l'oeil de la mer par avare canine' meaning 'the eye of the sea by canine avariciousness'. Ovason believes that the phrase means simply whirlpool and its underlying meaning Sicily. His reasoning for that is that classical mythology places a huge whirlpool, named Charybdis, off the coast of Sicily. Ovason sets out his reasoning: 'The Homeric reference has led to the famous phrase ... designed to represent two equal dangers –

in trying to avoid the whirlpool Charybdis, one falls into the maw of Scylla. In the Ovid telling of the tale, Scylla is the six-headed sea monster created by the enchantress Circe. She would eat the "dogs of the sea", as dolphins were called, along with as many mariners as she could entrap from passing ships. As she paddled in the sea, she found around her loins a belt of "dogs, ringed in a raging row", and round her feet she found "gaping jaws like Hell's vile hound", reminding us of the tradition that she herself had barked like a dog. It is not too imaginative to associate her with an avaricious canine, guardian of one of the two rocks in the straits between Sicily and Italy. Clearly, the Nostradamus line is referring to the whirlpool and the monster, rather than to any modern invention such as the periscope. Stripped of its Green Language obscurity, we see that the line is designed to indicate that the subject of the quatrain takes place in Sicily – probably near the Straits of Messina.'

Are the Nostradamus Predictions Useful?

Despite the plethora of books, television programmes, websites and general correspondences surrounding Nostradamus the evidence is surely that the Nostradamus prophecies offer very little guidance. There are so many interpretations and so many different 'code breaking' techniques used that the quatrains can be used to produce all manner of meaning. By using a complex system of changing letters by codes it has been argued that the quatrains spell out the names of Mikhail Gorbachev, the Princess of Wales, Robert Kennedy and so on (though other analysts appear not have seen this!) Frankly, a great deal of the literature purporting to translate Nostradamus' prophecies seems to be little more than speculative nonsense.

We surveyed as many books as we could on Nostradamus and saw very little commonality except where it appeared one author was content to rely on the analysis of others. In some cases the extension of the quatrain into English language, modern English and modern interpretation is so stretched that one can hardly see the original in the end product. Even that does not take into account the fact that the actual quatrains themselves require a good deal of interpretation even in their own language before they can begin to be interpreted.

But is it just that the quatrains are so deeply immersed in the Language of the Birds that they have only been amateurishly unravelled to date and that someone, perhaps as yet undiscovered or even unborn, will one day be able to translate them for the future benefit of mankind? Actually, it appears not. If Nostradamus had intended the prophecies to be as many believe them to be, i.e. very direct statements reflecting his visions of modern events, he could have made them clearer himself. He chose not to, either to protect himself from the Inquisition or because he believed that the information was so powerful that it simply could not be given to the uninitiated. If that is the case then we might presume that the future Initiate capable of interpreting them would come to the same conclusion and refuse to make the information available to the population as a whole.

Regardless of this we have great sympathy for the comments of Ovason who believes: 'There is also no doubt that Nostradamus did not intend these carefully crafted prophecies to be understood until *after* the historical events they each predicted.' Nostradamus himself commented, as already mentioned above: 'The whole work is therefore written in a nebulous rather than a plainly prophetic form ...' Ovason confirms that by saying: 'Although Nostradamus is the most famous clairvoyant in Western occult history, we cannot think of one single example in the whole of Nostradamian literature where a commentator has accurately unscrambled the meaning of the predicting verse prior to the event he predicted.'

George Bernard Shaw referred to the interpretations as having 'the elation of contemporary success', i.e. they work best when viewed from the position of the event having already come to pass. Charles Walker in *The Encyclopedia of Secret Knowledge* gives an example of a typical Nostradamus anagram. He cites three codes, PAU, NAY and LORON. These are an anagram of the name Napoleon (Napaulon) leaving the three letters ROY. Roy is French for king and therefore the anagram refers to King Napoleon (Emperor Napoleon) However, until Napoleon's name was known there was no way of interpreting the prophecies or of knowing that he would be king.

Another well studied prophecy states Roy-Roy will meet his death at the hands of Doux. (This is quatrain P58 from Nostradamus' *Presages*, quatrains published randomly in his various almanacs.) If Roy-Roy means King-King then Walker believes it refers to Henri III of France (1551–89) who was first king of Poland and then king of France and therefore twice crowned. He was murdered by a monk called Jacques Clement; *doux* means clement in French. Predictions that are only evident after the event has taken place are, at best, a scientific cheat and at worst useless. Can it be that all of this work by Nostradamus and all of the controversy that he has generated is entirely intended to prove only that he had the ability to see into the future and the wisdom not to release it to a public unready for the revelations? Perhaps so. However, we would speculate that the form of the quatrains, given Ovason's probably correct analysis, is that actually they have no meaning until the event has passed, and that that is their point. In short the quatrains are a form of Rorschach which allows the person to use the quatrains to acknowledge an event and then to see deeper into the true meaning of that event. In that, Nostradamus could be held to be the greatest ever exponent of the Language of the Birds. He produces a quatrain of such apparent clarity and such hidden meaning with so many 'occult blinds' and sets it to rest in time. An event comes to pass and an analyst of that time then ties the quatrain to the event. By reading deeper into the quatrain the person is then encouraged to read deeper into the event and to see its multilayered meanings and its consequences for the future.

We suggest that this is the true purpose of Nostradamus' work: to encourage people to think deeply about themselves and the world around them.

Nostradamus and the Titanic: an Experiment

The argument has been put forward that Nostradamus' quatrains are so vague that they can be made to fit any circumstance. We thought we would put this to the test by randomly selecting a circumstance for which Nostradamus had never been credited with prophecy and see whether we could find an appropriate quatrain. In fact it worked out quite well. We selected the sinking of the *Titanic* for no other reason than that we had just previously been to see the James Cameron film and there was a copy of the 'making of the film' book lying on our coffee table. It took a bit of hunting to find an appropriate verse but when we did find an appropriate quatrain it seemed very apposite. We chose VI.20.

> L'union feinte sera peu de duree
> Des uns changes reformez la plus part
> Dans les caisseaux sera gent endures
> Lors aura Rome un nouveau leopart.

This translates approximately as follows:

> Feigned union or false peace shall not last long
> Some shall change, most shall reform.
> In ships, people shall suffer
> When Rome has a new leopard (Pope?)

In order to analyse this with a view towards the sinking of the *Titanic* we need to set it in context in the period of 1912, when the sinking took place. Following the rules of the Language of the Birds where statements have overt and covert meanings of increasingly deeper significance we therefore believe we must also set the quatrain in the context of the impending First World War. This is not unreasonable since both incidents, the sinking of the *Titanic* and the social effect of the First World War, were to bring about major social reforms in the British class structures which would never be the same again.

Therefore, analysing the four lines individually:

Feigned union or false peace shall not last long
At the overt level, since we are considering the sinking of the *Titanic*, we must consider the union as being that between the British and the Americans. The ship itself was the result of such a union with both wealthy American and British companies engaged in its construction. But the 'false peace' did not last long after the sinking. There were enquiries in both Britain and America which pointed to the high loss of life of third class (steerage) passengers resulting from a combination of the lack of lifeboats and the physical design of the ship based on the British class structure which made it difficult for third class passengers to reach the boat decks. There was considerable dispute over whether another ship, the *Californian*, was near the *Titanic* and could have effected a rescue had its captain been more aware of the circumstances.

To examine the deeper meaning of the line we must consider that the reference to feigned union or false peace not lasting long could refer to the impending outbreak of the First World War. Certainly the foundations for the war which actually began in 1914 were laid down in the years previously and we might focus on the Balkan Wars of 1912 to 1913 as a major cause. These wars resulted in the quest on the part of Serbia to take over those areas of Austria-Hungary that were inhabited by Slavik peoples which strengthened Austria-Hungarian suspicion of Serbia.

Some shall change, most shall reform.
The *Titanic* disaster brought about significant changes. First, as a direct result of the sinking and the subsequent enquiries new laws were passed demanding a lifeboat space for every person on a ship, enforceable lifeboat drills, the maintenance of full-time radio watch while at sea and the formation of the International Ice Patrol which monitored the progress of icebergs. Other changes which the sinking brought about were related to the class and social structure; America was outraged that the British structure could have produced so clear a difference in the

survivor statistics of the second and third classes and in Britain it can be regarded, particularly with hindsight, as the point at which 'the working man' began to rebel against the idea of 'staying in his place'.

With the outbreak of the First World War this very theme was exacerbated. Soldiers coming home from the front were still very much immersed in the existing class structure (which in many ways still exists to the present day) but were rather more ready to assert their own demands on the basis of what they had given for their country. To some degree they had also seen 'their betters' in the roles of officers and had found that they were not that much different after all and even began to question whether the term 'betters' was appropriate.

We see therefore a clear link not just chronologically between the *Titanic* and the First World War but in the exact same effects on the social and class structures. The second line of the quatrain would seem to perfectly marry the two themes precisely as would be demanded by the hidden meanings of the Language of the Birds.

In ships, people shall suffer

This one is a bit obvious of course when related to the *Titanic* but we must deal with the existence of a plural. Clearly many suffered on the *Titanic* and we might stretch our luck and include the lifeboats. Many of these were adrift in the open sea for many hours after the *Titanic* foundered and certainly the people in them suffered from cold as well as the loss of their loved ones and the horrors of having watched the ship sink. But lifeboats are not usually called ships and this might be regarded as a bit of a cheat. We will therefore assume that the quatrain could have referred to both the *Titanic* and the *Carpathia*, the ship which came to their rescue. The survivors were brought aboard the *Carpathia* and it was on board that ship that many of them found out for certain that their loved ones had not survived with them.

Many people had 'gone to the boats' with the belief that the *Titanic* was unsinkable and that they were merely following some sort of strange regulation and would later be reboarding the ship.

Even after it sank, many in the crowded lifeboats assumed that the less crowded ones would go back for survivors floating in the water though in fact only one did and only a handful of survivors were pulled from the icy waters. We can therefore justifiably argue that there was suffering on both the *Titanic* and the *Carpathia*.

The application of this line to the First World War is fairly obvious. Prior to early 1917 the Allies were able to protect their lines of supply of food and raw materials by patrolling the sea lanes but the Germans used submarine warfare to inflict huge loss of life on the Allies' ships and of course huge suffering. As a result of this action the convoy system was created where warships protected troop and supply transportation. Naval warfare, needless to say, creates many situations where 'in ships, people shall suffer'.

When Rome has a new leopard (Pope?)
There was indeed a change of Pope in 1914. Pope Benedict XV reigned from 1914 to 1922, being made pope only shortly after being elevated to the Cardinalate. Of course, this is two years adrift from the sinking of the *Titanic* chronologically but we should not let that step in our way. Erika Cheetham, a well-known analyst of the prophecies of Nostradamus, linked a pope's reign of seventeen years as noted in quatrain V.92 to Pope Pius XII who actually reigned for nineteen years on the basis that Nostradamus was 'slightly out' by that margin in his prediction. So presumably two years is acceptable for our analysis.

However, just linking this line of the quatrain chronologically would hardly be fair so we must find in this appointment of a new pope some reason to link it to something relating to the *Titanic* if our argument is to work and, in keeping with the generally accepted theme of Nostradamus that his quatrains had deeper and deeper meaning it must be something that relates to an underlying significance for people generally and not just a coincidence of dates or events. And we found one!

The pope who took over the papacy in 1914, Giacomo della Chiesi, adopted the name Benedict XV. His predecessor had been

Pius X and his successor Pius XI. It is well accepted that when a pope adopts a name he intends that name to have meaning. For example, when Pope John Paul I adopted that name it was stated that he wished to reconcile the achievements of his immediate predecessor Paul VI and the worldwide love that had been given to Paul's immediate predecessor, John XXIII. John Paul II took the name clearly because he wished to indicate that he would continue the hopes that had been inspired by his predecessor John Paul I who died after only 34 days in office. Therefore we must look at the name Benedict and go back to the previous pope who had adopted that name, Benedict XIV. He had been pope between 1740 and 1758 and is noted for being one of the most learned popes who encouraged education and science, founding chairs of physics, chemistry and mathematics at the University of Rome. Here we have our link. The *Titanic* was held by many to be unsinkable or, as *The Shipbuilder* stated, 'practically unsinkable'. There were such declarations as 'this is the ship that God himself could not sink'. This was regarded as an affront to God and indeed the sinking was held by some to be a punishment for such lack of respect. More practically the sinking certainty was regarded as a punishment for humanity's increasing dependency on science and technology. Humankind, it was thought, was beginning to challenge the gods, at least in his own mind, by building machinery on an Olympian scale (the *Titanic*'s sister ship was called the *Olympic*). The Victorian era, which had only just ended, had promoted science, technology and rationalism, headed by Prince Albert, to a point where many felt that it was an affront to the natural order, and to the wishes of God. And the pope who took over in 1914 adopted the name of a pope known for his interest in science.

We must take this opportunity of reminding the reader that this whole exercise was not undertaken overly seriously and is a test of whether the quatrains can be adapted successfully to randomly selected criteria. We feel it worked quite well in this case, however.

For what it's worth the original quatrain has been interpreted in other ways. In one case as a warning to the present time in the late twentieth century when war will break out as peace around the world is unstable, when suffering on ships will inevitably arise from naval warfare and Pope John Paul II will either be assassinated or flee from Rome and be replaced by another Pope. We see no reason why that particular translation is any better than our own. Another analyst believes that this quatrain refers to the ascension of Pope John XIII as his coat of arms contains a lion which the analyst relates to the leopard.

Nostradamus as Tool of Propaganda During the Second World War

It is well known that the Germans under Hitler during the Second World War were deeply involved in astrology (see page 263) and the occult. Himmler, for example, maintained a group of clairvoyants and mediums, in addition to a professional astrologer, Wilhelm Wulff, on constant call to advise him. Himmler was also involved in Spiritualism, alternative medicines and other beliefs that were later encompassed by the phrase 'New Age'.

The Swiss astrologer Karl Ernst Krafft (1900–45) was employed by the Germans to produce edited and amended prophecies of Nostradamus which overtly predicted the triumphs of the Third Reich and of Germany in the Second World War. These were then distributed as propaganda. Not that this was a unique operation; the British had hired German refugee and astrologer Louis de Wohl (1903–61) to advise them on what astrological advice Krafft might be giving Hitler. De Wohl was later employed to create his own, faked, Nostradamus prophecies predicting the defeat of Germany. The RAF dropped booklets of faked Nostradamus quatrains.

A more specifc form of using Nostradamus for propaganda came in 1940 when the Germans wanted to clear the Paris roads so that they could cross into France from Belgium. Fake quatrains purporting to be those of Nostradamus were circulated which indicated that south-east France would not be affected by the Second World War. This, we are told, had the successful effect of causing a flight of civilians and refugees to that area, emptying the roads to the Channel ports.

Nor were the Germans and the British the only governments to use Nostradamus' quatrains to their own end. The US government used the quatrains in short films to promote America as the 'home of the free'.

Nostradamus, then, is not only believed to have predicted elements of the Second World War, even the rise of Hitler as some believe, but became a tool of that struggle.

A MODERN SEER: JEANE DIXON

The claims made for Nostradamus centre around his being able to see or predict the future (setting aside for a moment the criticism that only retrospective analysis is meaningful). This clearly overlaps with premonition and precognition, and a variety of other occult powers of 'seeing'. We should not be led into believing such abilities reside only with those in the distant past. There are many such powerful psychics who have had considerable success in the modern day; one of the most famous of these is Jeane Dixon. An examination of her prophecies reminds us that this history is not confined to the distant past but is a living history that we are experiencing up to the present day.

In 1952 Jeane Dixon was in St Matthew's Cathedral, Washington for her morning meditation when she had a vision of the White House before her. She had for some days felt 'an odd sensation of withdrawal' which she knew was often the forerunner of a significant vision. Above the White House the numerals 1960 appeared and a dark cloud spread from the numbers covering the White House. In front of the building she could see a young, tall, blue-eyed man with thick brown hair. An inner voice told her that it was a Democrat President elected in 1960 who would meet a violent death while in office. When giving an interview for *Parade* magazine four years later (11 March 1956) she stated that: 'A blue-eyed Democratic President elected in 1960 will be assassinated.' But the reporters preferred to say only that he would 'die in office'.

In the summer of 1963 she confirmed her vision, stating that she had 'seen' a large coffin being carried to the White House. 'This means that the President will meet death elsewhere and his body will be returned there for national mourning.' In October 1963 she told psychiatrist and parapsychology reseacher Dr F. Regis Riesenman that she had had a vision of Lyndon Johnson's name being removed from the vice-presidential door. The person who had caused the name to be removed had a two syllable name containing five or six letters, the second was s, the first was something like an 'o' or a 'q' and the last letter ended with a curve that went straight up (matching 'Oswald'). On 17 November 1963 she dined with John Teeter, Executive Director of the Damon Runyon Memorial Fund, Vicomtesse Fournier de la Barre and Miss Eleanor Bumgardner. But Miss Dixon was seen to be very distracted and confirmed that she kept seeing a vision of a dark cloud moving down on the White House and that tragedy was going to happen 'very, very soon'. She stated: 'In a very few days the President will be killed. I see his casket coming into the White House.'

On Wednesday 20 November Jeane Dixon was at a business lunch with Mrs Cope and Charles Benter. Again she was very distracted and told them it was because she knew the President was soon going to be shot. On the Thursday she confirmed her belief to one of the salesmen in her own office and told him that she had asked Kay Halle (who knew President Kennedy well and 'had his ear') to get word to Kennedy to cancel his trip to Texas. She believed that he had been informed but that he had gone anyway, which as it turned out was not correct.

On the Friday morning she met Charles Benter and told him, talking about the assassination: 'This is the day it will happen!'

At lunch-time Jeane Dixon was in the Mayflower Hotel having lunch with Mrs Harley Cope and Mrs Rebecca Kaufmann. Again she was distracted from eating and again confirmed: 'Something dreadful is going to happen to the President today'.

Suddenly the music from the orchestra ceased and the conductor, Sydney Seidenman, greeted the three women and told them that somebody had taken a shot at the president. Jeane Dixon commented: 'The president is dead'. Seidenman told her that he was not and that he may not even have been hit by the bullets but Mrs Dixon told him: 'You will learn that he is dead'. The first news which he had been able to report was that he was still alive and he was being given a blood transfusion. Mrs Dixon was adamant. 'The radio is wrong. President Kennedy is dead.' We now know of course that given the nature of his head wound his death was certain from the moment the assassin's bullet struck.

When Kay Halle was informed of what happened her own dreadful secret came out. She had known that the Kennedy clan were not given to psychic matters and that their image of a 'rough and tumbling', ball game playing, family was very much a reality. Kay had decided, 'I simply could not bring myself to deliver such a dreadful, nebulous warning. Frankly, I couldn't even convince myself that it was true, and knowing how brave and determined President Kennedy was, I realised that he would have been the last to give heed to such a warning. ... I knew that the Kennedys would consider it some kind of mumbo jumbo. The President would have laughed at the mere suggestion of it.' He had gone to Texas never having been told of the very many times Jeane Dixon had foreseen his death.

Jeane Dixon's successes had impact in her own life. One morning her husband Jimmy was due to fly to Chicago but Jeane warned him that she had 'seen' a plane crashing and told him he must take the train instead. Jimmy did not seem to want to hear of it and 'for the first time in her life she [Jeane Dixon] stamped her foot in frustration'. As her husband said afterwards: 'Like most husbands, I take the advice of my wife even though I don't like to have her think so. ... When the man and wife are in love, he pays her heed. I did not fly that day.' Just as well; the plane for which he held a ticket crashed outside Chicago killing all the passengers.

Roosevelt and Mrs Dixon

Jeane Dixon had been asked to visit the White House to speak to President Franklyn Roosevelt in November 1944. They apparently got on very well despite the fact that she was not always telling him what he wanted to hear. But perhaps the most painful message was one that he apparently was ready to hear. Indeed Jeane Dixon believes that he may have had his own premonition of his forthcoming death. He asked her: 'How much time do I have to finish the work I have to do?' Mrs Dixon touched his fingertips and told him: 'Six months or less'. In January 1945 she revisited the White House and confirmed that he had very little time left. They almost fell out over one vision she had of 'Uncle Sam reaching into another man's pocket, removing something from it, and giving it to a third country.' She warned him not to give away something which did not belong to America but noticed that he clenched both his fists and his body language indicated that whatever he had planned to do he believed it was for the good of the nation. In February 1945 Roosevelt, Churchill and the Soviet dictator Stalin met in Yalta and concluded an agreement which gave Russia control over half of Germany, the act which inspired Winston Churchill's comment that an iron curtain had fallen across Europe. Many believed that this was what Dixon had foreseen. Also as she had foreseen, on 12 April 1945 the president died of cerebral haemorrhage. It was in fact also on record that she had touched the fingertips of the vice-president Harry S. Truman and told him: 'You will become President through an act of God.' Truman took over on the death of Roosevelt.

Jeane Dixon's prophecies extended to the world of politics in a very specific way. At a time when China was regarded as an unimportant problem Jeane Dixon told President Roosevelt that it would become Communist. Indeed she referred to it as Red China. In October 1946 Jeane Dixon was at an ambassadorial reception at the Chinese Embassy in Washington when she announced: 'I see America fighting Red China in the future, not Red Russia.' She was challenged by the wife of Ambassador Loy

Henderson who commented: 'China isn't red, and with its rich cultural heritage it would never go for an alien ideology like Communism.' But Jeane Dixon was quite adamant. On 21 September 1949 Communists proclaimed The People's Republic and Chiang Kai-Shek moved into exile to the island of Formosa (Taiwan). China had become Red China.

It appears that Jeane Dixon also foresaw the partition of India and indeed announced in 1946 that the partition would be itself announced on 20 February 1947. That was indeed the date the announcement of the partition was made. In summer of 1947 Jeane Dixon was with management consultant Daniel Magner who mentioned New Delhi and she suddenly had a vision which she announced: 'Mahatma Gandhi will be assassinated.' She told them he would be killed within six months. He was assassinated on 3 January 1948 by a Hindu fanatic. She announced before the event the suicide of Marilyn Monroe (1962) and the plane crash that killed the secretary-general of the United Nations, Dag Hammarskjöld in 1961.

Predictions on TV

Jeane Dixon made some of her famous forecasts on live television. On 14 May 1953 she appeared on a NBC television programme along with her crystal ball. On air with her was a former ambassador to Russia, Joseph E. Davies. He asked her: 'How long will Malenkov be Prime Minister of Russia?' Jeane Dixon looked into her crystal ball and announced that he would be peacefully replaced by a man with an 'oval-shaped head, wavy grey hair, a little goatee, and greenish eyes.' She stated this would happen within two years. The ambassador poured scorn on her prediction, firstly stating that Russian leaders are not peacefully replaced and also that there was nobody up and coming who looked like the description she was offering. Indeed he was so scornful that he suggested she should read his book on Russia. She also indicated that the goatee-bearded gentleman would only rule briefly and then a short, bald-headed man would take over.

She also said that after that a silver ball 'would go into outer space.'

Joseph Davies was still ridiculing Jeane Dixon when the programme ended. However, within two years the last laugh went to Mrs Dixon. Malenkov was peacefully replaced as Soviet Premier by Marshall Bulganin who fitted her description exactly. However, the bald-headed Nikita Khrushchev took over as Communist party boss. Under his rule in 1957 the Soviets orbited Sputnik in outer space.

A most interesting example of vanity being punctured by Jeane Dixon's clairvoyance surrounded the incident of President Eisenhower's golf score. Jeane Dixon was to appear on a radio programme with the comedian Bob Hope. During recording the programme Bob Hope challenged Mrs Dixon. 'I've been playing golf with Ike this afternoon at Burning Tree. If you are so good, tell me what my golf score was.' Jeane Dixon looked into her crystal ball and stated: 'I'll tell you not only your score but also the President's. It was a 96 and a 92. You won.' Apparently Bob Hope was in distress. The President would believe that he had given out his golf score and this might well end their friendship. Bob Hope ordered that the golf score comments be removed from the tape before broadcast.

There has of course been enormous controversy since the assassination of President Kennedy about whether he was killed by a conspiracy and not by a lone gunman. When the Warren Commission announced that they believed it had been the work of a lone gunman two-thirds of the American people were scornful of the conclusion. In fact Jeane Dixon had entered this controversy in the month following the president's assassination. Ruth Montgomery, Jeane Dixon's biographer, wrote prediction columns of her psychic visions but omitted one in December 1963 in which Dixon told her: 'As I interpret my symbols, Fidel Castro believed that President Kennedy and Premier Khrushchev had gotten together on a plan to eliminate him and replace him with someone more acceptable to the United States and the U.N. Castro, in his conniving way, therefore arranged for the assassination of John F. Kennedy. Lee Harvey Oswald was the trigger man, but there were others involved in the plot.'

How It's Done

Perhaps more than most seers Jeane Dixon was able to explain the nature of the visions she had. And unlike many such seers she was apparently quite able to see numbers clearly. When she had accurately foretold the date of the announcement of the partition of India on 20 February 1947 her biographer explained quite simply: 'While reading for the Indian official the date had been shown to her in her crystal ball. The numerals, she amplified, were as clear to her as the prices listed on their luncheon menu.' This gives her considerable precision in some of her prophecies. She seems to have been psychic all her life. As a young child she was taken to see a gypsy who foresaw: 'This little girl is going to be very famous. She will be able to foresee world-wide changes, because she is blessed with a gift for prophecy. Never have I seen such palm lines!' She was given a crystal ball and was apparently able to see pictures in it immediately, almost as if she was watching television. Indeed she seems to have played with it almost like a kaleidoscope not realising that others could not see pictures as she did. One example of how she saw her visions was in her premonition of the death of the American actress Carole Lombard in 1942. Jeane Dixon encountered her in Los Angeles, shook her hand and was immediately able to tell her not to go on a plane over the next six weeks. Carole Lombard rejected the advice, replying that she was immediately touring by plane to promote the sale of war bonds. She was warned to travel by automobile or train only for six weeks. Jeane Dixon was later told that Miss Lombard had tossed a coin to see whether she should follow the advice or not and that the coin told her to continue flying. She died in a plane crash a few days later. Jeane Dixon described: 'As I touched her hand I saw the death symbol over her. It was high above the ground. I saw life on the ground around her, and thus knew that if she would keep her feet on the ground she could elude danger. It was a sort of inner voice that said, "six weeks". This voice comes to me frequently, and I always listen to it'.

On another occasion she was challenged to win a raffle. She had previously predicted the partition of India and an Indian official to whom she had given the prophecy took guests to the charity raffle commenting of an automobile being raffled off. 'I am going to win it. And then I shall drive you home in style.' Jeane Dixon heard someone say: 'If Mrs Dixon is so psychic, why doesn't she win the Cadillac?' She concentrated, holding several of the raffle books in her hand, selected one, wrote her husband's name on the ticket and announced that she had chosen the winner. The Indian official responded that if she was so certain would she be prepared to sell her present car to him at a bargain price. She agreed. And the following Saturday night received a telephone call confirming that she had won the automobile on, we are told, a 14,000–1 against chance. She also kept her promise in selling her own car to the Indian official who immediately obtained an $800 profit from it.

The Fátima Prophecy

Jeane Dixon believes that she was granted a vision of the undisclosed prophecy of Fátima in Portugal. At Fátima, a vision of the Virgin Mary appeared to three children. This vision told them only that she was 'from heaven'. The girls described her as a 'young lady, dressed in white'. The children were told there would be visions during the next six months, and were given a vision of hell that frightened them and several warnings to pass on about how humankind should stop offending God. Thousands of pilgrims went to Fátima to witness the visions. On the last day, October 13 1917, an estimated 50,000 to 70,000 pilgrims were present. Most saw the spectacular 'dance of the sun'; the sun broke through clouds and seemed to rotate and dive towards the earth in a blast of multicoloured light, and with much heat. This

255

lasted some ten minutes and was believed to have been seen as far as several miles away.

According to the Fátima story one of the girls, Lucia dos Santos, joined a convent and in 1927 reported that Christ had asked her to keep one of his prophecies secret until 1960. The secret had been placed in an envelope and conveyed to the pope in Rome. Catholics believed that in 1960 the secret would be revealed and indeed Catholic information centres all over the world were swamped with enquiries in that year. However, it was not then and has not yet been revealed. Jeane Dixon believes that she had a vision of what the revelation was. While kneeling at prayer in St Matthew's Cathedral she had a vision of the Virgin Mary and saw the word Fátima in the air above her. 'I read the word "Fátima" and sensed that the long secret prophecy of Fátima was to be revealed to me. I saw the throne of the Pope, but it was empty. Off to one side I was shown a Pope with blood running down his face and dripping over his left shoulder. Green leaves of knowledge showered down from above, expanding as they fell. I saw hands reaching out from the throne, but no one sat in it, so I realised that within this century a Pope will be bodily harmed. When this occurs, the head of the Church will thereafter have a different insignia than that of the Pope. Because the unearthly light continued to shine so brightly on the papal throne, I knew that power would still be there but it would not rest in the person of a Pope. Instead, the Catholic Church would blaze the trail for all peoples of every religion to discover the meaning of the Almighty Power; to grow in wisdom and knowledge. This, I feel sure, was the prophecy of Fátima.'

5

WORKING WITH THE CIRCUS OF ANIMALS

The previous two sections have examined the techniques and practices of trying to see the gods' intent by forms of divination. Nostradamus, and the many seers who have followed him up to the present day, have used varieties of devices to assist them (such as his scrying bowl), or none at all as in Jeane Dixon's case. But the final section of the book examines the claims and workings of the most famous and popular of all divination techniques: astrology.

CHALDEAN ASTROLOGY

It is the proposition of astrology that the astronomical bodies exert forces on people and the Earth below. Such influences may be calculated and even predicted by a knowledge of the positions of the heavenly bodies and their movements.

Astrology is arguably the most ancient of divination techniques. The most primitive people would have been aware of the bodies in the Heavens and perhaps attributed them to the realm of the gods – the divine. They might have believed that they saw, in the apparent movement of the stars, some sense of the gods' plan of events on Earth.

It is thought that astrology could date back around 40–50,000 years ago, when Cro-Magnon people related the objects in the sky to the seasons on Earth. In approximately 3000 BC astrology was first recorded as a system by the Chaldeans in the area of the

Middle East that is now Iraq. At around the same time it was practised by their near-neighbours the Babylonians and it is generally agreed by scholars that one of these groups, though it is not agreed which, formulated the first zodiac. Zodiac is the Greek term for 'circus of animals', and refers to the constellations through which the Sun, Moon and planets appear to pass, which are in the main named for animals. Ancient astrologers plotted the movements of heavenly bodies through the zodiac in order to predict the best times for waging war and to predict climatic or other situations.

The first two of three basic types of astrology were developed by the Chaldeans: **horary** astrology which is a system of predicting the best times for action and is the basis of the term 'horoscope', which is Greek for 'I look at the hour'; and **mundane** *astrology, which predicts large scale events in the world.*

Horary astrology is designed either to indicate the best time for action or to answer questions in much the same way as the Tarot or I Ching can be used to answer specific questions. A horoscope is cast at the moment of asking the question and the interpretation indicates the course of action or the answer. It also claims to be able to predict the future by the technique of progression, i.e. advancing the horoscope to a future time and examining it to see which will be the most favourable or unfavourable aspects for, say, a business venture, a new romance, a change of direction in life.

Mundane astrology is almost certainly the earliest form of astrological practice. It concerns itself with the prediction of forthcoming major events: disasters, wars, political upheaval. The reasoning behind it is that if the heavenly bodies exert an influence over the Earth then different areas of the Earth will be under different types of influence at certain times. By examining the influences in the heavens, mundane astrology seeks to determine which particular countries or regions would be under more or less pressure for expansion, defence, battle and so on. On the basis that all natural events such as earthquakes or volcanoes must have a cause, then mundane astrology seeks to identify which influences are most predominant, which might bring about that cause and at what times.

It is almost certain that early Babylonian astrologers used mundane astrology and indeed the political logic of using your astrologers to determine the fate of your nation is an inevitable early use of the subject.

It is believed that in the fifth century BC the Chaldeans related the position of the planets at the time of a person's birth to their life ahead and created the third type of astrology, **natal** astrology. In the modern day it is natal astrology which uses the horoscope developed by the Greeks.

The majority of modern astrology relates to natal astrology, the use of the birth chart of an individual to predict or interpret their life ahead. Astrology seeks to comment on talents, characteristics, relationships, business, family. It looks at character traits such as humour, perseverance, determination, aggression and so on.

Natal astrology is not confined to people, or even living creatures. A building, for example, is determined to have a 'birth date' when work on it begins or when its foundation stone is laid and a progression through the life of the building is said to be able to determine its characteristics, those who will be successful working within it and so on. In older times horary astrology was used to predict the best time to begin a building so that the building throughout its life would be in harmony with the cosmos.

It is known that the ancient Chinese practised astrology, around 2000 BC. Indeed the emperor was regarded as a high priest whose duty was to remain in harmony with the stars. Astrology, or knowledge of the stars, is also found in the cultures of the ancient Egyptians, Tibetans, the Indians, Mayans and indeed in all early developed cultures.

Being a bridge between mortals and the divine gods, astrology was a powerful tool and therefore kept secret from the general public. It is probably the first example of occult knowledge that was regarded as too powerful for the 'common man', and kept from him by systems of complex rules which were learned only by those so permitted. It was administered by the high priests and by royalty and as such represented an early form of political and spiritual power.

It was the Greeks around 500 BC who adopted Chaldean astrology and made it widely and publicly available. Some of the greatest thinkers such as Pythagoras, Aristotle and Plato accepted the link between the planets and the Earth, believing that astrology could predict better or less favourable times for certain actions.

In approximately 250 BC Greek slaves were the conduit by which astrology found its way to the Romans. The Emperor Augustus became the first Roman emperor to openly declare his belief in the power of astrology.

Modern astrology was probably born approximately AD 150 when Ptolemy the Greco-Egyptian astronomer (c. AD 90–168) wrote *The Four Books on the Influence of the Stars*, setting out an Earth-centred system of the Universe on which modern astrology is still based.

Not that astrology has always had acceptance. It was condemned by Christians such as St Augustine (354–430). The Christian convert Emperor Constantine (c. 274–337) in AD 333 regarded it as a demonic practice. As a result of Christian influence, astrology became disregarded in the West but it remained popular and in use in the East. Astrology found its way back into Western civilisation through Spanish Cabbalists around the twelfth century. During the Renaissance the greatest scientists, astronomers, philosophers and alchemists accepted the teachings of, or directly studied, astrology. Paracelsus (see page 41), the early sixteenth-century philosopher, regarded it important that no prescriptions or medication should be administered without regard to the stars.

The rise of science and the scientific principle in the seventeenth century and the gradual development of the science of astronomy began the process of driving astrology out of the public arena and into the backstreets of knowledge, where it was regarded more as a superstition or occult practice, a view probably relatively widely held in the present day.

Despite that, there have been leading modern figures who have supported astrology as a powerful tool. Revolutionary thinkers such as Jung did not disregard astrology, believing it to spring from the collective unconscious and accepting that for one reason or another an understanding of the horoscopes of patients allowed him to deal with their inner difficulties. He believed that astrology was in effect a symbolic language of the psyche and related it, as he did the *I Ching*, to synchronicity – a part of a connected universe.

THE NAZIS AND THE STARS

The Nazis and the Occult

It is worth diverting ourselves for a moment to examine the role of the occult in Nazi Germany. Astrology and the occult had an interesting role during the Second World War. According to Ellic Howe in his book *Astrology and Psychological Warfare during World War II* the German astrological movement was, from around 1920 to 1934, 'the largest and most efficiently organised astrological movement that has existed before or since'. Howe goes on to add: 'Once the Germans got to grips with astrology they did so with a dedication and energy unparalleled in any other country.' However, by 1941 the Nazis attempted to completely destroy astrological beliefs and practices for reasons we shall shortly come to.

It is said that Himmler kept two horoscopes, that of Hitler and of the Reich itself which coincided in predicting that April 1945 would be a turning point in Germany's favour. That month, of course, represented the death of Adolf Hitler and effectively the end of the Second World War but post-war analysis might well indicate that it was indeed a positive turning point for Germany's future. However, both Hitler and Goebbels believed that the death of President Roosevelt in April 1945 represented the fulfilment of that prophecy. In 1942 the Pendulum Institute was set up in Berlin. It consisted of astrologers and psychics who were to counter the 'Pendulum intelligences' of the British Naval intelligence who the Germans believed to be using map dowsing to divine the position of German submarines at sea. They employed the Swiss astrologer Krafft initially to analyse the horoscopes of the German and Allied commanders and key individuals. This would no doubt have been used to identify particular times for military operations when, astrologically, the stars indicated the most favourable and opportune moments.

Krafft had come to the attention of the Nazis in 1939 when, on 2 November 1939, he predicted an attempt on the life of Adolf Hitler between 7 and 10 November, around a week in the future. In Munich, on 8 November, an assassination attempt did occur and Krafft's prestige was established. Krafft came to an unfortunate end: he announced that General Montgomery's natal horoscope was stronger than that of General Rommel and got himself locked up in a concentration camp!

Ironically a German working as a British agent, Louis de Wohl, had planned to forge a letter and Krafft's signature informing a correspondent that Germany would lose the war and Hitler would die a violent death. The plan was to put the letter into the hands of the Gestapo, have Krafft arrested and thereby deprive Hitler of the services of a valuable astrologer. If the operation was undertaken, and there are no records to determine it either way, then it would have backfired since Krafft was already a prisoner at the time.

Howe attributes the surge of interest in astrology in Germany in 1920 to their defeat in the First World War. Defeated militarily, suffering runaway inflation and forced to review their own social perspective, they turned to the stars and divinity for comfort and guidance. One of the prominent astrologers of the time was Frau Elspeth Ebertin. In a book published in July 1923 she gave an astrological reading for Adolf Hitler, though without mentioning his name. It was as follows:

> A man of action born on 20 April 1889, with sun in 29 degrees Aries at the time of his birth, can expose himself to personal danger by excessively incautious action and could very likely trigger off an uncontrollable crisis. His constellation shows that this man is to be taken very seriously indeed; he is destined to play a 'Fuhrer-role' in future battles. It seems that the man I have in mind, with his strong Aries influence, is destined to *sacrifice himself for the German nation*, also to face up to all circumstances with audacity and courage, even when it is a matter of *life and death*, and a given impulse, which will burst forth quite suddenly, to a German freedom movement.

On 8 November 1923 Hitler and his followers enaged in a skirmish with the authorities which resulted in Hitler breaking his shoulder, being arrested and sentenced to five years in prison. (He was released after nine months having spent the time writing his first volume of *Mein Kampf*). The prediction was very shortly fulfilled by the onset of World War II.

Prior to 8 November, Hitler had rejected astrology. He apparently responded to Frau Ebertin's prophecy when shown to him: 'What on earth have women and the stars got to do with me?' Perhaps the success of her prediction was one brick in the wall of his subsequent astrological interest.

Actually it is unclear if Hitler genuinely believed in astrology or only in its propaganda possibilities, although it is equally clear that some members of the Nazi party such as Himmler did believe in astrology.

In 1941, however, the Nazi party suppressed astrology for one or both of two reasons: either the psychological uses for propaganda were turning against them or indeed the astrological predictions themselves were turning against them. If the latter then they were keen that no-one should have access to the power of astrology to predict the ill fortune ahead for the war.

The key incident in the turning point was the flight on 10 May

1941 of Rudolf Hess to Scotland in order to meet with the Duke of Hamilton and to be taken on to meet George VI and Winston Churchill with a view to brokering an end to the war. It was rumoured that Hess had become aware through astrology that 'Hitler's meteoric career was approaching its climax'. (An interesting but dubious story is related by Richard Deacon in *A History of the British Secret Service*. He suggests that a member of the Naval Intelligence Department, Ian Fleming [later to create the character James Bond] had false astrological information planted on Hess prior to the flight.)

Whether Hess was an astrologer, or indeed Hitler's astrologer as it has been rumoured, is unclear; certainly that was also put around as a piece of propaganda. Whether the flight to Britain was in part based on astrological information is equally uncertain. It seems to have played some role in the decision. One claimant reported that Hess was following astrology in his flight. Frau Maria Nagengast, a Munich astrologer, in 1954 claimed that she had received a letter from Hess in March of 1941. He had asked her what would be a good day for a journey abroad and she had suggested 10 May 1941 and been paid 300 Reichsmarks for her services. The flight was successful and so presumably she had done her work, though of course the mission was a failure and Hess was incarcerated for the rest of his life. However, since this revelation on the part of Frau Nagengast came many years after the war it is not certain if the claim is accurate.

Certainly shortly afterwards Martin Bormann, one of Hitler's close advisers, issued a decree referring to 'astrologers, fortune tellers and other swindlers'. They banned the public performances, as they put it, of 'an occult, spiritualist, clairvoyant, telepathic or astrological nature'. Prominent astrologers were rounded up and most were asked if they had any connection with Hess. For example, one astrologer who was arrested was Dr J. L. Schmitt, a Munich physician who was a keen astrologer and an advisor to Hess.

It was thought that Hess was also influenced by the political geographer Professor Albrecht Haushofer, a believer in astrology and a student of the works of Nostradamus. Rainer Hildebrand, Haushofer's biographer, commented:

> Hess's astrological foible strengthened his own conviction that everything possible must be done and hazarded in order to end hostilities without delay, because at the end of April and beginning of May 1941 Hitler's astrological aspects were unusually malefic. Hess interpreted these aspects to mean that he, personally, must take the dangers that threatened the Führer upon his own shoulders in order to save Hitler and restore peace to Germany. Time and again Hess's astrological 'advisor' had told him that Anglo-German relations were threatened by a deep seated crisis of confidence. ... indeed at this time there were very dangerous [planetary] oppositions in Hitler's horoscope. Haushofer, who dabbled a great deal with astrology, seldom left his friend [Hess] without a hint that something unexpected could 'happen' in the near future. (*We are the Last*, 1949)

ASTROLOGY IN PRACTICE

To continue our examination of astrology we must look at how a professional astrologer applies the complex rules of astrology to make determinations. In order to do this we consulted the computer astrology service 'The House of Jupiter' which has a worldwide reputation in the field. Their data is computer-stored and reads out complex combinations for each individual natal chart. The following explanations are from the 'component build-up' of that data.

How is a person's basic sign determined? Most of us know that a person born between, say, 20 April and 20 May is a Taurus, or between 21 March and 20 April is an Aries, and so on. But how is that determined?

It is determined by the Sun being in that sign. The band of sky called the ecliptic (the apparent orbital path of the Sun and planets from an Earth point of view) is divided into twelve sections which the Sun appears to pass through. These twelve sections are the zodiac signs determined by the constellations present within them. So when the sun appears to have moved into the band of sky containing that constellation, then that constellation is the 'current' one. We say 'appears to have moved' because of course it is the Earth, not the Sun, that is actually moving.

Therefore, anyone born anywhere in the world on, say, 30 April, is a Taurean because the sun appears in that segment of the zodiac band of the sky at that time. Sun signs are therefore the basic astrological division.

The Sun Signs

The Sun represents willpower, ego, personal identity, vitality, ambition, creativity, power, rank and esteem; the sense of 'self'. We start by looking at the basic characteristics of the twelve Sun signs.

Aries the Ram: 21 March–20 April; Ruling Planet: Mars

Arians have a strong sense of individuality. The idea of living a life of obscurity doesn't appeal to them. They are self-assertive, which can be positive or negative: positive when used to speak against injustice, negative when lack of tact creates disharmony. Arians can be anti-social and impatient. They are a law unto themselves, being oblivious to the world around them, and acting according to their own feelings and beliefs, sometimes ignoring the needs of others. They set their own standards. They can be idealists. They can have enormous energy and can create both support and disharmony at work by doing twice as much as those around them. Colleagues feel well supported; superiors can feel threatened by a combination of natural leadership and driving energy. Arians have a great sense of enthusiasm. They are dynamic. Much of this drive comes from being ruled by Mars, the god of War.

Taurus the Bull: 21 April–21 May; Ruling Planet: Venus

Taureans are steadfast and loyal. They seek those qualities in their partners also, and indeed often attract similar qualities to them. They are home loving and home based. They value their relationships with their family and enjoy being at home together with them. They can be incredibly stubborn; they know they are right and the act on that knowledge, standing their ground even when fiercely challenged. They have strong sensuality; they must express their feelings physically by touching the things they love, and by surrounding themselves with people and objects which prompt in them an affectionate response. The purpose of money to a Taurean is as a way of attaining beautiful things. At work, they oscillate between hard working and lazy. Their work places are either spick and span, or small disaster zones; there is rarely any middle ground. They are punctual and have good time management capabilities, are very methodical, meet deadlines, fulfil quotas, and save on expenses. They can shape vague ideas into practical proposals.

Gemini the Twins: 22 May–21 June; Ruling Planet: Mercury

Geminians are often accused of being 'two-faced' and superficial. People have difficulty knowing where they stand with a Geminian. But the positive side of this is that they are versatile and adaptable. While many find change threatening, Geminians find it refreshingly challenging. They are intellectual; have a good mind and use it to the full. Their judgement is generally very sound. They are perceptive people, and often one step ahead of others. They have a good sense of right and wrong, in themselves and in others. Their adaptability comes through in their social life; taking all kinds of lifestyles in their stride. Their social 'reach' is often very adventurous, but this can lead to difficulties. They can become foolhardy. They are tolerant, and liberal, in their outlook. They have a great need for partners; to be 'twinned'. They are concerned with 'best friends', with who likes whom, and they live life seeking their true 'soul-mate'.

Cancer the Crab: 22 June–23 July; Ruling Planet: the Moon

Cancerians are homelovers and homemakers. Home is somewhere they can retire to, a real haven to get away from it all. Their attitude to outside life, to their work, etc is coloured by the prevailing atmosphere in their home at any given time. They seek to avoid, and protect others from, potentially adverse influences. They might be accused of being overprotective, preventing others from living through normal experiences. This derives from a desire to keep things as they are; Cancerians do not easily embrace change. They can be moody; for a short time or for days, and it is not easy for others to judge when the mood will pass. They can be ruthlessly ambitious, and form alliances for convenience, breaking them when the need has passed. They are tenacious in their pursuit of their goals and are often admired by others for this.

Leo the Lion: 24 July–23 August; Ruling Planet: the Sun

Leos are the party-lovers of the world, seeking the good and fun times. They are escapists who enjoy stories and banter and social interaction at its most 'fun' level. They are proud, have great personal dignity and self-esteem, and do not suffer fools gladly. If they have a fear, it is of public embarrassment; anyone causing a Leo such humiliation can become an enemy for life. They are attracted to the theatre, to flamboyant displays, to strong emotions, and to larger-than-life characters, and the elevated language which often accompanies such performances. They have a great respect, even worship, for heroes and heroines, real or fictional. They are not great theorists, getting bored with too much 'heavy' debate. They are ideas people but they seek to translate them into action. They can be impetuous and impatient, sometimes resulting in reckless decisions or actions.

Virgo the Maiden: 24 August–23 September; Ruling Planet: Mercury

Virgos are, on the positive side, people who consider and attend to the minute detail of matters. On the negative side they can become the nitpickers who annoy others and reduce morale. They are good at watching the purse-strings; they believe in expressions such as 'look after the pennies and the pounds will look after themselves' and 'mighty oaks from tiny acorns grow'. They never begin a project without thinking it through first. They are often fascinated by diet and nutriton, continually seeking new ways to deal with the body's requirements for nourishment. They enjoy natural, simple foods and indeed support a natural, untamed environment. They can be a complex mix of mind and body, of intellect and physicality. They express themselves at work both mentally and physically. Exercise and sport are therefore an important part of the Virgoans' lifestyle. They can be shy, even withdrawn, and miss out an opportunities and social events, regretting what they have missed.

Libra the Balance: 24 September–23 October; Ruling Planet: Venus

Librans have a seemingly endless supply of energy, both mental and physical. They often 'burn the candle at both ends' and get away without suffering the usual ill-effects. They seek and enjoy, indeed flourish from, social interaction and involvement with others. They are creatures of self-display, putting on a show for the boss in one situation, perhaps 'flirting' in other, social, situations. They thrive on being noticed and on provoking reaction. They are slaves to the latest fashions. They are people of extremes; they work hard and play hard. They usually find a place in their mind to find the balance they need because of their extremes; and find peace in poetry, or other art – the more tranquil the better.

Scorpio the Scorpion: 24 October–22 November; Ruling Planet: Pluto

Scorpios like things to run according to design. They form a plan and then expect everything and everyone to follow that plan; they become very unsettled if things veer off course. They persevere to the end come what may; they have great focus and singularity of purpose. They can be very intense. Such rigidity can lead to missing out on opportunities because they have not been incorporated into 'the plan'. Scorpios need to find the balance between purposefulness and obsession. Scorpios often seek money, and are often determined in their pursuit of it. They can be ruthless savers and accumulators of wealth. They are emotional; their smallest feelings capable of becoming surges of power. When high-running emotion does not find an expression, Scorpios are apt to turn on the innocent in anger and frustration.

Sagittarius the Archer: 23 November–21 December; Ruling Planet: Jupiter

Sagittarians can be very self-centred. They live in their own heads, and often trample over the feelings of those around them in pursuit of their own goals, which are often quests for pleasure. They enjoy good conversation but are not necessarily good conversationalists; they are more interested in what they themselves are saying than in what others are saying. They seek the heady, social whirl and can easily feel constrained. They veer away from those who might make them feel claustrophobic. They have a highly developed sense of morality and principle. They react instinctively to humanitarian issues, and have a passionate belief in freedom on all levels: physical, mental and spiritual. They can be overtly religious, overwhelmed by the feeling that a greater power is watching over them.

Capricorn the Goat: 22 December–20 January; Ruling Planet: Saturn

Capricorns are ambitious and fight hard to climb to the top of every mountain they encounter. They are very principled and do not sell themselves short just to please others. They have a high sense of morality. They are natural teachers in the broadest sense of the word; perhaps 'guru' would be a better word, implying not just factual teaching but an understanding of the rules that go with it. They have a cool manner and a controlled emotional disposition which earns them the respect of many, who see in them the evidence of the maturity others so often desire.

Aquarius the Water Carrier: 21 January–19 February; Ruling Planet: Uranus

Aquarians are the great humanitarians, the dispensers of love and knowledge. They 'wear their hearts on their sleeves', giving freely of the wealth of their heart and head sometimes for little or no reward. They get their pleasure from helping and advising others. They can seem detached and disinterested in matters more emotional and intimate. Conversely, they often have a wacky, individual and unusual sense of humour. Taking the broader view they care that society is ever moving forward, that it does not stagnate or regress. They champion ideas and organisations which others might dismiss as 'merely institutionalised'. Indeed, they view institutions not just as impersonal labyrinths serving only those who 'belong' but as having potential value to everyone.

Pisces the Fish: 20 February–20 March; Ruling Planet: Neptune

Pisceans can form attachments that others do not always understand or appreciate. They have a freewheeling, almost 'scatty' view of life which they take in their stride. They find life a fascinating journey; less important is any thought of destination. Money is only seen as a means to an end; the ability to acquire what is needed on the journey.

Many people believe that being born 'on the cusp', i.e. on the dates where one sign changes to the next, gives them the qualities of both. Professional astrologers discount this and rely on the Sun sign and other arrangements of the stars to define an individual's basic qualities. 'On the cusp' means very little when compared to the data available.

The twelve signs of the zodiac are divided up between the four elements: Earth, Air, Fire and Water.

- **Aries**, **Leo** and **Sagittarius** are Fire signs; fiery people who have the 'shortest fuse'.
- **Taurus**, **Virgo** and **Capricorn** are Earth signs; practical, down-to-earth people.
- **Gemini**, **Libra** and **Aquarius** are Air signs; unpredictable and changeable people.
- **Cancer**, **Scorpio** and **Pisces** are Water signs; the most emotional of people.

But it stands to reason that everything outlined above is absurd at face value; far too general. It would not be logical to assume that each twelfth of the world's population would conform to these broad criteria. So what are the modifications?

The first, and major, modification is the position of the Moon. The moon orbits the Earth once a month and so appears to move rapidly in and out of the zodiac signs, spending only a couple or days in each. The Sun is masculine and the Moon feminine; each dictates those qualities in any person. So male or female have masculine and feminine qualities accentuated and balanced by the position of Sun and Moon at birth. Astrologically the Sun and Moon are both luminaries, they give us light. (There is a distinction that the Sun generates light and the Moon reflects it.) We will look at the Moon signs in general in the division below.

The second important modification is the rising sign, or ascendant. This means that at the point of birth another constellation is 'rising'; a Taurean born on, say, 1 May 1998 at midday in London will have the Moon in Cancer and Leo as a rising sign. (The ascendant will be Leo rising.) In an astrological chart the ascendant is the sign just coming over the horizon at the point of birth. To be more specific, to quote Cordelia Mansall in *The Astrology Workbook* (1985), the ascendant is 'the point where the Eastern horizon intersects with the Ecliptic judged according to sunrise each day'. As the Earth turns once every twenty-four hours and there are twelve zodiac signs, this means that the ascendant changes round about every two hours.

We therefore find that each Sun sign has 144 possible combinations of Moon and ascendant. The Earth's population is therefore not divided into twelve types but into 12×144 types, i.e. 1,728 types. And we are still at a very basic division with many more modifications to consider.

If our Taurean above had been born at 5.45 a.m. BST, more or less at dawn, he would be a Taurean with Taurus as his rising sign; he would be a 'double Taurean' which, in effect, means that his Taurean characteristics will be enhanced, making him more typical of the basic Sun-sign texts above. Anyone born at dawn has a double helping of their Sun-sign characteristics.

The Moon in Your Life

The Moon governs emotions, habits, maternal instinct, feelings, moods, receptiveness, memory and nostalgia and is of great importance in the compilation of emotional sensitivity.

General characteristics of Moon signs are an 'emotional' reflection of the corresponding Sun sign. Moon in Aries, for example, brings Arien characteristics to anyone of any Sun sign whose Moon is in Aries. You will need to consult an astrologer or an ephemeris to discover where your Moon is placed, but we shall set out the general characteristics which will assist in the reader understanding how just these two sets of qualities – Sun and Moon signs – can create a balance and combination in people so born. And as we further explore the specifications we see that the combinations produce a very large number of combinations.

General characteristics of Moon signs, then:

Moon in the dominant and impulsive sign of Aries

Such people are naturally persuasive, drawing others into their circle, and giving them a feeling of power. In an emotional context, they can use their qualities to conquer the opposite sex at will. They react very quickly to emotional stimuli, and always seem to have enough stamina to carry them through demanding situations. Others appreciate their directness, and also their single-minded approach once they have decided where their affections lie. They can be volatile and touchy, but sincere and demonstrative. They convert feelings into actions, which gives others a sense of being in fresh and exciting company. Sometimes they get too extreme with their enthusiasm and dive head-first into a relationship where more caution and judgement should have been wise.

Moon in the placid and comfortable sign of Taurus

The embodiment of the expression 'slow and steady wins the race'. Emotionally, such people play a waiting game, observing and weighing up the fundamental value of a person or situation before committing themselves one way or the other. Their feelings come from a deep source, as if they rose up from an underground well. Their dependability is a virtue, and they tend to stand by their partners through thick and thin, whatever the cost. This dependability and sincerity can cloud their better judgement and they can become the victim who suffers. They are, however, very clear-headed, with good judgement and insight into the dynamics of their relationships. At the root of this awareness is probably the oldest of human instincts, self-preservation: they give their all but do not allow it to destroy them.

Moon in the restless and nervous sign of Gemini

Friends give these people a sense of belonging, and it is this security which bestows upon them their greatest emotional strength, for it makes them feel part of something special. Their dream is one of being twinned to someone with whom they can walk through life hand in hand, bound in the first instance by a vow of mutual friendship, out of which love proceeds to grow.

It is very important for them to have some element of intellectual trade between themselves and their partner as this is a source of emotional stimulation. Words and conversation spark in them certain trains of thought which create inroads into their emotions. Understanding their own inner nature gives them a platform from which they can oversee the actions of others. They must resist the temptation to set themselves up as a standard against which they measure others; the purpose of self-education is not self-adulation, but to disseminate gifts of the spirit.

Moon in the sensitive sign of Cancer

Such people are very emotional. Feelings rule their lives. They have a strong receptivity to atmosphere, often responding to the hidden qualities of people and situations. They react by feeling, and can often only offer this as justification for their actions. Regardless of their actual sex or sexuality, they are open to what are often called the 'feminine', tender, sympathetic, sides. They are often self-protective, and protective of others, avoiding contact with harmful and emotionally damaging influences. They hide their sensitivity by constructing an impenetrable emotional wall both to avoid appearing too soft in the eyes of others and to screen out their own vulnerability.

Moon in the proud, warm and loyal sign of Leo

These are warm-hearted people with full, demonstrative, feelings. Their partner is never in doubt of their loyalty nor, indeed, the depth of their affection, as they show their emotions naturally and willingly. Their partners are usually of a similar type; they need their open displays of emotion reciprocated. Once a partnership has been established they settle in for the duration. They flourish by staying with one person, which allows them to delve deeper into their own feelings.

Moon in the conscientious and shy sign of Virgo

Emotionally, such people keep themselves to themselves. They are very private and self-protective, giving away very little in public, or to others generally. But in safe and secure relationships, out of the public eye, they let down their defences and reveal rich and warm gifts of the heart. Being a 'private person' means that others misjudge these people, thinking them cold, even aloof.

Moon in the charming and social sign of Libra

It is very important for these people to be in a relationship. They need people at the deepest, emotional, level. Through somebody close to them, they can see their own reflection, giving them greater confidence to face the world at large. Being naturally communicative and chatty, these people need to find an element of intellectual compatibility with their partners in order to establish a broader base for expression. Such exchanges allow them to develop mutual rapport. Mental and emotional understanding and communication encourage respect, a necessary part of any meaningful relationship.

Moon in the intense and possessive sign of Scorpio

Here are people whose rivers of emotional life run deep. There's nothing shallow about their feelings, and nothing lightly given. Because they experience emotions so intensely they frequently find themselves bottling things up and keeping their feelings to themselves; to express them could be too exhausting. They are naturally sympathetic, responding to many things which others might pass by. They have an excess of emotion which needs an outlet. They are moved by others' misfortune. They laugh with others, and they know how to cry as well. Those who do suppress their anger or emotional expression find that this powerful Moon sign can bring on stress-related illness and a severe breakdown in the natural bodily defence mechanisms. Emotional intensity can make such people very possessive, for the object of their affections is also the object of desire. Jealousy can easily rear its head.

Moon in the optimistic sign of Sagittarius

Such people are a blend of loyalty and independence. They will tend to support even the most hopeless-looking cases, convinced that good will come in the end. They can be prone to extreme emotional mood swings. They can be extremely excitable, often flaring up to defend allies, or their own integrity. In the heat of the moment their emotions boil over, and they often express themselves with greatly exaggerated gestures, making sudden and alarming movements which can seem frightening. They are hot-blooded, and incurable romantics who seek adventure.

Moon in the reserved and cautious sign of Capricorn

Sensitive people whose feelings are easily hurt. They often respond by withdrawing and pretending that they are not hurt, or that they do not have feelings. They do not express themselves with confidence and should try to be more trusting and less rigid in their approach. They are loyal and devoted people. When tired they are apt to become very moody and ill-tempered, taking out their feelings on others, particularly their partner.

Moon in the friendly and impersonal sign of Aquarius

These people have a good social life; the key to their emotional balance. Party conversation and the free trade of ideas are as much an emotional fillip to them as quiet evenings in with a loved one. They are thought, by others, to be emotionally detached and undemonstrative. They have a reputation for remaining uncommitted and stand-offish. Cautious they might be – because they think before they act – but they are not uncommitted. Once they attach themselves to someone, that person becomes their *cause célèbre*.

Moon in the psychic and vulnerable sign of Pisces

Soft-centred and easily wounded, such people are the champions of causes, great and small. They give their feelings freely. As such they can become emotionally tired, and seek to avoid issues knowing that once drawn in they will not be able to stop their emotions pouring out. Others might accuse them of being elusive, even devious in their chosen 'causes'.

The Ascendant

Having looked at Sun and Moon signs an astrologer would now go on to look at the ascendant, or rising sign. It is important in forming personality and character, indeed some astrologers believe that the effects of the rising sign can be stronger than those of the Sun signs. We shall not set out all of the general characteristics of the ascendant however as again they are a reflection of the general Sun sign qualities but applied to personality and character. As an example, for someone whose ascendant or rising sign is Aries, they would have typical Arian qualities applied to forming their personality. A typical 'reading' for such an ascendant would be:

They have a powerful sense of individuality, and will avoid situations in which they fear they might become just one of the crowd. They forge their own personal path through life, despite often flying in the face of conventional wisdom. It is a challenge for them to ensure their choice of direction succeeds, for success on these terms will make them feel they can plant their flag in the field of individual achievement. Suceess is, for them, measured according to how true they remain to their own ideals. Being naturally impatient, they are quick to anger, but just as easy to placate. Moods come in rapidly-changing waves, and they are not inclined to brood. They can be outspoken, regardless of possible consequences – they have what others might call a 'publish and be damned' attitude. This unapologetic and fearless characteristic ensures that there will be many occasions when they will be accused of being nothing but a troublemaker. But without people like them, fewer lies would be exposed, and fewer liars would go unpunished, for they often combine fearlessness with a high moral tone. Of course, they can just as easily be an unprincipled, anti-social rogue, careering from one enterprise to another without a thought for those whom they encounter; they set their own level of morality. (House of Jupiter)

The Planets

There are other elements to the astrological puzzle. The next component relates to the planets, which rule over each Sun sign. The planets orbit the Earth along the ecliptic (see page 268) and so weave in and out of the zodiac constellations just as the Sun does. We shall summarise their contribution only briefly:

- **Mercury** defines how people communicate and relate to other people, and to some extent relates to journeys and to travel.
- **Venus** defines an individual's love and affection, and personal magnetism.
- **Mars** defines passion, desire, aggression, drive and enthusiasm, and motivation.
- **Jupiter** defines philosophy, religion, education, spiritualism, travel, business, commerce, legal and financial affairs.
- **Saturn** defines responsibility, restriction, stability, security and insecurity.
- **Uranus** defines changeability and erratic behaviour.
- **Neptune** rules the psychic, the subconscious, fears and phobias, deception, enlightenment and disillusionment.
- **Pluto** is the planet of births, deaths and regeneration.

It is the position of the planets in the signs and houses (see below) which further refines the strengths and weaknesses of the individual. So, for example, our Taurean born at midday (above) has Venus in Pisces. This suggests an affectionate, loving, romantic character when we combine the qualities of Venus and Pisces. And so on for all the planets.

The Houses

In Equal House Astrology each house represents 30 degrees of arc (12 × 30 = 360) and in this case corresponds exactly to the Sun signs. This is the type of astrology generally used by newspapers which produces bland generalisations. In effect they take just one element of all the components discussed here and apply it across the board to the whole population. However, in Topocentric or Placidus Astrology – the main types of astrology used for detailed and specific readings – the twelve houses are not of equal arc and therefore do not correspond exactly to each sign.

The houses do not correspond to a physical construct, but are an intellectual concept. They dictate the following:

First House: rules the self, who I am, how I relate to the world and life and how the world and life sees me.

Second House: money, material possessions and the ability to acquire wealth and possessions.

Third House: communication, talent, short journeys, local travel.

Fourth House: home, how I see my home environment and how it sees me; also the relationship with parents.

Fifth House: my creativity, my maternal instincts, sexuality, artistic abilities, children.

Sixth House: my health, my work and profession and service – how I do or do not serve the community.

Seventh House: marriage, relationships, partnerships.

Eighth House: legal matters, divorces, legacies, wills and inheritances, lifestyle.

Ninth House: the mind, education, travel, philosophy, religion and spiritualism.

Tenth House: career, profession, status.

Eleventh House: friendships, the social side of our lives.

Twelfth House: the hidden, inner depths; a house of restriction and confinement.

Just as each of the planets has to be in a sign so it has to be in a house. For example, someone with Mercury and Venus in their third house combines the characteristics of communication, talent, their affectionate side, and so on. They would make good artistic communicators – a good TV presenter perhaps.

If Jupiter is in the ninth house then that individual's interests are likely to be religion, philosophy, education and so on. Perhaps they would be a good teacher.

Aspects

The growth of the complexity of 'choice' for individuals becomes clear; it is far from a broad brush of twelve sets of characteristics. And there are still more refinements to be considered.

A further refinement comes from looking at the planets in aspect or, as astrologers would put it, how the planets communicate with each other. There are harmonious communications and disharmonious communications. The harmonious are the **trines** and **sextiles**, the trines being an angle of 120 degrees between planets, the sextiles 60 degrees. The two planets involved in a trine would be in the same category of Earth, Air, Fire or Water signs. The disharmonious ones are the **oppositions**, where planets are opposite each other at 180 degrees, and the **squares** where planets are at 90-degree angles to each other. These relationships are plotted on the birth chart.

These aspects determine how the qualities of the planets are displayed in our characteristics positively or negatively. To give an example, someone with Mercury in Gemini at birth (and Mercury is the 'ruler' of Gemini) would normally be expected to be chatty, inquisitive and nosy. However, if the same planet, Mercury, were squared with or opposed by a restricting planet such as Saturn, the person would have restricted communication ability and be inhibited. They would not seem to be chatty, but when you got to know that person their natural chattiness would come out.

Another example would be someone with the Moon in Cancer (and the Moon is ruler of Cancer). They would normally be a homeloving and maternal and emotionally-giving person. But if their Moon was square to or opposing Saturn then that person would be very inhibited and lacking in confidence emotionally.

An example of a positive situation: a person with Mercury in Virgo (Mercury rules Virgo) would be expected to be a precise, accurate, and eloquent person who takes care in their communication and the way they conduct themselves in the world. They would have positive organisational skills. If Mercury was in trine to a changeable planet such as Uranus that person would then have the same precision but with broader horizons, less fixed and focused. The trine allows them to let go more than they otherwise would.

A **conjunction** is where two planets meet close together in the same house and sign. This can be good or bad, depending on the planets. For example, if the Moon is conjunct Venus this would be a positive characteristic giving a great ability for love and affection and to outwardly show it. But if the Moon or Venus were conjunct Saturn it would give emotional restriction or the inability to show affection.

Every sign has a positive and negative quality. It depends on the planet, the sign, the house and the aspect as to whether the negative or the positive quality of that individual will be displayed.

Progressions

The natal chart is a description of the person – who they are. The chart can be progressed to any time and it will show how that person's life is progressing and the likely events in that person's life. A predictive forecast can be based on either progressions or a transit forecast. A transit forecast shows where the planets are in the heavens at any given moment in relation to their position at the time of the individual's birth.

Taking a different use of astrology, a person may cast a chart (or engage an astrologer to cast one) and find out the best time for an interview. This is predictive astrology. The astrologer starts with the birth time, date and place of the client. By looking at both the progression of the natal chart and a transit forecast he or she would find both favourable and unfavourable times for the interview. If there are bad aspects in a given month the potential interviewee would be advised to avoid that month, and be guided to a better month for the interview.

APPLICATION OF HORARY ASTROLOGY

In horary astrology, the natal chart is not of consequence. It is the chart at the time the request is made. For example, at 16.31 on 1 May 1998 an individual might request an astrologer to find out whether a job interview soon to take place will be successful. It is not the time of the interview that matters in this instance, but the time that the question is raised. Using the house of Jupiter's complex astrological programme the following reading was evident based on this time and date.

Jupiter is in the sign of Pisces, which it ruled in ancient astrology, before the discovery of the more watery planet Neptune, and the Moon is in Cancer which is its natural ruler. Moreover Jupiter is situated in the sixth house (work and service) and the Moon is in the tenth house of career, ambition and profession. Venus in the sixth house is also helpful. In essence, there is a trine between Jupiter and the Moon denoting that the Moon would make the interviewee shine to the interviewer.

Jupiter also rules business, commerce, work, industry. Therefore one would expect a very favourable outcome to the interview. If the interview was for promotion it would almost certainly be successful because the Moon is in the house of long term careers.

TESTING ASTROLOGY

With all the various permutations mentioned above we end up with a situation where there is almost a unique set of criteria for each minute of time, for each position on the face of the planet. Readings combine many factors. Astrology, then, is a much more precise field than just a division into twelve types. However, do all these various refinements mean anything? Is it just an illusion, a game played by astrologers? Or is there 'something to it'?

Throughout history many leading people are said to have consulted astrologers before taking important decisions, including Julius Caesar, Henry VIII, Napoleon, Winston Churchill, Ronald and Nancy Reagan and members of the British Royal Family. They presumably believed that there was 'something to it'. The fundamental questions for astrology in a scientific age are: Is it real? Does it work?

The Gauquelin Experiments

Probably the most famous attempt to study astrology, and indeed he set out to disprove it, was made by the French statistician Michel Gauquelin in 1949. He embarked on a study with a view to disprove the claims of French astrologers who argued that they had statistically proven their case. In fact he did successfully show that their statistics were faulty; however, in the course of his work, he found aspects that he himself could not explain. He therefore continued his work more deeply working with large, statistically significant test groups and in consequence discovered that there were indeed certain correlations between the natal charts of certain individuals and the professions or activities they adopted in their life. For example, scientists and doctors were likely to be born with Saturn on the ascendant, soldiers and athletes tended to be born with Mars on the ascendant and so on. In some cases the statistical odds against such charts were millions to one against.

Going through the files of The House of Jupiter – they have over 10,000 horoscopes on file and we viewed them with appropriate confidentiality and anonymity – it was clear that, for example, there were similarities in the charts of those with similar health problems, of achievers, of leaders and so on. The similarities within any group were so striking that, even viewing them unscientifically, it was clear that astrological patterns were similar for those who had lived similar lives or undergone similar problems or achievements. The variety was obvious also; there were no two horoscopes that were the same or even nearly so; such is the variety of components involved.

Scientists unable to disprove Gauquelin's work, but unwilling to accept something which was abhorrent to them, argued that there must have been some sort of huge coincidence at work. Some even argued that it was something to do with the French character since all of Gauquelin's subjects were French. The work was repeated in four other European countries; all produced the same statistically significant support for the connection. The final conclusion was that there was statistically no possibility that chance was the explanation for the skewed statistics. There was indeed a connection between people's birth signs and their later lives. Gauquelin's later work also showed that statistically there were significant connections in planetary relationships between parents and their children.

Gauquelin also tested the hypothesis that people born in the odd-numbered Sun signs (Aries being number one and so on round the zodiac) were more likely to be extrovert while those born in the even-numbered star signs were more likely to be introvert. Again the statistics proved this to be quite beyond the range of chance. Other people have furthered the work and there is now a considerable body of statistical evidence in support of astrological relationships and correlations between planetary movements and events on Earth. Gauquelin's work has been tested by the British psychiatrist Hans Eysenck who, like Gauquelin originally, expected to disprove the statistics but found them quite unarguable.

These statistical tests prove only a small aspect of what is claimed for astrology and science has not yet been able to statistically demonstrate all the claims of interaction, character traits and so on for which astrology sets out guidelines. However, the fact that the very basics of astrology are now proven within scientific rigour is reason enough that scientific study of astrology should continue.

There are many first-rate and free-thinking scientists who are therefore looking at astrology not particularly with a view to proving it to be real but to finding out which aspects of it might be genuinely significant and how or why that should be so. However, lesser minds in the scientific community have refused even to consider astrology worthy of study. It was Gauquelin's work which initially inspired the formation of CSICOP, the Committee for the Scientific Investigation of Claims of the Paranormal. This organisation is a collection of scientists, sceptics and magicians who see it as their role to debunk any claim for the paranormal – often, it seems, regardless of evidence. Indeed in 1981 when CSICOP set out to disprove Gauquelin's work a former member of CSICOP accused them of falsifying data.

Births, Marriages, Deaths and Astrology

Other studies have supported the connection between astrology and human characteristics. Over a two-year period a team of scientists and statisticians analysed a million people in Switzerland. They recorded the hour of birth of each individual since 1875 and then conducted a number of other tests. They studied all marriages in Switzerland over a seven-year period looking at over 700,000 people, also studying divorce statistics. They were able to show a distinct relationship between partnerships which lasted (Capricorn man/Pisces woman, Pisces man/Scorpio woman, Gemini man/Taurus woman) and the three relationships which were most difficult (Libra man/Aries women, Aries man/Leo woman, Gemini man/Capricorn woman). By examining over a million deaths in Switzerland over a twenty-five-year period they discovered that there was a proneness to certain illnesses on the part of certain birth signs: Leo suffered strokes, Leos and Librans suffered lung cancer, Scorpios and Capricorns suffered stomach cancers, Pisceans suffered breast cancer and were susceptible to accidental death.

A study of the make-up of the British House of Commons demonstrates the skewed balance of birth signs. It is often, as recently, dominated by Arians (leadership is a defining characteristic of Arians) and Taureans. Aries and Leos frequently dominate the Cabinet and Shadow Cabinet, again as recently. Arians and Taureans also typically dominate the back benches. John Major and Neil Kinnock (resigned 1995) are both Arians; Tony Blair is Taurean.

Such a predominance of classic characteristics in such a classic situation can hardly be put down to chance. Combined with other statistically significant surveys the link between astrological signs and characteristics seems certain.

We must, however, be aware of other possibilities. One might simply be that because the star signs also relate to certain times of the year that factors relating to hours of sunlight, humidity, temperature, etc affect children in their formative years and help mould certain characteristics. In addition perhaps there is a tendency for certain people to either fulfill their anticipated Sun sign expectations or indeed for parents to drive children into certain patterns of behaviour because they themselves believe in the Sun signs. Neither of these seems to be likely to create such patterns that they would be statistically significant, but they may be influences.

The real problem for science is a very simple one: astrology works. It may be that there is no link between the heavens and people; it may be that people cannot foretell their future by reference to astrological chance. Nonetheless time and time again, intuitively, people demonstrate that – in some way – astrology works. We know of one woman who with just a few minutes with anyone is highly accurate in 'guessing' their Sun sign. Many other people have found that they have liked or disliked, been charmed by or turned off by, people and discovered that just that reaction is typical of the interaction between their own and the other individual's sign even though it may be some time later when they discover just what the other person's sign is.

So: it seems to work and there is statistical evidence to show that there is genuine correlation. But then how far can it be taken? Does the fact that the time of your birth correlates to your characteristics also mean that individual fortunes can be told for individual days for individual people? Just how far can the link be pushed?

Sir Martin Rees, the Astronomer Royal, took the standard line for astronomy – which is affronted by astrology – and commented that: 'There is no place for astrology now in a scientific view of the world'. His article, published in the *Sunday Telegraph* of 28 December 1997, may be inspired partly by pique. He states: 'I was talking not long ago with a leading Indian industrialist, and felt flattered by his eagerness to probe my views on the financial markets and international politics. But his interest plummeted when he realised that I was a mere astronomer, and not the Queen's astrologer. In India, Cabinet ministers are routinely guided by horoscopes.' He also adds: '... In Britain, however, astrologers outnumber, and massively out-earn, astronomers'.

He does, however, have meaningful things to say on the subject of why astrology and paranormal studies are so popular today. He points to the 'perceived failure of mainstream scientists to deliver the advertised benefits; many people uneasy about research, about where research may be leading. ...' He takes the view that religion offers certainty but at a moral price, demanding certain standards and comments that astrology and 'pseudo-sciences' provide merely comfort, with all the benefits of religion without any of the demands placed on the individual.

In fairness to Sir Martin Rees his comment that: 'Its [astrology's] predictive claims cannot stand any critical scrutiny' is not unreasonable as he seems to be commenting on the very general 'populist' exposure of astrology through the media.

But astrologers argue that, given sufficiently precise knowledge of the date, time and place of birth of an individual, their astrological readings are very specific and indeed some have been strikingly so. There have been spectacular failures, of course. Such failures could mean the system does not work or it could mean that, like dentists, accountants and physicists, there are good astrologers, bad astrologers, and a whole lot who think they are better than they really are.

In 1998 the *Daily Mail* published a survey of 1,092 interviewees which purported to discover whether people's personal characteristics matched their Sun signs. The people were shown twelve different personality profiles without being told which Sun sign was related to each. The summary of the survey was impressive: 'A sceptic would expect no correlation between star signs and star sign characteristics. But interviewees belonging to all twelve signs showed a powerful and unmistakable connection with the personality trait usually attributed to their star sign.' Individually people related to their own Sun signs. For example, 34 percent of people questioned said they had characteristics normally associated with Libra but 46 percent of Librans claimed so. Similarly 30 percent identified with Pisces characteristics but 41 percent of Pisceans did. Every star sign produced the same result. Nick Sparrow, the managing director of ICM who conducted the survey, commented: 'Our findings demonstrate a link between star signs and personality'. However, there is an inherent problem with the survey in that the high interest in astrology means that people are frequently familiar with their Sun sign and its 'classic' characteristics. They could easily have picked out their own sign from their own knowledge of their Sun sign characteristics.

Scientific Studies

There are indications of physical links related to astrology, and people, and the world about us which – while tenuous and not statistically proven – are thought provoking. It is inevitable that good scientific work in these areas should be done and it may well be that proof of the validity of astrology is yet to be forthcoming. Gauquelin himself in *The Cosmic Clocks* (1969) examines the suggestion that humans are influenced by the Sun and the Moon. There is a connection noted by many doctors between the Full Moon and the activities of patients of mental homes, for example. Dr Leonard J. Ravitz of Duke University has indicated from his studies that electrical potential in the human bodies of emotionally disturbed patients changed according to phases of the Moon and indeed that the greatest changes were in those patients who were the most disturbed.

Other researchers have made significant connections. Maki Takata found that the flocculation index of human blood (the degree of curdle of blood albumin) is influenced by sun spot activity. Piccardi noted connections between chemical reactions in the body and sun spot activity in lunar cycles. Rocard has indicated that human beings seem to be sensitive to the fluctuations in the Earth's magnetic field (which he believed related to dowsing) and certainly it has been suggested that pigeons and other animals have a strong homing instinct based on the Earth's magnetic field. Since the Earth's magnetic field is also subject to cosmic influence there is the potential link to astrology. There is little doubt that the Sun, the Moon and the planets do have physical effects on the Earth, not least gravitational effects. To what degree they can affect individual human beings is unclear and seems remarkably unlikely but nonetheless there is too much evidence to be dismissed without further study.

For the influence of the Moon there have been some studies which indicate that there seems to be a genuine link. Dr Frank Brown of North-Western University was interested by the fact that oysters opened and closed their shells according to tidal rhythms which are in turn caused by the Moon. The question was whether or not the shells were responding to the physical effects of tides or to the lunar influence. He removed oysters from their Atlantic home, taking them to darkened pans in the centre of landlocked Illinois. In two weeks the oysters had changed the rhythm of their opening and closing to a pattern which indicated that the oysters were responding to the lunar cycle rather than to the physical tidal action (which was not present).

Other work also suggested connections. Brown had a rat placed in a darkened cage where it could not in any way see the Moon. Yet the rat was twice as active when the Moon was above the horizon as when it was below.

The effect of the stars themselves on the Earth or individuals seems much less likely. Their enormous distance seems to make them mere points of light in the sky and no more than reference points as far as astrology is concerned; but perhaps we do not yet know all of the influences in the cosmos. This is still only the twentieth century and we are still grappling with the physics of Newton and Einstein; perhaps there are discoveries yet to be made of more exotic influences which will be better discussed in the thirtieth or the fortieth century.

Another important analysis of astrology was conducted by Maurice Cotterell (and reported in *The Mayan Prophecies* [1995] which was co-authored with Adrian Gilbert). Engineer and computer scientist Cotterell used to work in the Merchant Navy and noticed that his colleagues seemed to play to their astrological signs ('fire' signs, 'water' signs, and others). These signs were also studied by Professor Hans Eysenck who had worked on Gauquelin's statistics. Eysenck worked with astrologer Jeff Mayo looking at large samples of people to see if indeed they did respond to their earth, water, fire or air signs. The conclusion was that there was a clear statistical significance proving that they did. Cotterell, however, wanted to know why. He began with the assumption that the Sun, which was the most obvious influence on the Earth, had fluctuations in its magnetic field and that the Sun's productivity might affect children prior to birth. Cotterell discovered that the Sun changes the type of radiation it emits monthly due to its fluid, plasma, construct and indeed that there are four types of solar radiation which are emitted in a sequence. These types correspond to the astrological 'signs'. Believing that the magnetic field influences both human cell structure and DNA, Cotterell argues that he has identified a connection between the Sun and humans at the time of the conception and birth. In fact Cotterell was at odds with astrologers on that point; Cotterell believes that his identification relates to the human being at conception whereas astrologers tend to look at the time of birth. There is a case for both. The human is alive from the point of conception and subject to whatever influences exist. By the same token it is only at birth that the human becomes an independent entity severing its most obvious influences; the attachment to the inside of its mother's body.

Russian scientist Dr A. K. Podshibyakin discovered that there is a four-fold increase in road accidents the day after a solar flare and indeed studies in several European cities show not only increases in accident rates but also in suicide and violent crime. Perhaps most interesting from the astrological point of view is the work of radio engineer John Nelson who believes that the magnetic disturbances in the Earth's atmosphere which relate to solar flares can be predicted according to conjunction and aspects of the major planets. Magnetic disturbance is highest when the planets line up unharmoniously and lowest during harmonious line-ups.

How refined?

The complexity of refinements mentioned earlier may be the basis of why astrology, against all scientific wishes, seems to work. These refinements mean that the differences between individuals can be quite striking. Let us take the example of twins. We know that there are many twins who exhibit very similar characteristics, however they could have differences if their births were reasonably far apart. Twins born within, say, five minutes would be so similar that their horoscopes would probably be almost identical. That their lives might overlap or mirror each other is hardly a surprise astrologically, whatever other factors are involved.

But twins born, say, ten minutes apart could be quite different astrologically. If one was born in the last minutes of Virgo and the next in the first minutes of Libra; if the Sun is in those respective signs for the time of birth, then the twins will each have different basic characteristics based on their Sun signs. The same could apply to the 'changeover' between signs in ascendant.

The two charts on pp 296 and 297 relate to twins born on, respectively, 16.20 and 16.30 on 1 May 1998; just ten minutes apart.

The main differences are that the first twin will be Virgo rising giving a strong characteristic of being precise, having a critical eye for detail, punctual. The second twin is Libra rising and is likely to be indecisive, requiring extreme emotional stability and a yearning for harmony. The first will be practical; the second very emotional. Twin two will be more attention seeking.

However, two children born hours apart in different parts of the world might be more similar than twins. Because the Earth is moving in space it is possible for one person to be born under the same set of signs as another if the Earth has shifted position so that the second birth is in the same 'location' spatially as the first. It would be remarkable if all the planetary and other features lined up, but the basic characteristics might. Such people are called astro-twins; astrologically twinned by their birth characteristics.

KEY FOR CHARTS ON PAGES 296-297, AND 299-300

Planets ☉ *Sun* ☽ *Moon* ☿ *Mercury* ♀ *Venus* ♂ *Mars* ♃ *Jupiter* ♄ *Saturn* ♅ *Uranus* ♆ *Neptune* ♇ *Pluto* ☊ *Moon's Nodes*

Star signs ♈ *Aries* ♉ *Taurus* ♊ *Gemini* ♋ *Cancer* ♌ *Leo* ♍ *Virgo* ♎ *Libra* ♏ *Scorpio* ♐ *Sagittarius* ♑ *Capricorn* ♒ *Aquarius* ♓ *Pisces*

DATE: 1 May 1998 AD Fri	MC 29 18 ♊		☉ 11 03 ♉	8
TIME: 16 20 00	ASC 29 28 ♍		☽ 19 58 ♋	10
ZONE: 1 00 E	— Plac —		☿ 14 43 ♈	7
LATITUDE: 51 31 N	11. 5 24 ♌		♀ 27 35 ♓	6
LONGITUDE: 0 06 W	12. 5 32 ♍		♂ 13 46 ♉	8
CITY: London	2. 23 17 ♎		♃ 19 40 ♓	6
	3. 23 18 ♏		♄ 25 39 ♈	8
			♅ 12 39 ♒	5
	☊ 7 20 ♍ R 12		♆ 2 10 ♒	4
			♇ 7 24 ♐ R	3

Aspects Radix-1/Radix-1

☉ ☌ ♂	2 42	+0 14	☿ △ ♇	7 18	−0 50	♄ ⚹ MC	3 40	−0 46
☉ □ ♆	1 35	+0 57	♀ ☌ ♃	7 55	−0 55	♆ △ ASC	2 42	+0 42
☽ □ ☿	5 15	−12 21	♀ ⚹ ♆	4 35	+1 7			
☽ △ ♀	7 37	+12 3	♂ □ ♆	1 7	−0 43			
☽ △ ♃	0 18	−12 58	♀ □ MC	1 44	+0 13			
☽ □ ♄	5 41	+13 2	♀ ☍ ASC	1 53	+0 25			
☿ ⚹ ♆	2 4	−0 48	♄ □ ♆	6 31	+0 8			
☿ Q ♆	0 33	−0 49						

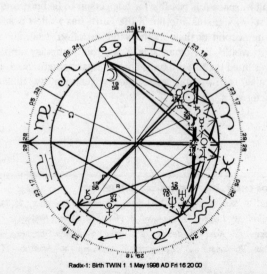

Radix-1: Birth TWIN 1 1 May 1998 AD Fri 16 20 00

Radix-1

DATE: 1 May 1998 AD Fri	MC 1 37 ♋	☉ 11 04 ♉ 8
TIME: 16 30 00	ASC 1 14 ♎	☾ 20 03 ♋ 10
ZONE: 1 00 E	—— Plac ——	☿ 14 43 ♈ 7
LATITUDE: 51 31 N	11. 7 35 ♌	♀ 27 35 ♓ 6
LONGITUDE: 0 06 W	12. 7 31 ♍	♂ 13 46 ♉ 8
CITY: London	2. 25 16 ♎	♃ 19 40 ♓ 6
	3. 25 28 ♏	♄ 25 39 ♈ 8
		♅ 12 39 ♒ 5
	☊ 7 20 ♍ R 11	♆ 2 10 ♒ 4
		♇ 7 24 ♐ R 3

Aspects Radix-1/Radix-1

☉ ☌ ♂ 2 42 +0 14	☿ △ ♇ 7 19 −0 50	♆ △ ASC 0 56 +0 42
☉ □ ♆ 1 35 +0 57	♀ ☌ ♃ 7 55 −0 55	
☾ □ ☿ 5 20 −12 21	♀ ⚹ ♆ 4 34 +1 7	
☾ △ ♀ 7 32 +12 3	♂ □ ♆ 1 7 −0 43	
☾ △ ♃ 0 23 −12 58	☾ Q ASC 0 49 −12 28	
☾ □ ♄ 5 36 +13 2	♀ □ MC 4 1 +0 13	
☿ ⚹ ♆ 2 5 −0 48	♀ ☍ ASC 3 39 +0 25	
☿ Q ♆ 0 33 −0 49	♄ □ ♆ 6 31 +0 8	

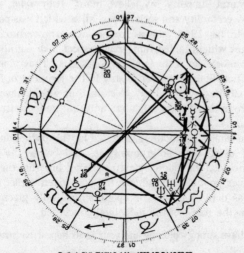

Radix-1: Birth TWIN 2 1 May 1998 AD Fri 16 30 00

The two charts on pp 299 and 300 are of two people, the first born in London, and the second in Tokyo. Their charts are almost identical.

Put to the Test

It was irresistible to put the computers at the House of Jupiter to the test! We provided them with a specific time, date and place of birth and asked for a read out. We gave them: Edinburgh, 6 May 1953, 6.10 a.m. The House of Jupiter did not know the subject, which was in fact Prime Minister Tony Blair.

He had already been featured in *Old Moore's Almanack, 1996* before, of course, he became Prime Minister. That article certainly highlighted features that we have since come to recognise: stating that his birth chart indicated 'a decidedly intellectual combination but one that is also practical, consistent: he can back up his rhetoric and high ideals with hard work'. They describe him as 'a philanthropist who aspires to bring humanitarian values down to earth ... Blair is genuinely concerned about steering a *morally sound* course, one that both empowers and supports his fellow man.' They refer to his 'popularity, versatility and social grace' all of which was perhaps embodied in his 1998 address to the French government, in French, and which gained him great respect in a country not always comfortable with English politicians. They correctly predicted that 'Blair seems set to stay in the forefront of British politics' (had he lost the 1997 election that would have been much more in doubt than it is now) and that he is 'courageous and stubborn'.

House of Jupiter's computers, accessed for this purpose in May 1998 but using data programmed in well before the 1997 election, included the following extracts. They are from the same very complex pool of material that the data given earlier in the section was derived from. The operator was only given birth details, not the name of the individual concerned.

- You have strong opinions and your ideas appear consistent.

Radix-1

DATE: 1 May 1998 AD Fri	MC 0 50 ♉	☉ 10 53 ♉	10
TIME: 12 18 30	ASC 17 01 ♌	☾ 17 45 ♋	11
ZONE: 1 00 E	—— Plac ——	☿ 14 34 ♈	9
LATITUDE: 51 31 N	11. 10 30 ♊	♀ 27 23 ♓	8
LONGITUDE: 0 06 W	12. 17 52 ♋	♂ 13 38 ♉	10
CITY: London	2. 5 06 ♍	♃ 19 38 ♓	8
	3. 28 48 ♍	♄ 25 37 ♈	9
		♅ 12 39 ♒	6
	☊ 7 21 ♍ R 2	♆ 2 10 ♒	6
		♇ 7 25 ♐ R	4

Aspects Radix-1/Radix-1

☉ ☌ ♂	2 44	+0 14	♀ ☌ ♃	7 45	−0 55	♄ ☌ MC	5 13	−0 54
☉ □ ♆	1 45	+0 57	♀ ✶ ♆	4 46	+1 7	♅ ☍ ASC	4 22	−0 41
☾ □ ☿	3 10	−12 27	♂ □ ♆	0 59	−0 43	♆ □ MC	1 20	+1 2
☾ ✶ ♂	4 7	−12 31	☉ □ ASC	6 7	+0 16			
☾ △ ♃	1 53	+13 3	☿ △ ASC	2 27	+0 6			
☾ □ ♄	7 53	+13 7	♂ □ ASC	3 23	+0 2			
☿ ✶ ♆	1 56	−0 47	♄ Q ♆	0 59	−0 7			
☿ Q ♆	0 25	−0 48	♄ □ ♆	6 33	+0 8			
☿ △ ♇	7 10	−0 49						

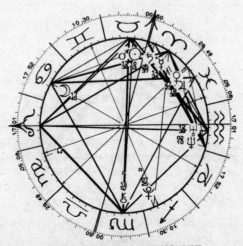

Radix-1: Simon UK Born Baby 1 May 1998 AD Fri 12 18 30

Radix-1

DATE: 1 May 1998 AD Fri	MC	9 14 ♉		☉	10 32 ♉	10
TIME: 12 00 00	ASC	16 15 ♌		☽	12 52 ♋	11
ZONE: 9 27 E	— Plac —			☿	14 17 ♈	9
LATITUDE: 35 42 N	11.	13 58 ♊		♀	26 59 ♓	8
LONGITUDE: 139 46 E	12.	16 53 ♋		♂	13 22 ♉	10
CITY: Tokyo	2.	9 11 ♍		♃	19 34 ♓	8
	3.	6 45 ♎		♄	25 35 ♈	9
				♅	12 38 ♒	6
	☊	7 22 ♍ R	1	♆	2 10 ♒	6
				♇	7 25 ♐ R	4

Aspects Radix-1/Radix-1

☉	✶	☽	2 20	–12 28	♂	□	♆	0 44	–0 43	♆ □ MC	3 24 +0 59
☉	☌	♂	2 50	+0 14	☉	☌	MC	1 18	+0 2	♆ ☍ ASC	3 37 –0 47
☉	□	♆	2 6	+0 57	☉	□	ASC	5 42	+0 10	♆ □ MC	7 4 –1 0
☽	□	☿	1 25	+12 39	☽	✶	MC	3 39	–12 26		
☽	✶	♂	0 30	+12 42	☿	△	ASC	1 58	–0 1		
☽	△	♃	6 42	+13 14	♂	☌	MC	4 8	+0 16		
☿	✶	♆	1 39	–0 46	♂	□	ASC	2 53	–0 4		
☿	Q	♆	0 8	–0 47	♄	Q	♆	0 56	–0 7		
☿	△	♇	6 52	–0 48	♄	□	♆	6 35	+0 8		
♀	☌	♃	7 25	–0 55							

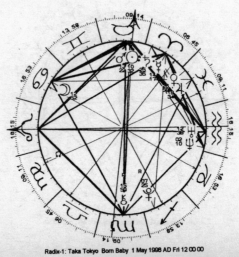

Radix-1: Taka Tokyo Born Baby 1 May 1998 AD Fri 12 00 00

DATE: 6 May 1953 AD Wed	MC	26 03 ♑		☉ 15 23 ♉	12
TIME: 6 10 00	ASC	4 49 ♊		☽ 11 29 ♒	10
ZONE: 1 00 E - SCO DST	—— Plac ——			☿ 26 24 ♈	12
LATITUDE: 55 57 N	11.	17 27 ♒		♀ 15 02 ♈	12
LONGITUDE: 3 13 W	12.	26 16 ♓		♂ 3 28 ♊	12
CITY: Edinburgh	2.	24 58 ♊		♃ 29 12 ♉	12
	3.	10 10 ♋		♄ 22 20 ♎ R	6
				♅ 15 17 ♋	3
	☊	7 27 ♒ R 10		♆ 21 54 ♎ R	6
				♇ 20 47 ♌	5

☉ □ ☽	3 54	+12 57	♂ ☌ ♃	4 16	−0 28	♃ △ MC	3 10	+0 42
☽ ⚹ ♆	0 6	−0 56	☽ △ ASC	6 39	−12 29	♃ ☌ ASC	5 37	−1 12
☽ □ ♇	5 24	+0 58	☿ □ MC	0 21	−0 48	♄ □ MC	3 42	−1 0
☽ ⚹ ♀	3 33	+13 51	♂ △ MC	7 26	+0 14	♆ □ MC	4 9	−0 57
☽ ☍ ♄	4 4	−1 48	♂ ☌ ASC	1 21	−0 44			
☽ ☍ ♆	4 30	−1 45	♄ □ ♆	7 3	+0 6			
☽ △ ♇	5 37	−1 44	♄ ☌ ♆	0 27	+0 3			
♀ ☍ ♄	7 19	+0 8	♄ ⚹ ♇	1 33	+0 4			
♀ □ ♆	0 15	+0 2	♆ □ ♆	6 36	+0 3			
♀ ☍ ♆	6 52	+0 5	♆ ⚹ ♇	1 7	+0 1			
♀ △ ♇	5 46	+0 4						

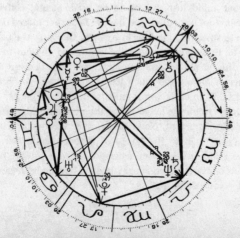

Radix-1: Tony Blair 6 May 1953 AD Wed 6 10 00

However, you can at times slide into dogmatism and an unwillingness to change. Good powers of concentration and endurance ensure that your determination remains as strong towards the end as it was at the beginning.'

- 'You are ... one of the most stubborn creatures alive! Being one of those people who always knows they're right – because unfailing instinct tells you so – you'll always stand your ground when challenged, with little regard for personal danger.'

- 'You have a knack for attracting people who are recognisably different, even eccentric. It's as if you deliberately – if unconsciously – seek out those who possess these qualities, for they fascinate you. In fact, the more unconventional they are, the more attraction they have for you. Perhaps part of this attraction is motivated by you yourself having a tendency to deny these same unconventionalisms in yourself. Therfore, because everything needs an outlet, your own anti-social behaviour finds a healthy release by living through that of others.'

- 'You have a great need to find your way to the top. It's more than just ambition – it's almost an emotional desire. If you didn't get to the top of the highest ladder, you'd feel as if you'd forsaken your life: as if you'd been presented with special opportunities which you'd then failed to live up to.'

- 'You are a brainbox. Ideas always seem to be floating around in your mind just waiting to be used. Mental activity is therefore not something you have to force; nor indeed do you have to strain too hard for inspiration. Of course the point is that all these goodies should be formulated and put to good use; this is not always the case, however. Perhaps it's a matter of having too much too often; perhaps you become overloaded. In other words much of this mental energy often continues to bubble under rather than become fashioned into something coherent. Nevertheless, once the nut is cracked, there's no limit to the precision of your mental skills. An active mind makes for an active body; hence you are nearly always on the go, even when you don't have to be. Others get tired – you get strong!'

- 'Things have a way of happening easily for you. Goals and opportunities which may elude others often come to you overnight. This is both good and bad. The good is that you're saved unnecessary hardship and suffering in the pursuit of objects which often, in fact, are yours by right. The bad – or perhaps it's more appropriate to say "negative" – side of things is that, because of the facility with which you achieve your ends, a certain complacency can set in and, with it, a lack of awareness of what it's like to be on the outside looking in. This does not reflect how you really are for, if truth be known, equality of opportunity is something you'd like to see for all.'

(Note: The reference to complacency is interesting. During the 1997 election night, victory for New Labour was devastatingly obvious from the outset. Indeed, Michael Heseltine virtually admitted that from early in the evening. Yet when Blair took to the stand during the night he commented that 'he never liked to be complacent' – to which there was much raucous laughter! – only commenting that 'it does look good, though'. Perhaps he was aware of, and had even been criticised for, acting complacently and felt the need to make clear his alertness.)

- 'You co-operate well with those in authority in your working life. You use all that surrounds and is available to you to further your own material status. Advancement and worldly success are things which you want and strive for. Everybody knows that you'll get them.

THE MEDICINE WHEEL

While looking at the system of astrological divination above, which we might call Chaldean astrology, it is worth comparing it to the ancient mythology of the Native North American Indians which has come down through time by oral tradition. It is known as the 'Medicine Wheel' or Earth Medicine. There are many striking parallels with the astrology more familiar to us.

However, this system of astrology is more directed towards self-development than the Chaldean version. Whereas Chaldean astrology suggests that character and influence are almost set in stone from the moment of birth, and perhaps even the inevitability of certain illnesses, career paths, and so on, Earth medicine indicates the influences that have arisen since the time of birth, emphasising the opportunity for self-development from that point. As such therefore it is an astrology well in tune with the mood of the time; a time when people are looking towards their own self-realisations; the individual seeking to become the person they are capable of becoming. Earth Medicine is also not predictive in the way that Chaldean astrology is.

The mythology of the Medicine Wheel is long-standing in native American Indian lore, though much of it is shrouded in mystery. Medicine wheels are large stone circles set out on the plains by Indian tribes. Archaeological evidence suggests that they related to the calendar and were either astronomical or astrological in purpose, perhaps in a similar way to that speculated for such monuments as Stonehenge. Generally the Plains tribes were nomadic and not particularly given to building lasting structures, so these medicine wheels must have had considerable importance. There are approximately fifty remaining such 'wheels' scattered across the plains of Canada and the United States. They vary greatly in size; the smallest just a few feet across but the largest nearly two hundred feet in diameter. They are made up of tons of rock, individual rocks of around a foot across laid out to form the circles and the central cairns and sometimes connecting 'spokes'. The largest cairns are thirty feet across and ten feet high. Some of the wheels also have cairns positioned around the perimeter.

The best known of the medicine wheels is the Bighorn Medicine Wheel in Wyoming, which is believed to be around two hundred years old. Native Americans regard it as a 'holy site' of their culture.

Astronomer John Eddy began investigating the medicine wheels in 1972, and in particular the Bighorn. He believed that the layout reflected the summer solstice and that it could have been used as a reference point for the rising of prominent stars such as Sirius and Rigel. Although there was no obvious lunar connection some analysts have argued that the twenty-eight spokes might represent the lunar cycle of twenty-eight days. Investigation of another prominent wheel – the Moose Mountain Medicine Wheel in Saskatchewan, Canada – showed that it too represented the summer solstice alignments. Dating suggested it was extremely old and may date back two to two and half thousand years. Carbon dating in the central cairn produced readings of 440 BC. Such findings have provoked an interest in both the antiquity of Indian culture and also its astrology. Modern medicine wheels are constructed with great ceremony and ritual as a focus for spiritual development and medicine power.

Kenneth Meadows, who published his own explanations of the Medicine Wheel culture in his book *Earth Medicine* (1989) states: 'Earth Medicine can help us find meaning and purpose in our lives. It encourages us to accept responsibility for our own life and offers us greater freedom and responsibility. Instead of being victims of circumstance, we can gain mastery of our own destiny'.

The Earth Medicine Explanation

As in Chaldean astrology the year is divided into twelve, month-long divisions represented by an animal totem. These periods fairly closely correspond with the Chaldean cycle. The period of time to which the totem relates is also characterised by its time in nature and by elements which correspond to the alchemical elements identified by Aristotle; fire, earth, air and water.

The elements relate to the individual's birthtime and govern emotions, spirituality and psychology. Air is the realm of thought, and is transformative. 'Airy' people are not very attached to the Earth, can be rather vague, but are 'ideas' people. Fire is dynamic energy for change; it governs passion, sexuality, enthusiasm and tends towards the extrovert. Earth is stable, solid; the realm of the dependable and of abundance. The element of caution and prudence. Water is fluid, changeable and governs the emotions. Water creates sensitivity, and tends towards the introvert. The divisions and their main characteristics are:

Falcon Awakening time March 21 to April 19

Falcons are visionaries and initiators but they can lose interest quickly in their own schemes; can be hasty. Optimistic, determined, independent, sometimes self-important. Can be prone to exaggeration, fantasy and tactlessness.

Health: Prone to headaches, stress, high blood pressure, sudden illnesses.

Opportunity for growth: To learn discernment; to be themselves and not respond to others. Learn to finish what has been started. Curb impatience and restlessness.

The Falcon's element is fire.

Beaver Growing time April 20 to May 20

Shapers, doers. Practical and reliable, with a strong sense of purpose and duty. Strong sense of perseverance. Not great risk takers. Home loving and nature loving. Flourish in a positive and loving atmosphere but highly sensitive and anxious in a tense environment. Seeing is believing would be their motto.

Health: Prone to heart conditions, kidney complaints and urinary infections. Subject to many sore throats.

Opportunity for growth: Shed need for material wealth. Need to learn to form relationships without possessiveness.

The Beaver's elements are earth and fire.

306

Deer Flowering time May 21 to June 20

Happy and buoyant people, eager for change. Up one minute and down the next. Easily bored, though keen to be involved in everything. Good communicators, make a lot of social connections. Tendency to be snap decision-makers. Not very punctual.
Health: Prone to ailments of the lungs and bronchial passages. Can be subject to liver complaints.
Opportunity for growth: Need to better balance logic and intuition. Try to find opportunities that have true value rather than mere interest.
Deer elements are air and fire.

Woodpecker Long days June 21 to July 21

Emotional, sensitive. Family instincts are strong; they value the security of hearth and home. They put on a hard exterior and only open up to those close to them. Will tend to prey on the sympathy of others. They tend to worry unnecessarily, and with the slightest reason. Can be moody.
Health: Low pain threshold. Prone to stomach disorders.
Opportunity for growth: Know that love must be given out if it is to be taken in. Worry, it has been said, is a dividend paid on problems before it is due; learn not to worry too far ahead of time. Woodpecker element is water.

Salmon Ripening time July 22 to August 21

Extremists, proud, vain, self-confident. Arrogant but congenial so that others allow them to interfere where perhaps different personalities would not get away with it. Dogmatic though not always consistent. Rational, but prone to be persuaded by flattery.
Health: Rarely ill; and they recover well. Suffer from stress and high blood pressure in later life. Circulation problems likely to develop.
Opportunity for growth: Need to find a deeper purpose in life. Must learn to stop 'using' other people. Need to learn to be more goal-based.

Salmon elements are fire and water.

Brown bear Harvesting time August 22 to September 21

Plodding, eye for detail, cannot hold 'the big picture'. Nitpickers. Hard workers. Not able to express themselves openly. Can get taken in by others. Comfortable with routines and familiar patterns. Prefers planning to surprises.

Health: Stomach and bowel problems. Stress-related illnesses abound, particularly ulcers.

Opportunity for growth: Need to learn the difference between what is nice to do/know and what is needed to do/know. Should try to trust their own instincts more.

Brown bear elements are earth and water.

Crow Falling leaves time September 22 to October 22

Restless, artistic. Crows enjoy change, new horizons, new experiences. Pick up and respond to atmosphere; if the mood turns dour, so do they. Go from enthusiastic to lazy in a short space of time. Easy-going and able to shape themselves into other's needs. In trying to avoid disharmony they sometimes try to please everyone and end up pleasing none.

Health: Muscular problems and problems of the lower back.

Opportunity for growth: Know that integrity is sought in all actions; do not be led into areas of dubious moral purpose. Learn to work with other people, but avoid dependence on others.

Crow elements are air and earth.

Snake Frost time October 23 to November 22

People of extremes. Can get very distressed, but quickly get back to normal. Nevertheless can be trying for those who do not understand them. Deep, mysterious, intense people. Great charisma. Good analytical abilities. Generous with time and possessions. Respond well to a challenge. Like to be surrounded in luxury.

Health: Bottling up emotion causes stomach and various nervous disorders. Need to channel high sexual energy.

Opportunity for growth: Try to develop self discipline and emotional security. Trust creativity and develop it.

Snake elements are earth and water.

Owl Long nights November 23 to December 21

Warm and jovial people. Adventurous. Need and seek freedom of mind and body to expand themselves. Jack of all trades, master of none. Very enthusiastic about their own passions, but tend to relegate the passions of others to a lesser value. Can be prone to explosive outbursts and sarcasm. Attracted to dangerous pastimes. Explorers and visionaries. Cannot distinguish between greed and need.

Health: Prone to becoming overweight. Some tendency towards stress-related disorders.

Opportunity for growth: Must be goal-based in all areas of work and life. Avoid over-indulgence.

Owl elements are earth and fire.

Goose Renewal time December 22 to January 19

Ambitious, practical, determined. Interested in themselves far more than others. Wary of making relationships but fiercely loving and loyal when they do. Love of nature. Idealistic, which can make them get problems out of proportion and suppress humour. Can become embittered easily.

Health: Nervous rashes. Rheumatic complaints. Tend to keep going when others would have 'crashed'.

Opportunity for growth: Learn to be adaptable. Let go of the past. Learn to conquer pessimism.

Goose elements are air and earth.

Otter Cleansing time January 20 to February 18

Independent and dynamic. Artistic. Humane. Great love for the world in general. Lovers of freedom; unable to conform to sets of rules. They have flair, but can be impractical in application. Broad-minded and happy to break taboos. Eccentric. Unpredictable. Intuitive. Feelings tend not to run deep so they make good people to confide in; they don't hold onto or spread around what they are told.

Health: Keep themselves in pretty good shape. Tend to suffer from circulation problems; varicose veins.

Opportunity for growth: Make an effort to turn ideas into realities which are ultimately fulfilling.

Otter element is air.

Wolf Blustery winds time February 19 to March 20

Compassionate and generous. Understanding and warm. They take a lot in from others often to the point of draining, even harming, themselves. They make decisions based on instinct and feeling, not on logic. Self-expressive, freedom-loving. Gullible. Cannot stand criticism. Take things very personally.

Health: High blood pressure, problems, circulation problems.

Opportunity for growth: Cultivate intuition which is already a valuable asset in the Wolf. Avoid procrastination, the 'thief of time'.

Wolf elements are air and water.

What becomes apparent is that the translation of character traits and other aspects of the individual are very similar in both Chaldean and Earth Medicine astrology. As these two strains appear to have developed without 'contamination' or contact between the originating groups it adds to the suggestion that there is a reality behind astrology, demonstrated by many scientific studies. However, we must acknowledge that there have been no such studies done on the more precise aspects of Earth Medicine as there have been on Chaldean astrology.

Nor does this overlap indicate what the reality is. Perhaps proponents of astrology are correct in attributing these effects directly to the stars, or perhaps there is a third factor unidentified which is common to both human birth times and astronomical movements and which is the true reason for the commonalities between 'types'. For the future, we believe this is a rich area for true scientific study, moving beyond proving 'that it works' which seems well demonstrated to all but the most stubborn disbeliever, but aiming to find out why it works, and what the true influences are.

IN CONCLUSION

We started this book by pointing out that the material contained in it, though something of an encyclopedic journey through the history of the occult and magic, was relevant to the modern day because of the similarities of the youth revolution we call the 'sixties' – which has, of course, continued through to the present day. But what of the future?

We stand at the beginning of a new Millennium, but despite a number of books and newspaper debates on the subject – most of which have concerned themselves with trivia about the Millennium Dome in London, or other unimportant matters – there has been little public presentation or recognition of how the move into a new Millennium will affect human thinking. Yet the effects of Millenarianism are quite profound.

Firstly there is the question of attitude. At the change of a year people generally look forward to the year ahead. The fact that a **year** is changing tends to make people think of what the year ahead will bring; one step up the promotion ladder, perhaps, some family arrangements or a significant family birthday, and so on. At the change of a decade the fact that it is a **decade** that is changing leads people to thinking of what the decade ahead will bring. Even that change of perspective is quite telling; a decade ahead certainly means that even fairly young children will have become adults or nearly so, they will have changed schools and might have entered into higher education. People look at their careers and ask themselves where they will be in ten years time. People look towards the stages of life; perhaps the next ten years holds growth, the chance to reach the peak of your career. Perhaps retirement is looming with all its attendant changes. At the turn of a **century** a major change of thinking is inevitable. Few people alive today can remember what it is like to live through the change of a century, most of those that were alive to experience it are unlikely to have been old enough to remember it directly. As human individuals we cannot think a century ahead in our lifetime, most of us will be dead before the next change of century, and in any case all we can guess is that the majority of our lives, and all of our career, will be past. What we can do is expand our thinking into two areas; the family, and society. In the family we think of the future of our children, and perhaps our grandchildren. What will their world be like? We can extrapolate from our existing society and guess at the changes they will have to take in in their lifetimes. This also encompasses our thinking for society. What will society look like over the next hundred years and how will changes in society affect our descendants?

But the change of a **millennium** is of a quite different order. Needless to say no-one alive today was alive at the change of the last millennium and no-one alive today will be alive at the change of the next one. Few people apart from those from the old aristocracies and a few diligent family researchers have any idea what their own families looked like in the year 1001, and few would give much time to considering what actual descendants they will have alive in the year 3001. The focus of our thinking for one thousand years ahead is entirely society-based. We attempt to take in a view of the changes that will affect humans for the next thousand years, and because of the detachment from personal values, it is a unique perspective.

Inevitable is the desire to make comparison. What was life like around the turn of the year 1001, compared to today? And what has taken place in the last thousand years?

United States Around the turn of the millennium, Norse explorer Leif Ericsson was just setting foot on the continent that would one day be known as North America, naming it Vinland. He is credited with being the first European to do so. A

Viking-type settlement, matching his description, was discovered in Newfoundland.

England In 1013 king Canute II completed the Danish conquest of England. Within a few years he had become king of England, Denmark, and Norway. The next few decades represented a struggle between his two heirs for control of England. Arguably the most important battle in English history, even in European history took place in 1066 near Hastings. William, Duke of Normandy, invaded, claiming the English crown. The Saxon king, Harold was killed in the battle, William – the Conqueror, as he became known – took the English throne. Modern day England reflects the influences of the following Norman conquest.

Japan was enjoying its Golden Age of Art. A secure, aristocratic society rejected Chinese artistic influences and flowered in its own culture. The world's first great anthologies of poetry were compiled, the world's first novels written (by, for example, Murasaki Shikibu and Sei Shonagon who chronicled court life of the time). Art and architecture flourished, particularly supported by the powerful Shingon and Tendai sects of Mahayana Buddhism, who commissioned the Buddhist temples. But the military dictatorships of the shoguns were soon to arise; they would rule throughout most of the millennium, to 1867.

In **China** the Song Dynasty had commenced in 960 and would last until 1279. This had followed over fifty years of internal strife and civil war. Central government was established, tighter control of the army, and Confucianism became the dominant ideology.

In 1206 Genghis Khan came to power as the Mongol leader of what would soon become the world's greatest empire. In 1279 his grandson, Kublai Khan completed the conquest of China and ended the Song dynasty.

In **Africa**, around 1000, the Zimbabwe culture was the most influential in the south. Archaeological remains including a fortified acropolis of stone indicate how advanced this society was. Zimbabwean merchants traded as far away as China. The Kingdom of Ghana is known to have flourished around this time as an advanced civilisation which included metalworking and a widespread trading network. In roughly AD 50 the Aksum kings of Ethiopia emerged and extended their reach across the Red Sea to southern Arabia.

Shortly after the year 1000, the Berbers of the western Sahara set out on a period of conquest and expansion, invading Moorish Spain and Ghana. Moorish Spain was the centre of learning of the time, and greatly influenced the development of Europe. The city of Cordoba had a library with 400,000 books. Medical studies and teachings began in Muslim Spain. Other Muslim kingdoms were established in Asia and Africa. In 999 Mahmud of Ghazni established a Turkish Islamic empire in Afghanistan.

End of Rome The effects of the fall of Rome (AD 476) started a chain of events that moulded the shape of Europe for the next thousand years, to the present day. The period after the fall of Rome in western Europe was known as the Dark Ages. Rome had brought the region efficient channels of communication, stable government, a uniform currency, schools, libraries and a common language. After the fall of the government which had maintained this, Europe was at the mercy of nomadic invaders who destroyed the libraries, damaged trade agreements with petty local warring, and replaced the efficient system of currency with an inefficient and imprecise one of barter. Towns, cities, and the famous Roman roads fell into disrepair and decline. The rich inheritance of art from Greece and Rome was largely pushed aside. With the loss of centralised control small feudal states prevailed. Ruled by a lord and a group of knights the states were small self-sufficient farming communities. The world view that Rome had offered was lost; most ordinary people lived their entire lives without venturing more than a few miles from their homes. Gradually the lords attempted to extend their grasp, resulting in many local wars and infighting, all of which served to retard any overall progress of civilisation.

Gradually however, the emergence of larger states did result in the consolidation of government and the re-establishment of trading and culture on a broader scale. Interestingly the successors to the power of Rome found themselves in awe of those who had come before them. Rome had left its mark in architecture and in its cities and roads and those who had conquered Rome became influenced by both the splendour that had been Rome and the fact that they had been unable to equal it.

Christian monasticism dominated the next centuries, from around the third century. In the sixth century St Benedict founded a Christian community at Monte Cassino which became the prototype for the monastic way of life in Europe. Monks would undertake teaching, record history, and safeguard libraries while working the land and devoting themselves to Christ.

The power of the papacy reigned supreme at the turn of the millennium. The pope was often the most powerful man in medieval Europe. Pope Gregory VII, who reigned from 1073 to 1085, challenged European royalty for supremacy and in 1076 excommunicated the Holy Roman Emperor, Henry IV (1050–1106) who had opposed him. The pope's power won through and Henry was forced to don penitent's rags and go to Pope Gregory in Canossa, Italy, to beg for forgiveness. (Henry got his own back later.)

The Crusades of the early centuries of the 'new' millennium brought Europe back from the economic wilderness by combining trading, spirituality and cultural exchange. As we have seen in this book the Crusades and the Knights Templar are inseparable both in actuality and in their influence.

Inventions that arose were driven by change. As the cities flourished again so there developed a need for more food to feed the populations. To meet increasing demand farmers had to learn to fertilize fields and to rotate crops to make the best use of land. New crops were cultivated. New technology was imported from the Muslims (who had got it from the Chinese) – the windmill and wheelbarrow, for example.

Increased trade involved shipping; one invention that came to the fore was the magnetic compass. The rudder replaced the steersman's oar enabling the building of heavier ships capable of longer and more arduous travel.

There was even an early attempt at arms limitation. Around the turn of the millennium a new weapon had been invented that was so powerful it struck fear across nations. The crossbow could fire a bolt over 300 metres and pierce chain mail armour. It was regarded as so deadly that it was outlawed by Catholics for use against Christians by the Lateran Council of 1139. But it could not be 'uninvented' and remained in use until the fifteenth century, when it was superseded by the longbow and firearms.

Most of these events barely take us past the first few centuries of the 'new millennium' yet could hardly have been foretold by the peoples of the world at the time of 1001.

Did Rome really believe it could fall? Did it have any vision of what was to follow? Did the citizens of the Roman Empire, seeing the splendour of the civilisation they lived in, believe that the future would hold greatness, and an extension to that splendour as art and architecture developed? Did they really imagine that those who could defeat them could plunge their world into a Dark Ages of feudalism? And do we not think in terms of development and progress rather than retrograde steps into a feudal past? Even when we try to learn by history do we not think in terms of either development or destruction – perhaps by atomic warfare – when perhaps there are alternative futures we have yet to conceive of?

Could Leif Ericsson have conceived of the future of the land he was standing on in 1000? Can we be sure where our own explorations of space and the deep oceans will lead in the next thousand years?

Of the progress of technology we can obviously see a pace that seems too rapid even to measure. In the last hundred years alone we have progressed immeasurably, with almost everything in common use today almost unthinkable when Queen Victoria was on the throne: the CD, the internet, reusable spacecraft, communication satellites, and so on, and so on. Extrapolated at that pace, one thousand years into the future could bring a world as impossible to dream of as this world would have been to a feudal serf of 1000. Though we also know that great and developed civilisations have been here before, and gone almost without trace.

All the great kingdoms, empires and civilisations that have flourished in past times have fallen in time. The question of whether that will happen to the countries and civilisations we now know is irrelevant, the only question is when and how will they fall. And what will replace them. But do we, in, say, England or the United States really believe that one day we shall be swept aside by a march of culture, or technology, or something we have yet to imagine.

This book is a history of the way people thought, of the way they lived, and tried to influence others to live. It is a history of belief and counter-belief. Of what was fashionable, and what was suppressed at different times. Millenarianism is about trying to think into the next thousand years to see how we shall think as a species. What values we shall hold dear. What shall be suppressed, and why (because something surely will)? The idea that we shall use the experiences of the last thousand years to learn how to do it better in the future is an illusion; it is an old adage but true that 'the one thing we learn from history is that we never learn from history.'

But we have a duty to guess, even knowing that we shall almost certainly be wrong. The upsurge of thinking that has characterised the last quarter of the twentieth century and therefore the last years of the present millennium (at the time of writing), and which includes a rediscovery of Hermeticism, of the spirituality of alchemy and the occult, of the nature-care of paganism, is still in conflict with 'conventional' religion but it is possible that these odd bedfellows will learn to accommodate each other. New religions have a habit of taking in facets of the old religions that they replace; many Christian churches have pagan symbols in them that have been adopted and adapted by Christianity. Generally such changes take much longer than a lifetime, and the reason is clear: people do not change their minds about their beliefs generally speaking, but they do die off and are replaced by younger, fresher people who hold different views. In this way religion and belief mutate down the generations.

But the likely conflict looks more set to be with a new, intransigent religion that is consciously trying hard to refuse to accommodate all others, believing itself to be the One True Faith. That is the fundamentalist religion of science. Having evolved from the very beliefs that we have described in this book; astrology into astronomy, alchemy (at face value, anyway) into chemistry, and so on, science is now seeking to challenge those who would promote a Hermetic, holistic, approach to the future. It believes in compartmentalising, in specialisation, and in the isolation of its parts; the opposite of the holistic principles. Science should not be rejected; it has brought forth great advances and promises to develop many more. It is our future. But the imposition of morals and ethics, of recognising that it is a part of a whole rather than a discipline which can stand alone, must be a part of its evolution.

It is likely that the next *Jihad* will be between adherents to divided viewpoints over the future direction of science.

And the challenge of the next thousand years will be to avoid the Holy War, and to unify the science of the future with the wisdoms of the past.

REFERENCES AND
RECOMMENDED READING

Baigent, Michael & Leigh, Richard, *The Elixir and the Stone*, Viking, 1997

Baigent, Michael & Leigh, Richard, *The Temple and the Lodge*, Jonathan Cape, 1989

Barrett, David V, *Runes*, Dorling Kindersley, 1995

Bourne, Lois, *Dancing with Witches*, Robert Hale, 1998

Cavendish, Richard (ed), *Encyclopedia of the Unexplained*, Arkana, 1974

Cavendish, Richard, *A History of Magic*, Weidenfeld & Nicolson, 1977

Crowley, Vivianne, *Wicca; The Old Religion in the New Age*, Aquarian, 1989

de Givry, Grillot, *Witchcraft, Magic & Alchemy*, Dover Publications, 1931

Dening, Sarah, *The Everyday I Ching*, Simon & Schuster, 1995

Fenton, Sasha, *Fortune-Telling by Tarot Cards*, Thorsons, 1994

Fenton, Sasha, *Understanding Astrology*, Thorsons, 1991

Fairley, John & Welfare, Simon, *Arthur C Clarke's World of Strange Powers*, Collins, 1989

Franklyn, Julian (ed), *A Survey of the Occult*, Tynron, 1935

Goodman, Felicitas D, *How about Demons?* Indiana University Press, 1988

Guiley, Rosemary Ellen, *Encyclopedia of Mystical and Paranormal Experience*, Gange, 1991

Hill, Douglas & Williams, Pat, *The Supernatural*, Bloomsbury, 1989

Howe, Ellic, *Astrology and Psychological Warfare during World War II*, Rider & Co, 1972

Hutton, Ronald, *The Stations of the Sun: A History of the Ritual Year in Britain*, OUP, 1996

Kalweit, Holger, *Shamans, Healers and Medicine Men*, Shambhala, 1992

MacNulty, W Kirk, *Freemasonry*, Thames & Hudson, 1991

Mansall, Cordelia, *The Astrology Workbook*, Aquarian Press, 1985

Marshall, Richard, *Witchcraft – The History and Mythology*, Crescent, 1995

Masello, Robert, *Raising Hell*, Perigee, 1996

Matthews, John (ed), *The World Atlas of Divination*, Headline, 1992

Meadows, Kenneth, *Earth Medicine*, Element Books, 1996

Montgomery, Ruth, *A Gift of Prophecy: The Story of Jeane Dixon*, Arthur Barker, 1966

Ovason, David, *The Nostradamus Code*, Arrow, 1998

Robinson, Enders A, *The Devil Discovered*, Hippocrene, 1991

Rutherford, Leo, *Principles of Shamanism*, Thorsons, 1996

Sakheim, David K & Devene, Susan E, *Out of Darkness – Exploring Satanism & Ritual Abuse*, Lexington, 1992

Singer, André & Lynette, *Divine Magic*, Boxtree, 1995

Spencer, John and Anne, *Powers of the Mind*, Orion, 1998

Steiger, Brad, *American Indian Magic*, Inner Light, 1986

Valiente, Doreen, *Witchcraft for Tomorrow*, Robert Hale, 1978

Walker, Charles, *Encyclopedia of Secret Knowledge*, Rider, 1995

Wilson, Colin, *From Atlantis to the Sphinx*, Virgin, 1997

Wilson, Colin, *Dictionary of the Occult*, Geddes & Grosset, 1997

Wilson, Colin, *Mystics and Prophets*, Paragon, 1997

Wilson, Colin, *Ritual and Magic*, Paragon, 1997

INDEX